Youth Culture
and
The Generation Gap

Youth Culture

and

The Generation Gap

Gerhard Falk and Ursula Falk

Algora Publishing
New York

Library of Congress Cataloging-in-Publication Data —

Falk, Gerhard, 1924-
The youth culture and the generation gap / by Gerhard Falk and Ursula
Falk.
p. cm.
Includes bibliographical references and index.
ISBN 0-87586-367-1 (trade paper: alk. paper) — ISBN 0-87586-368-X (hard
cover: alk. paper) — ISBN 0-87586-369-8 (ebook)
1. Youth. 2. Conflict of generations. I. Falk, Ursula A. II. Title.

HQ796.F32 2005
305.235'0973—dc22

2005000281

Front Cover: Woman Showing Tattoo to Friends
© Corbis
Date Photographed: 2000

Youthful couple
© Jack Foley/CORBIS
Photographer: Jack Foley
Date Photographed: May 20, 1999

Printed in the United States

The authors are indebted to our son Clifford Falk for his invaluable help in dealing with the vagaries of the computer and for proofreading the entire manuscript.

TABLE OF CONTENTS

INTRODUCTION

This book seeks to relate the development of the youth culture from the 16th century to the 21st century. Beginning with the life of children and adolescents in the Puritan colonies of New England, the discussion moves to more recent times and compares the influence of parents and peers on the young in America.

There is and has indeed been a generation gap in this country and everywhere. However, that gap is not as great as proposed by the media; most young Americans do accept the values of their parents.

Seeking to develop their own identity, adolescents live at a risk-taking age that serves to divorce them from the controls of the adult world. The effort to attain some sense of self-direction is heavily influenced by the school and by the ethnic group to which a youngster belongs.

Not all young Americans go to school, despite the law demanding this. Migration, homelessness, poverty and minority status affect school attendance. We fully explore the fate of those who are excluded from that vital aspect of youth experience.

Because adolescence is the age at which humans first experience the demands of the sex drive, the "sexual wilderness" of the United States makes sexual encounters most confusing and difficult for many youngsters. Single motherhood, disease and emotional consequences of sexual encounters are discussed.

Despite the "separation of church and state" doctrine and despite the freedom of or from religion enjoyed by Americans, religion still has a powerful influence on young and old. This influence cannot be overlooked if we want to understand American adolescents and particularly those who belong to minority religious communities.

More powerful than religion in the lives of the young is the entertainment industry. Consuming millions of dollars, that industry also spends an inordinate amount of the adolescent's time in the form of sports, electronic devices, magazines and music. The music is centered on the rock and roll, hippie, and punk subculture that first developed in the 1950s-1960s but is still very influential in shaping the tastes and opinions of the young.

A good part of the language used by young people is derived from the counter-culture, although the widespread failure to read, write and understand good English extends to all ages and social classes in America. Even the college educated are often deficient in the use of the language; great efforts have recently been made to reverse this trend.

Finally, we recognize that young Americans are very much influenced by the social class system endemic to American society. Students create a social class system of their own and some are unable to master the class-related demands of the public schools.

In sum, this book reveals the lives of American young people as they have been and as American society shapes them now.

Part I. From the Puritan Child to Millennial Youth

CHAPTER 1. THE YOUTH CULTURE FROM THE PURITANS TO THE MILLENNIALS

PURITAN CHILDHOOD

The history of childhood in the United States begins with the Puritan settlements in New England in the 17th century. The Puritan community, which had arrived in Massachusetts from England and the Netherlands in 1620, was settled on the assumption that they and their children would be "saved" because they had demonstrated an act of faith by coming to the wilderness that was North America.

Whatever the meaning of "saved" may be, the early Puritans believed that their children had strayed from the truth and were exhibiting conduct that was threatening the entire Puritan experiment here.[1]

An important Puritan concept was "grace." The reception of God's grace was believed to depend on a number of actions the Puritans took to insure this state for themselves and their children. They therefore built schools and colleges, demanded that families promote literacy and instituted apprenticeships for their older children, all designed to bring about the salvation of the young.[2]

The purpose of Puritan education was to create an adult infused with God's mercy and grace. This terminology may have no or little meaning to 21st-century Americans, but it was viewed as vital in the New England of the 17th

---

1. Michael Zuckerman, *Peaceable Kingdoms: New England Towns in the Eighteenth Century*, (New York: Vintage Books, 1972).
2. Edmund S. Morgan, *The Puritan Family*, (Westport, Con. Greenwood Press, 1980) :185.

century. Accordingly, those who applied to full membership in a seventeenth century Puritan congregation were asked to demonstrate they had successfully converted to the "true" religion. Believers were certain of their own damnation unless they became believers and rejected all "sin" by living according to God's commandments. Education therefore served the purpose of radically transforming a child into such a believing adult, capable of self analysis. Since Puritanism as a form of Calvinism taught that salvation is pre-destined, any effort on the part of man to attain salvation himself seemed useless. However, the American Puritans taught that man can at least prepare for his own salvation by means of the kind of education they fostered upon their children.[3]

The Puritans, like all cultures, sought to teach their children the ways of their society so that their children could function within that society. This process is called socialization by sociologists, and in the case of the Puritans, created "the civil man." The "civil man," according to Puritan norms, respected authority, obeyed the laws and accepted responsibility for his family. In addition, the Puritans also demanded that each child internalize the values of the Puritan community. Sociologists call this the enculturation process. The Puritans sought to develop in each child an inner compulsion to think, feel and act in ways acceptable in their culture. This process exists, of course, in all cultures.[4]

Adolescence did not exist in the 16th century, just as it still does not exist in many cultures around the world today. Instead the teens were viewed as a prelude to maturity, which they still are. However, farming was nearly the only occupation open to men and housework and child rearing the only occupation for women, and people could assume adult roles at a far younger age than is possible for those wishing to earn a livelihood in our high-tech culture today. We define adolescence as the time beginning with biological maturity and ending with economic independence. In 21st century America that is a period of about nine years. In 17th century New England and everywhere else such a period did not exist because those old enough to reproduce themselves were also old enough to work at lucrative employment.

As the 17th century progressed, the population of Massachusetts became larger and more heterogeneous than it had been in earlier years. Therefore, the

---

3. Howard M. Feinstein, "The Prepared Heart: A Comparative Study of Puritan Theology and Psychoanalysis," *American Quarterly*, 22, (Summer, 1970):168.
4. Frederick Elkin, *The Child and Society: The Process of Socialization*, (New York: Random House, 1960) p.4.

earlier consensus concerning the education of children was no longer supported by everyone in the community. In fact, a good deal of the Puritan culture came under scrutiny at the end of the 1600s, leading to the Great Awakening at the end of the century.

The Great Awakening consisted of a number of revival meetings all over the United States, including New England and the other states. This revival movement was induced by the publication of Isaac Newton's *Principia Mathematica*, which challenged established beliefs despite the preoccupation of Newton with Christianity. This book by Newton laid down a mechanistic interpretation of the universe. This meant that human beings have some ability to discover the secrets of the universe and are therefore capable of controlling their own destiny. This view, although promoted by the pious Newton, corroded the established Puritan orthodoxy, which held that one's destiny was predetermined by God and could not be altered. Consequently, religion itself became more rational and less emotional. All this threatened the Puritan dominance of New England even as it also threatened religion in other parts of the country. Hence, the Great Awakening sought to reverse this trend even as the rate of children born illegitimately increased, as did other signs of "moral corruption." More important was the introduction of the idea that the individual could actively seek salvation. That was certainly a direct challenge to the Calvinist doctrine of predestination.[5]

At least one outcome of these huge social movements was the introduction of dissent from established truths. Greater emphasis was now also placed on education, with the evident result that the educated began to challenge belief. One such belief was the Puritan theology, which focused entirely on what God had done for man by insuring his salvation in the next world and his livelihood in this one. Now, education led to the view that the responsibility for salvation is man's and not only God's. Consequently, the theocracy of New England and other states dissolved as democracy made religion accessible to all people and not only to the "elect" few. Religious consensus failed as well, as the "New Lights" or revivalists sought to adapt religion to changing times and circumstances while the "Old Lights" sought to hang on to the old order. In sum, all this meant that the "younger generation" had defied the older generation while using these religious developments as a vehicle for this defiance. Such defiance was

---

5. Marshall W. Fishwick, *Great Awakenings: popular religion and popular culture,"* (New York: Haworth Press, 1995).

similar to the rock and roll music or the "60s revolution" that defied the rigidity of the 1950s. Likewise, marijuana is the signal for joining the youth culture of the early 21st century.

Despite the gradual development of a distance between the Puritan ideal child and the real child, the 18th century still viewed American children as miniature adults and treated them as such. This may be seen by the clothes worn by children in those centuries. Their clothes resembled those of adults. As the historian Kiefer writes: "as children of Colonial times were expected to behave like adults, they quite logically wore clothes appropriate for the role."[6]

John Demos, an astute student of Puritan life, has written: "Colonial society barely recognized childhood as we know and understand it today."[7]

There are those who deny that the Puritans of the 17th century viewed their children as "miniature adults." The historian Ross W. Beales disputes this notion and holds that even in colonial America adolescence was recognized, even if not labeled as such, and that the Puritans recognized "the four ages of man," including the young adult.[8]

There may be continuous dispute concerning the position of youths in early America. Since all colonies were not the same in ethnic origin, religion and occupation, nothing much can be said about all colonial Americans.

There are, however, some writings dating to the 18th century that depict children of that day as corrupt and unmanageable, a complaint as old as the age of Socrates. The historian David Stannard quotes a French writer, Guy Miege, who commented in 1707: "the indulgence of mothers is excessive which proves often fatal to their children ... and which contributes much to the corruption of the age" and went on to say that children "at last grow unmanageable."[9]

Miege evidently did not include the Puritan child in his observations. According to Puritan doctrine as exemplified by the writing of John Robinson in 1628, "there is in all children...a stubbornness and stoutness arising from natural pride...which must be broken and beaten down." There can be little doubt that Robinson meant that literally. Evidently, some Puritans viewed their children as

---

6. Monica Kiefer, *American Children Through Their Books, 1700-1835*, (Philadelphia, The University of Pennsylvania Press, 1948)pp. 1, 94, 225.

7. John Demos, "The American Family in Past Time," *American Scholar*, 63, (1974):428.

8. Ross W. Beales, Jr., "In Search of the Historical Child: Miniature Adulthood and Youth in Colonial New England," *American Quarterly*, 27, No.4, (October 1875):379-398.

9. David E. Stannard, "Death and the Puritan Child," *American Quarterly*, 26, no. 5, (December 1974):456-476.

depraved and damnable creatures. These Puritans thought that their children would "go astray as soon as they are born" and that therefore one cannot begin religious instruction too soon. Emphasizing the wickedness of children, the Puritan Benjamin Wadsworth wrote that "their hearts naturally are a nest, root, fountain of sin and wickedness."[10]

The writings of Robinson and Wadsworth are of course not the only diaries and letters still in existence since the 17th century. There are others that seem to disagree with Robinson's and Wadsworth's assessment of children. One of these is the diary of Samuel Sewall, which many historians have viewed as "an unparalleled window of late seventeenth and early 18th century Boston." It must be emphasized that this diary represents a time in the Puritan experience when more and more people had immigrated to the Massachusetts Bay Colony who were not Puritans.

According to the historian Judith Graham, who tested the commonly accepted view that the Puritans lived a "joyless, repressive and even brutal" family life, the Sewall diary reveals no such trend. Instead, Graham finds that Sewall had "a loving, mutually respectful relationship with his wife" and that "the Sewall daughters and sons were raised in a warm, moderate and 'open' household." Graham includes a discussion of Sewall's religious attitudes and his rejection of physical punishments. In short, Graham seeks to rebut the work of Phillip Aries, David Hunt and Lawrence Stone, whose work reflects European culture and was applied to New England by others.[11]

The Puritans expected children to be obnoxious and badly behaved. Because that which people believe is real in all cultures is real in its consequences, a generation gap was of course the anticipated and real consequence of these beliefs.

We recognize, therefore, that the youth culture and the generation gap are only in part the product of nature in that the young are by definition beginners on the road to membership in the adult community.

Because life expectancy has changed so much between the 17th and 21st centuries, not much of a youth culture was possible in the earlier years. The differences between the New England mortality in the 17th century and that same rate today may be understood by recognizing that 12% of all children born in 17th

---

10. Ibid. p. 461.
11. Judith S. Graham, *The Diary of Samuel Sewall*, (Boston: Northeastern University Press, 2000).

century New England died before they reached one year of age. Many young mothers also died in childbirth because infections killed them. Because of these early deaths the total life expectancy of the 17th century community appeared to be only about 40 years. However, an adult who had reached age 30 could expect to live to be fifty-nine years old even then. This is still quite distant from our expectation in the 21st century, when a male child who was born in 2003 can reasonably expect to live at least 75 years and a female child can expect to live 82 years.[12]

Because so many children died of the childhood diseases now commonly controlled by immunology, children were confronted with the fear of their own death throughout their childhood. In addition, the Puritans believed that failure of any member of the community to obey the numerous religious strictures they enjoyed would result in divine punishment for the whole community because they, the elect, were in a binding "covenant" with God. God's anger became visible to the Puritans in the form of comets, earthquakes, crop failures and other natural signs and events. Since children were viewed as "depraved and ungodly" they became the targets of God's wrath and therefore posed a real danger to the whole community. This belief in turn led parents to make every effort to "beat the devil out of him" and to keep children at a distance. The effort to place emotional distance between a child and adults was of course also motivated by the certainty that parents could expect to bury a number of their children.[13]

The Puritans were most insistent on modeling their lives on the Old Testament, and they tended to take literally many of the admonitions to children about the debt children owe their parents and the consequences of failing to be obedient to parental direction.

Max Weber, in his famous essay concerning the protestant ethic and the spirit of capitalism, writes that "it is important to note that the well-known bibliocracy of the Calvinists held the moral precepts of the Old Testament..., on the same level of esteem as the New." Weber goes on to say that the Proverbs and Psalms were the most read by the Puritans of the books of the Bible and that the contents of these books influenced the Puritan mind set and their emotional life more than anything else.[14]

---

12. Borna Brunner, Editor, *Time Almanac 2002*, (Boston: Information Please, 2002):119.
13. Stannard, *Death and the Puritan Child*, p. 467.
14. Max Weber, *Protestantische Ethik und der Geist des Kapitalismus* translated by Talcott Parsons as The Protestant Ethic and the Spirit of Capitalism, (New York: Scribner, 1958) p. 123.

There are numerous Proverbs bearing on child rearing, which may be viewed as having a direct influence on Puritan opinion. Among these is undoubtedly Proverb 10:4 which exemplifies the Puritan rejection of luxury and "conspicuous consumption" and the importance of the work ethic. "Lazy hands make a man poor, but diligent hands bring wealth" (Prov. 10:4). Another example is Proverb 1:7: "The fear of the Lord is the beginning of wisdom, but fools despise knowledge and discipline." Self control, another important Puritan virtue, is the subject of Proverb 25:11: "Like a city whose walls are broken down is a man who lacks self control."

Added to these admonitions is the 5th Commandment, which not only pre-scribes that children must honor their father and mother, but also promises a long life to those who do so.

Armed with this literature, and in the absence of any other reading material, the Puritan child was indeed impressed by these strictures, so that the kind of youth culture and generation gap known to us in the 21st century was inconceivable to the 17th century Puritans.

SOCIAL CHANGE AND THE 18th Century

As the 17th century passed into the 18th century the generations which had been born to the founders of the Massachusetts Bay Colony passed away and new generations were born and came from England and other parts of the world. These new generations were agents of social change, as all generations must be. It is of course understood that history does not present itself in distinct slices but in overlapping forces, so that change is not always and immediately visible to those who undergo it.

Sociologists have studied two and three generation families for some time and have been able to locate some of the changes which generations create. These studies usually concentrate on value gaps between the generations and often include immigrants, among whom such gaps are particularly visible.

The impact of immigration on the values of the host population is great. This is so because the new arrivals belong to groups who have experienced dif-ferent conditions than the native hosts. Furthermore, many immigrants come together with their families, often consisting of three generations. These genera-tions differ even among themselves in terms of their experiences and values and do not present a unified front to the natives. In fact, immigrant families can include babies and octogenarians. More changes come about as the immigrants marry natives and undergo both structural and functional assimilation.[15]

All of this impacted the Puritan communities in 18th century New England. In the early 17th century John Winthrop had led 20,000 Puritans from England to Massachusetts. One hundred years later, all the American colonies combined had 400,000 people, which soon became 2 million as Germans and others came to the US in greater and greater numbers. This meant that the Puritan view of the world was being challenged by people who had no connection to that life-style and who did not know the language in which it was being lived.

The challenge to the Puritan view came from English immigrants and from immigrants from other cultures. A look at the colonial population at the time of the American Revolution reveals that in 1776 the colonies had a population of 2,587,200. New England had a population of 654,100 at that time. More than 70%, or 461,400, of these New Englanders had come from England, 4000 were native Americans, 14,800 were African and all the others came from Northern Europe, i.e. Scotland, Ireland, Germany and numerous other European countries.[16]

At the beginning of the 21st century, it may seem that these countries of origin are so close and similar in culture that the new Americans who came from there must have felt a sense of community with one another. That, however, was not the case. Among the English themselves there were many subcultures caused by different religious beliefs. These subcultures led to a good deal of social insulation and endogamy because religion was much more important in the America of the 18th century than it is now. It is necessary to avoid judging the past by contemporary opinion and in this case it is important to recognize that the Puritan attitudes were threatened by these new immigrants, including those who had come from England. It is further necessary to recognize that all Africans were not the same and that this was also true of native Americans. Furthermore, some immigrants who had come to the United States in the 18th century could not speak English. In New York, Dutch and French were widely spoken.

As immigration into the US became a flood and an estimated 5 million came into the US between 1820 and 1860, no group could predominate, so that

---

15. David I. Kertzer, "Generations as a Sociological Problem," *Annual Review of Sociology,* 9, 1983):141.

16. US Bureau of the Census, *Colonial and pre-Federal Statistics,* Series Z I 132.

the Puritan influence declined considerably after having been continued here for more than a century.

Religious diversity also increased during the eighteenth century. In 1775, one year before the American Revolution and over 150 years since the landing of the Pilgrims, colonial America had become the home of numerous denominations, all of whom established houses of worship and schools designed to insure the survival of each religion. Not only were there numerous Protestant sects in America by the 18th century, but there were then two Jewish and 50 Catholic places of worship in the colonies.

In fact, by the 1730s an African culture had also evolved in the US In fact, by 1790 the Afro-American population reached nearly 20% of the US population, although it declined proportionately thereafter.

All of this agitated to undermine the uniformity once attained by the Puritans and therefore created differences of opinion concerning child rearing and the expectations of young people themselves.[17]

The British colonies in America were of course not only located in Puritan New England. There were also the Middle colonies and the Southern colonies, whose lives were quite different from those of Massachusetts, Connecticut and Rhode Island.

For example, Wolf analyzed the German families who had settled in Germantown, Pennsylvania at the end of the seventeenth century and found them to be a heterogeneous, very mobile and individualistic people. Unlike the Puritans of New England, the German-American settlers of Pennsylvania were opportunistic and interested in their private ambitions. Even patriarchal control was far less in Pennsylvania in the 18th century than was common in New England.[18]

The Southern colonies were even more distinct from New England than the Middle colonies. In seventeenth century Maryland and Virginia parents died young due to typhoid and other diseases. There were therefore many orphans and step-parents. Families were often held together by widows and sons, not daughters, achieved early autonomy, making their own marriage and career decisions.[19]

---

17. Vincent Parrillo, "Diversity in American: A Sociohistorical Analysis," (Sociological Forum 9, No. 4, 1994):526.
18. Stephanie Grauman Wolf, *Urnab Village: population, community and family structure in Germantown, Pennsylvania, 1683-1800*, (Princeton, N.J., Princeton University Press, 1976).
19. Lorena S. Walsh, "Now-wives and sons-in-law": parental death in a seventeenth-century Virginia county," in: Thad W. Tate, Editor, *The Chesapeake in the Seventeenth Century*, (Chapel Hill: The University of North Carolina Press, 1979) pp.153-182.

It is commonly believed that early American families had innumerable children. The reason for this belief is that there were indeed some men who had upward of fifteen children, with two or three wives as so many young mothers had died in childbirth. However, most early American families had no more than six or seven children (still a large family by the standards of 2005). Furthermore, it must be understood that there was not one kind of colonial family but that there were considerable regional differences in mortality and population growth rates in colonial America.

Historians have discovered that in Southern colonial families there was "an emphasis on parental indulgence, training for independence, and, especially for boys, freedom of movement beyond the plantation."[20]

There has been considerable controversy among historians concerning the role of girls and women in colonial America. Here, too, New England differed from the Middle colonies and the Southern colonies in the manner in which women were perceived. No doubt, Puritan women had little identity other than their nearest male relative, i.e. their fathers and husbands. While in New England women had little economic power, this was not true in other areas. Evidently, in the Middle colonies and the South, women performed important work such as working in the fields and almost always inherited their husbands' estates. Because so many men died young, widows held a good deal of property and also supervised their children's education.[21]

All of these arrangements, whether in the north or the south, underwent a most profound change after 1800, particularly in the northeast, where wage-earning men entered factories and wives assumed the almost exclusive position of household guardians. With the increasing ascendancy of mothers over absent, working fathers as child supervisors, child rearing became more emotional and more sentimental. The family therefore became more child centered. Furthermore, the American Revolution (1776-1783) had left many women alone while their husbands were fighting the war for independence. That meant that women were running businesses and farms and they gained access to, and responsibility for, the family finances. It meant that the rigid role distinctions

---

20. Philip J. Greven, *The protestant temperament: patterns of child rearing, religious experience, and the self in early America*, (New York: Alfred A. Knopf, 1977)p. 265.
21. Lois Green Carr and Lorena Walsh, "Planter's Wife," *William and Mary Quarterly*, 34, no.3, (1977):556-557.

between masculinity and femininity were becoming blurred; and contraception and divorce initiated by women were slowly developing, at the same time.[22]

When the Treaty of Paris led to the recognition of the United States of America as a new nation, the 18th century was coming to its end and the social changes the revolution precipitated were taking hold in the minds of men. The revolution promoted self-esteem in a whole generation of women, leading to the attainment of education and economic and public activities among women. This does not mean that all women suddenly left the domestic area of work and became students and working wives in the manner of 21st century Americans. In fact, the majority of women continued for years to follow in the footsteps of their mothers and grandmothers. This was particularly true of the northern states, including the erstwhile Puritan colonies. Nevertheless, in the middle states and in the south a good number of women attained freedom of choice in marriage and economic autonomy.[23]

In these families, "children became the center of indulgent attention," as modernization began to be felt in America while the "pre-modern" family was gradually coming to an end. There are of course no single dates in history on which one epoch ends and another begins. Therefore, even the authoritarian family continues to exist among some Americans even in the 21st century. Two examples are the ultra-orthodox Chasidic Jews of Brooklyn and their Christian counterparts, the Amish, the River Brethren and other sects mainly concentrated in Pennsylvania.[24]

Puritanical attitudes continued well into the 18th century. It appears, however, that Jacksonian America was dominated by Victorian virtues, not so much because of Puritan convictions but because numerous contradictory ideologies had gained adherents in the United States, so that dominant men feared the loss of their control over their families and particularly their children. It was this fear of loss of control that led to sexual repression during most of the 18th century.

It was during this time that the great American value cleavage first became visible. This is the struggle between American individualists and "tradition-

---

22. Mary Beth Norton, *Liberty's Daughters: The Revolutionary Experience of American Women,1750-1800*, (Boston: Little, Brown, 1980).
23. Daniel Blake Smith, *Inside the Great House: planter family life in eighteenth century Chesapeake society*, (Ithaca, N.Y. Cornell University Press, 1980):pp. 281-299.
24. Tamara K. Hareven, "Modernization and Family History: Perspectives on Social Change," *Signs: Journal of Women in Culture and Society*, 2, (1976):pp.190-206.

alists," a struggle that is by now emblematic of American culture. In the early and middle 19th century, as today, there were those who glorified individualism even as others sought to emphasize the traditional family and its patriarchy.

At the beginning of the 18th century, New England was still governed by a hierarchy. The family and the church dominated that world and controlled everything. The family was then still the agent of production and was also responsible for training young people in every occupation from farmer to doctor or businessman.[25]

Nevertheless, the early 18th century saw considerable changes in America. The population of the country grew from 0.25 million in 1700 to 8.5 million in 1815. This led to the growth of American manufacturing. Furthermore, many sons never inherited their fathers' farms because the farms went to the oldest son, leaving younger sons to move West or to enter occupations other than farming. Therefore, more and more young men lived outside the family and outside the control of small communities.[26]

That loss of control was underscored by the rootlessness and increasing violence of many of the unskilled and unpropertied young men who were now loose from their families and communities. This led some to indeed become as "loose" as others imagined them to be. Yet, public perception, then and now, always exaggerated and now exaggerates the danger reputedly deriving from such young men. Jacksonian Americans (1832-1840) imagined dangerous young men drinking heavily, engaging in ferocious sexual escapades, seducing young women, and fighting hostile animals and a hostile Western environment. All this made culture heroes of these men and created the myth of the Western frontiersman as the paragon of independence and American freedom. Hence adolescence was born.

At the end of the 18th century and the beginning of the 19th century the movement of women into wage-earning occupations led to mobility and autonomy in the mill towns of New England. Now women and girls were beginning to taste freedom as well. Some young women and boys became partial supporters of their families with the money they earned in factories and mills and thereby altered the status of adolescents and children, particularly as the lifespan of the New England population increased.

25. Philip Greven, "Historical Demography and Colonial America," *William and Mary Quarterly*, 23, (April, 1966): 234-256.
26. James Henretta, "Families and Farms: Mentality in Pre-Industrial America," *William and Mary Quarterly*, 35, (January 1978):23-31.

The changes in attitudes toward children were grounded in the influential work of John Locke, who published *Some Thoughts Concerning Education* in 1693. By 1740 this book and his *Essay on Human Understanding* had become the foundation of educational thinking in England and America. Locke argued that parents should develop in their children the ability to reason by influencing children to practice self-denial and suppress the passions as well as the imagination. Locke thought that learning should be based on these principles but that it should also be a pleasant experience and could even be disguised as play.[27]

The 18th century also saw the production of numerous medical treatises aimed mostly at fathers, but sometimes also at mothers, which promoted the use of reason in child rearing. Works of this kind were located in the library of the Pennsylvania Hospital and other places and became important sources of conduct towards children.

Benjamin Rush, who was known as the foremost physician in 18th century America and who was also a signer of the Declaration of Independence, was concerned with the education of children. He related the education of children to republican principles. Included in his principles of education was the teaching of Christianity to all children, which Rush thought would lead to "virtue and restraint," which he deemed essential for the survival of liberty.[28]

Rush also advocated female education. Today, when 61% of college students are women, this may seem quaint. However, in the late eighteenth century, female education was almost unknown. He did not see such education as leading to the independence of women in the work force but rather as a means by which mothers could have a positive influence on the education of their boys. Rush included the Christian religion in his proposed curriculum. He also drew up rules for his proposed schools which were mainly concerned with learning reading, writing and arithmetic but not much more.[29]

These early schools were not compulsory. They were imitations of English schools and were the beginning of universal child schooling in America. Eventually, in the nineteenth century, schools became youth ghettos and now share

---

27. Lawrence Stone, *The Family, Sex and Marriage in England, 1500-1800* (New York: Harper, Row, 1977).
28. Benjamin Rush, "A Plan for the Establishment of Public Schools and the Diffusion of Knowledge in Pennsylvania," in Frederick Rudolph, Editor, *Essays on Education in the Early Republic,* (Cambridge, Mass. Harvard University Press, 1965) p.10.
29. David Freeman Hawke, *Benjamin Rush: revolutionary gadfly,* (Indianapolis: Bobbs-Merrill, 1971)p.359.

in the production of the "independent" adolescents so commonly seen in all American communities.

Since the 16th century, Puritan schools had concentrated mostly on Bible reading and were not that much interested in teaching children writing. Of course, not all children went to schools in 16th century New England because fathers were encouraged to teach their children at home. This changed somewhat in the 19th century because by then a good number of fathers were working outside the home and Puritanism was in any event on the decline in America. Therefore, mothers were now entrusted with the task of teaching children at home.[30] The end of the 18th century also saw secularization, leading to changes in religious and moral authority within the family and the general community. This came about mainly because of the influence of the French *philosophes* on American values and opinion. Thomas Jefferson (1743-1826), the third president of the United States, had lived in France as had Benjamin Franklin (1706-1790). Both men were greatly influenced by the writings of the Swiss philosopher Jean-Jacques Rousseau (1712-1778), who was, without question, one of the most prominent forerunners of the French Revolution and, in particular, secularization. He was of course not the only writer favoring a secular rather than theocratic community. By the end of the 18th century, secularization theory had a long history including the writings of the most ancient Greek and Latin authors such as Epicurus (343 B.C.E. – 271 B.C.E.) and Lucretius (99 B.C.E. - 55 B.C.E.), whose works had been revived and translated into modern European languages by the secularists of the eighteenth century. Moreover, the 18th century saw the publication of books by Fontenelle, Montesquieu, Voltaire, Condillac, Diderot, Morelly, Mably and others. All of these French writers promoted a secular point of view which became the focus of American political leaders and authors. Montesquieu was particularly influential in this country, as his book The Spirit of the Laws led to the development of the tri-partite American government with its built in checks and balances. Of course, secularization of American life was not only attained by developments in literature and philosophy. The scientific revolution begun in the 17th century by such men as Galileo, Bacon and Kepler caused men to question the assumptions of religion and the repression it had imposed upon the family and its child rearing practices. Together with the diffusion of science came the ever-increasing interest in education and its consequences.

---

30. Ann Louise Kuhn, *The mother's role in childhood education,* (New Haven: Yale University Press, 1947).

These consisted at the very least of questioning all erstwhile Puritan assumptions and led to that great revolution which gave women and children more rights and more power than they had ever seen before at any time or in any place.[31]

Of course, the vast majority of Americans did not then read French philosophy any more than they do today. However, the leading politicians of the day did so and they were the men who had the greatest influence on the direction the United States took with the establishment of the government in 1789.

The 19th century saw a number of changes in the education and status of children in American society. These changes were the consequence of a growing secularization of America in the 1800s. Therefore, secular reasons were advanced for the education of children after the Great Awakening had destroyed religious unity in the US and secularization was gradually laying hold to the minds of men.

In the 19th century, urbanization, industrialization and immigration led to the abandonment of Puritan principles and the creation of publicly funded schools, particularly in Massachusetts. There, and in other states, the state sponsored schools for those children who could already read and write. This meant that children who could not do so because their poor parents could not send them to a private school to learn reading and writing were not eligible to be schooled in a public facility. Yet, by 1818 the City of Boston had assumed responsibility for educating children aged four to six and home education was gradually dwindling in number and importance. One room schools now became the vogue in this country because such schools were cheaper than larger, graded schools as is the general rule now. Private education was beginning to decline in numbers of children in attendance. Meanwhile public schools were increasing their enrollment, including the enrollment of very young children. [32]

Nineteenth-century education in America was also greatly influenced by the writings of the Swiss writer Johann Heinrich Pestalozzi. He sought to implement the ideas of his countryman Jean Jacques Rousseau and stressed the importance of the physical development of the child. This led to an under-

---

31. Gerhard Falk, *Man's Ascent to Reason,* (Lewiston, N.Y. The Edwin Mellen Press, 2003) p. 245.

32. Dean May and Maris A. Vinovskis, "A ray of millennial light: early education and social reform in the infant school movement in Massachusetts, 1826-1840" in *Family and Kin in American Urban Communities, 1800-1940,* Tamara K. Hareven, (New York, Watts and Co., 1976).

standing of the more gradual development of children and militated against the schooling of very young children as had been practiced in the early part of the nineteenth century. Thereafter, age six became the age at which most every school would accept children, although parents had often sought to send their children to school at a younger age because they wanted to use the schools as a baby sitter or child custodian. [33]

The need to send children to school early increased as more and more fathers and mothers worked outside the home after the Civil War (1861-1865). Then mass immigration to the United States forced many women to go to work in domestic or factory employment and made the newly developed kindergarten movement popular. The idea of the kindergarten came from the German educator Friedrich Froebel, who had spent several years with Pestalozzi at the Pestalozzi school in Yverdon, Switzerland. These schools began in America only among the German speaking immigrants but became popular after 1860 when Elizabeth Peabody established the first English speaking kindergarten.[34]

Although the kindergarten became a permanent feature of American education, it contributed far less to the youth culture emerging at the end of the 19th century than the two forces which shaped school enrollment of older children, i.e. those 14-18.

These two forces may be identified as the rural Protestant beliefs concerning the value of education and the social factors associated with industrialization and urbanization at the end of the 19th century, i.e., after 1870.

In 1870 only 2% of young Americans graduated from a secondary school. There were then only 160 high schools in the US. By 1890, 74% of all American children ten to fourteen years old attended grammar school. But schooling past the age of fourteen continued to be unusual. Yet, by the end of the century there were over 6,000 high schools in America. Twenty years later, in 1920, 16% of high school age children obtained a diploma although there were then still 190,000 one room school houses in operation in the country.[35]

33. Will S. Monroe, *History of the Pestalozzi Movement in the United States*, (Syracuse, N.Y., C. W. Bardeen, 1907).
34. Ruth M. Baylor, *Elizabeth Palmer Peabody: Kindergarten Pioneer*, (Philadelphia: University of Pennsylvania Press, 1965).
35. United States Department of Commerce, *Historical Statistics of the United States, Colonial Times to 1970*, (Washington D.C., United States Government Printing Office, 1975).

THE 20TH CENTURY EDUCATION EXPLOSION AND THE GENERATION GAP

The two forces which we have said influenced the growth of education, schooling and therefore the youth culture in America were cultural beliefs and industrialization. This may be seen by the speed with which schooling grew even before the Civil War while urbanization was only advancing gradually. For example, in 1860 only 20% of Americans lived in cities with populations over 2,500 although school enrollment was already quite high. The reason for this educational growth was the belief in individual achievement coupled with the view that children should be taught moral values, discipline and thrift.[36]

At the beginning of the 20th century an additional belief fostered the ever increasing attendance at school. That was the belief that there is a distinction between childhood and "Youth," a distinction that did not theretofore exist. As life spans increased and more time could be allotted to education, more and more Americans sent their children to school even before industrialization and urbanization made that mandatory. Nevertheless, the growth of cities and the increase in industrial labor contributed immensely to the invention of the youth culture and the development of the youth ghetto known as the school.

Looking back at the 18th century, we note that in 1790 only 5% of the American population lived in cities. In 1850 this had increased to 15% and then jumped to 40% by 1900 and 51% by 1920.[37]

By 1900 this great growth in urbanization and its re-definition of youth had led to the creation of the first juvenile court in Chicago subsequent to the Illinois Juvenile Court Act of 1899. Similar legislation spread throughout the country. Nothing demonstrates more dramatically the arrival of the youth culture than these developments.[38]

The increase in school enrollment was also fostered by the increased need to specialize and learn skills needed to fill new and more complex jobs than were available in a rural society. This was particularly true of the growth of "white

---

36. David B. Tyack, "Ways of seeing: an essay on the history of compulsory schooling," *Harvard Education Review*, (46): 355-396.

37. Frank J. Coppa and Philip C. Doles, *Cities in Transition*, (Chicago: Nelson Hall, 1974) p. 220.

38. Larry J. Siegel, Brandon C. Welsh and Joseph J. Senna, *Juvenile Delinquency*, (Belmont, Ca., Wadsworth/Thomson, 2003)

collar" occupations including the professions. This led to an increase in creden-tialing or "diploma chasing."[39]

Therefore, diplomas of all kinds became barriers to job entry and that also contributed to the rise in school enrollment at the end of the nineteenth and beginning of the 20th century.

Despite the growth in schooling the vast majority of school-aged adoles-cents did not go to school but worked at anything they could find. This was par-ticularly true of the industrialized northeast.

At the end of the 19th century the status of parents and grandparents still determined much of the schooling and economic opportunities of children and grandchildren. However, the 20th century saw great social changes which led to alterations in the transmission of socioeconomic status between the generations and usually permitted the rise of succeeding generations in the status hierarchy of American society.

The change in values from one generation to the next is called "the gener-ation gap." This involves not only education, occupation and preferences for lines of action, but also family size, the statusVietnam of women, the secular-ization of American society and the enhancement of minorities in the American social scheme. The latter may be called "expanded universalism" which, together with new child rearing values, from obedience to autonomy, became a function of alternative family structures and changing gender roles.[40]

During the 20th century the effect of the status of parents on their children's occupational outcome declined in each successive generation. A gen-eration is any birth cohort at a 20 year interval.

The sociologist Sobel found that grandparents born between 1896 and 1911 generally inherited their parents' socioeconomic position. This was true because those born in those years entered into farming, as had 85% of all Americans for generations. During the 20th century, however, farming declined considerably while the proportion of professional, technical, administrative and clerical occu-pations increased. Greater equality of opportunity existed after 1960 because the last forty years of the 20th century have made more non-manual jobs available.[41]

39. Burton Bledstein, *The culture of professionalism: the middle class and the development of higher education in America*, New York: Norton Publishing, 1976).

40. Vern L. Bengtson, "Generation and family effects in values socialization," *American Sociological Review*, (40, 1975):358-371.

41. M. E. Sobel, "Structural mobility, circulation mobility and the analysis of occupational mobility: a conceptual mismatch," *American Sociological Review*, (48, 1983):721-727.

Because of the rise in opportunity and because of the decline in the birth rate, child rearing practices in the United States have changed from a demand for obedience to autonomy and independence of children. This became particularly accentuated as more and more middle-class children left the parental home for college and then never returned. The high rate of divorce also contributed to the change in child rearing practices in this country. This has resulted in a large number of female headed families and in families involving stepmothers and stepfathers. Therefore the old paternalistic control model of the family could not be maintained, leading to the substitution of the youth culture for the authority of the family. Parental discord undoubtedly makes children's mobility out of the family more likely.

Furthermore, the Great Depression of the 1930s undermined paternal authority because men who could not support their families lost prestige within the family; women were more often able to find work than men because they were willing to work for less money, and had traditionally worked in occupations men would not consider. Working women and unemployed men created a role reversal in the family which broke down many paternalistic stereotypes.

The 1960s were a unique epoch in American history. The Sixties were the years of the Vietnam war and the civil rights movement and also saw the beginning of the women's liberation effort. These three "movements" demanded the overhaul of the entire American social system. This did not occur. Instead, in the latter part of the century the radical efforts of the Sixties were modified to alter the existing social institutions to fit the values of the '80s and 90s without throwing out all the achievements of the American past.

All of these events, i.e., universal public education, the Depression, the Second World War, the Korean and Vietnam wars, the revolt of the Sixties and the high divorce rate contributed to the development of the generation gap which now exists in American families.

The generation gap is ubiquitous; it exists in all American social classes, ethnic groups, income levels, regions and occupations. The reason for this is the invention of adolescence at the beginning of the 20th century and its continuing influence to the beginning of the 21st century. The adolescent experience guarantees the generation gap.

One means of investigating the generation gap is to look at college students. College students are in their late-adolescence and experience a considerable amount of change in their lives as they leave the parental home and suddenly face a great diversity of people they never saw before.

The psychologists Brooke Jacobsen, Kenneth Berry and Keith Olson conducted a study of the generation gap as it affected their students at Colorado State University. This study was conducted in 1971 and therefore affected students born in the 1950s.

The researchers asked students to assess four social issues then receiving widespread attention and subject to considerable disagreement between the generations. These issues were: sexual behavior; economic problems; social problems and political problems.

Disagreement between the generations at that time centered mainly on abortion, inflation and drug use. Disagreement between the generations of these issues became more pronounced as education proceeded so that seniors were far more likely to disagree with their parents on these and other issues than was true of freshmen. Nevertheless, there is a pronounced value agreement between the generations despite disagreement on specific issues.

Gender also influences agreement or disagreement between the generations of various issues. Daughters are more likely to agree and sons more likely to disagree with parents concerning abortion, sexual morality, inflation, pollution, drug use, campus life, war and segregation. Disagreement concerning these issues is particularly pronounced between fathers with only a high school education and holding blue collar jobs and their college educated sons. Evidently, college students with working class origins experience a greater amount of social change than college students with a middle-class background. The researchers in this study also found that fathers with advanced education who disagreed with their children on the issues here discussed were usually professionals who had always adhered to strict standards of ethics concerning their patients or clients and who would not therefore subscribe to the "new" morality of the 1960s.[42]

Age Stratification

In the United States, both in the past and at present, there has always existed a system of age stratification which resembles social stratification based on economic condition. This is true because members of various age strata have differential access to rewards and status-roles. The young, the middle-aged and

---

42. R. Brooke Jacobsen, Kenneth H. Berry, Keith F. Olson, "An Empirical Test of the Generation Gap: A Comparative Intrafamily Study," *Journal of Marriage and the Family*, (37, no. 4 November 1975): 841-852.

the old clearly do not have the same opportunities in the job market, while in the family parents have more power than their children.

Unlike economic stratification, which usually locates individuals in one strata for life and which seldom allows any one person to move through all of the economic strata available in his own lifetime, age mobility is universal. This means that with the increase in longevity more and more Americans live through more life strata than ever before.

It is also noteworthy that the size of the American household has shrunk over the years. In 1870 a family or household contained an average of 5.1 persons. In 1973 this had shrunk to 3 and has remained there for the past thirty years. The proportion of large households was also higher in the 19th century than in the 20th. In 1901 more than 20% of American households contained seven or more persons. After 1973, only 4% of American households were that large. In the 19th century marriage was attained rather late. Furthermore, many recently married people were unable to establish their own home right away. Therefore, about 20% of people in their late teens and early twenties lived in their parental home in the 19th century. Today only 10% of that age group live with their parents.[43]

This widespread emancipation also contributes to the generation gap so evident in the US of the 20th century. At the beginning of the 21st century American assumptions and values have changed. This has come about as life expectancy has increased and, with the exception of a minority who die young, letting everyone move through all ages of man from infancy to old age. Since age changes all individuals and alters the roles all men play at different ages, some distinctive attitudes and behaviors may be related to the aging process. No doubt each cohort resemble one another in role playing and behavior, as aging is a dynamic phenomenon.

As people proceed through the stages of age, they are either upwardly or downwardly mobile. Therefore. it is possible to receive greater or lesser rewards as age progresses. In the US this usually, but not always, follows a curve. There is increasing reward in middle age compared to the young and a decline in power, prestige and income in old age.[44]

The age structure changes constantly as one cohort is replaced by another. Therefore, no cohort ages in exactly the same way. Surely those who became

---

43. US Bureau of the Census, *Current Population Reports,* (Washington, D.C., The United States Government Printing Office, 1979) p. 43.
44. Joan M. Waring, "Social Replenishment and Social Change: The Problem of Disordered Cohort Flow," *American Behavioral Scientist,* (19, November 1975):237-256.

adults in the depression had quite different experiences than those who became adults in the 1950s or those who reached adult life at the turn of the century.

We have now seen that the youth culture and the generation gap are the product of value changes which have altered American life immensely during the century just past. In the 16th century it was assumed that all men lived in a predictable universe presided over by a benevolent God and governed by immutable natural laws. This in turn led to the view that in human affairs all things were either right or wrong, good or evil, civilized or savage. Sex, in particular, was regarded with suspicion and religious conformity was an aspiration of Europeans and Americans alike.

The early 20th century saw major changes in these attitudes. These changes came first from the physical sciences. Until then, Newton's mechanics were regarded as the final explanation and description of the universe. Then, Albert Einstein showed that time and space were elements on the same continuum and were not distinct entities. Together with developments in the sciences and arts, modernists denounced religion and all certainties and sought to free men from Victorian proprieties.

Numerous other changes also led to the generation gap now so evident in American life.

First, there is the increase in longevity. This has created two generation gaps in that the "middle aged" are distinct from the "old" even as their children, now in their twenties, regard the "middle aged" as antiquated. All this came about because of medical advances, including antibiotics, more precise operation procedures and better aftercare. As a result, the average life expectancy in the United States has increased to 75 for men and 82 for women. This means that Americans now live 30 years longer than was true one hundred years ago.

In view of these developments the US population is becoming older and older even as the number of children born each year has declined from about 4 million annually to only 3.9 million in 2002.

Third, more women than ever are now employed. Of the 135 million employed adults in the United States, 47%, or 63 million, are women. This means that a large number of children are "on their own" after school and subject to the youth culture, as we shall see.[45]

The kind of work available has changed dramatically over the past half century. Farming is conducted by only 5 million, or 1.8 % of the American popu-

---

45. Borgna Brunner, *Time Almanac 2000*, (Boston, Mass. Information Please, 2001)p.345.

lation, and even industrial labor is now shrinking rapidly. Instead service types of occupations have grown immensely, so that two thirds of all employees are engaged in service work.

All these changes militate in favor of a youth culture and a generation gap separating the young from the adult middle aged world and more and more independent of the generation preceding them. Age peers become more and more significant in such circumstances, as we shall see in the next chapter.

Summary

The Puritan view of childhood was greatly influenced by beliefs in predestination and Biblical admonitions. Adolescence was not understood. As the 18th century progressed, numerous non-Puritan immigrants challenged these beliefs. Immigration, religious diversity, the rise of Newtonian physics, the growth of industry and the loss of paternal control over the family all contributed to the gradual development of the youth culture in America. These forces were augmented by the influence of secularization and the promotion of the public school. As adult female employment grew the school became a youth ghetto reaching into the college years. This led to the employment of young people outside the home even as farming became the rarest occupation in America. The young therefore earned money and asserted the power that money provides into developments that are commonplace in Western culture generally. The next chapter will deal with these developments.

CHAPTER 2. THE COMPETING INFLUENCE OF PARENTS AND PEERS

TWO VIEWS

There has been a longstanding dispute between those social scientists who believe that the "youth culture" has so overwhelmed the young that they are unwilling to be influenced by parents and other adults and listen only to their peers and those who believe that parents are still the primary influence upon their children.

This dispute is half a century old. The reason for this ongoing dispute lies in the effort of investigators to discover whether one group, parents, or the other group, peers, is the source of influence to the exclusion of the other. It is our contention that such an approach must fail because the extent of influence from peers and adults depends on the issues involved.

There are of course children who are so wedded to the youth culture that they take all their cues only from other youngsters. We will see why this occurs. In the context of this study we will demonstrate that these influences vary and that the same adolescent who is interested in the opinions of his peers today may well conduct his life according to the views of the adults in his life tomorrow.

The pressures that drive adolescent conduct depend on the content of the behavior considered, so that drinking alcohol may well be produced by peer pressures while at the same time school achievement may be related to the wish to find approval among adults.[46]

---

46. L.S. Anderson, T.G. Chirisos and G.P. Waldo, "Formal and Informal Sanctions: A Comparison of Deterrent Effects," *Social Problems* 25 (1977):103-14.

"Pressure" can have more than one meaning. It can mean that the sources of the "pressure" are those who can apply sanctions or punishments if their views are not obeyed. Another view holds that "pressure" to conform to any reference group comes about because the adolescent (or anyone) has internalized the demands of significant others. Internalization of such "pressure" is achieved by socializing a child into accepting the norms of his culture.

> Linda is the middle child of a family of three girls. The oldest, Sabina, is an attractive, very bright teenager who has always excelled in school. The youngest, Diane, or "Deedee," is a beautiful blue eyed vixen who charms everyone who meets her. She is her father's favorite and she can do no wrong. Linda, although she is of slight stature with curly light brown hair, considers herself the thorn in the rosebush. As a young child she was always very helpful, clung to her mother for solace and struggled with schoolwork. She had difficulty competing with her siblings and made up for her perceived lack by being very accommodating and being there when she was needed to do tasks that the others did not want to do. For this she received praise from her mother. The mother spent as much time with this child as she could in spite of her very hectic and consuming profession. Linda received a great deal of negative attention because of her poor grades in school, and the chasm between the sisters and this youngster became deeper as she grew older. Much time and money was spent in getting tutors for her, and her father's attention centered around her lack of knowledge and her poor grades. He would frequently laugh and ridicule her when he was not chastising her for what he considered her lack of effort. (Incidentally, this child was of normal intelligence, as measured by standard IQ tests). It appeared that studying was not a part of Linda's interest. She was a people pleaser who made friends readily. She was easily exploitable and was taken advantage of by her peers. At home as she got older, Linda would frequently retreat into her bedroom where she would sleep for hours. This was her retreat from what she felt to be a difficult position. She obviously considered herself a "lesser" person than those of the others in her family. For her retreats she was chastised, especially since her room looked like a war zone. Clothing were dropped on the floor and lay in bundles everywhere including under the bed; food particles decorated the sheets and her bed was always unmade with rumpled sheets gracing the mattress. A mixture of cheap perfume and decayed food was a familiar odor in this unpalatable cocoon. The only time this haven was superficially cleaned was when the teen was repeatedly badgered by her frantic mother. With a great deal of persuasion, Linda obtained a part time job as cashier in a small grocery store not far from her home. She managed this position remarkably well and was promoted to the office to balance the books and do some fairly complicated and very responsible tasks for that business. It proved to her that she was competent and could achieve. She spent her money freely and was motivated because of the pleasure the income brought her. Linda did graduate from high school but did not attend the graduation ceremony. Since she did not receive any public

honors, she had the feeling that her parents would be disappointed since her older sister had been lauded and admired when she graduated two years previously with honors. Linda did enter college and performed fairly well. She turned to her peers for solace. The girls who became her friends were heavily engaged in the alcohol and marijuana culture. Although Linda did not drink at home, it did not take long before Linda followed suit and joined this group of peers, indulging herself and "having fun" belonging. Being "caught" by her mother only reinforced her anger and distanced her even more from her family. The alienation from them involved leaving town to take on a menial job, accompanied by others who also escaped from parental guidance and perceived criticism.

Margaretta was a child born to a wealthy Protestant American family of old English descent. She was born into "old money"; her grandfather was an aristocratic gentleman whose financial and business interests were on top of his list together with the retention of his good name and that of his two adult offspring. His older son, a very mannerly gentleman, was the father of young Margaretta. This child was properly brought up by her mother and a nanny and was always surrounded by attention. She had an exquisite wardrobe, every imaginable toy and others of her status as playmates. Every activity in her life was scheduled and structured. There was play time, tutorial time, classes in an exclusive private school and always lessons in etiquette. Her upbringing and her role models were expected to create a refined desirable human being, taught to bring pride and honor to herself and her people. As an older teen Margaretta looked outside of what she considered her gilded cage. In her travels she met some youngsters who seemed very interesting and enticing. They seemed to be "natural," and to have fun. They seemed to be free spirits without the fetters of affected behavior; loose revealing garments; hair that was multi-colored, without the restriction that she had been experiencing. She somehow disappeared and joined this group of rebels. Her frantic parents searched endlessly for her, to no avail. They believed her to have been kidnapped and were beside themselves with grief and fear. In the interim Retta had joined the LIBERATED, a group of street "kids" much older than Margaretta. These individuals took her in and trained her in their ways. Like these individuals, she began to steal and engage in innumerable lawless behaviors. She felt love from this gang of hoodlums and assisted them in enriching themselves at the expense of some wealthy people with whose ways she was familiar. This gang exploited Margaretta in any number of ways. Her knowledge of when and where to rob her erstwhile circle led to a round of break ins and other crimes. Retta had found a perverted joy and satisfaction in feeling accomplished and being a leader and a "needed" one for a pack of criminals that seemed to appreciate her and allowed her the unfettered freedom that had heinous unforeseen consequences for its victims. As an adult, many years later, the woman Margaretta did not have to face the same fate that would have been rightfully hers because her very wealthy family interceded in her behalf, although the stigma of this situation could never be erased.

A "norm" is an expectation which any group has of its members. When such norms are not met and one or more members reject the norms of their erstwhile reference group and seek out a new and different reference group then the result is norm conflict. This development leads to an emotional gap between the group and its erstwhile member. This is what has happened countless times in the US in the 20th and 21st centuries. [47]

Because human life is complex and there are innumerable issues with which all men must deal, the young as well as the middle aged and old have to make decisions concerning the manner in which they want to respond to their needs, their drives and their expectations.

Issues which particularly influence the relationships between parents and their children and at the same time influence peer relationships range from sex to economic behavior and school achievement to alcohol and drug use. It is therefore necessary to investigate a number of issues if we are to explain the youth culture and the generation gap.

The social psychologists Bruce J. Biddle, Barbara J. Bank and Marjorie M. Martin studied these issues in the 1980s. Their analysis concluded that "any discrepancy between parental and peer pressure is likely to pose problems for the adolescent." They further found that peer behavior is more likely to affect the adolescent than parental behavior while parental norms are more likely to affect adolescents than peer norms. This discrepancy is explained by suggesting that parents have had much more time in which to promote norms or standards for their children than peers have. Peers can therefore influence immediate conduct but have difficulty imposing standards or norms of a wide ranging kind. This means that what parents say is more important than what they do. Such a finding runs counter to public opinion but is well supported by the research of Biddle et al. [48]

These researchers also found that adolescent drinking behavior is less affected by either parental or peer pressure than is school achievement. This may be caused by the lesser opportunity of both peers and parents to observe drinking than school achievement. Furthermore, parents are more likely to pressure children concerning their school achievement than their drinking of alcohol.

---

47. Robert J. Brym and John Lie, *Sociology: A compass for a New World,* (New York: Wadsworth, 2003)p.495.
48. Bruce J. Biddle, Barbara J. Bank and Marjorie M. Marlin, "Parental and Peer Influence on Adolescents," *Social Forces,* 58, no.4 (June 1980): 1072. 65 no.1

The conduct of adolescents is much more subject to the consequences of such behavior than to norms or general expectations in American culture. This is significant and demonstrates that norms are and have been quite weak and very confusing since the 1970s in the United States. We have already seen that in earlier centuries Americans were able to live their lives according to universally accepted norms first introduced by the Puritan communities of 17th century New England. We further described how these norms were challenged and eventually abandoned so that since the middle of the 20th century anomie is the rule and certainty the exception. Therefore, it is not surprising that immediate preferences are more likely to influence adolescent decision making than abstract norms.

The work by Biddle et al. indicates that the topic or the category of behavior is very important when seeking to discern whether parental or peer pressure is more or less influential on behavior. The fact that school achievement is more likely to be subject to parental influence than drinking can certainly be explained by the evidence that school failure can have very severe consequences such as failure to be admitted to higher education or failure to earn a living. Drinking, on the other hand, is normative in America. Alcohol consumption is in fact so normal that in 1999 the average American drank 32 gallons of beer but only 24 gallons of milk and/or 23 gallons of coffee. Beer is of course not the only source of alcohol consumption in the United States. Moreover, 42% of American children consume alcohol before they are thirteen years old.[49]

The reasons there is so much alcohol drinking among adolescents are first, that the use of alcohol is normal in our society, Furthermore, it is within the means of most adolescents and it is associated with maturity and friendship.

The same is not true of school achievement. First and foremost, school achievement requires effort. That is certainly not true of drinking alcohol. Adolescents are also warned a great deal more about school failure than of the dangers of using alcohol, which their parents are most likely using all the time.[50]

Parental influence on adolescents extends, of course, a good deal beyond school or the use of alcohol. The political opinions of adolescents are also subject to the influence of parents and peer groups.

Adolescents are notorious for having little or no interest in politics. We use the word notorious deliberately because it means "widely known." Yet, what

---

49. http://www.nbcsd.k12.pa.us/sadd%20facts.htm
50. Biddle, *Parental and Peer Influences*, :1075.

is widely known may not be entirely true. Adolescents, that is those over age 18, do not vote in very great numbers. Yet, most political campaigners have succeeded in bringing young people into the political process and have employed the enthusiasm engendered among college students in particular in furthering their political ambitions.

The political scientists Kent Tedin found that party identification of college students is more likely influenced by parents than by peers. Yet, when it comes to the marijuana laws, peers have a good deal more influence than parents. Tedin found that college students are a good deal more "liberal" than their parents concerning marijuana use and that they are more influenced by peers than parents regarding marijuana use because that issue is important to them. That is not usually the case regarding other political issues.

On the contrary, most political issues are more important to older people than to younger people even if they affect younger people directly. In part, this is due to the life cycle effect. Therefore, adolescents are more likely to learn the political views of parents than of their peers, particularly because political issues are seldom a topic of discussion among children or adolescents or anyone under the age of 21.

The relationship between parents and children is a long one. Friendships, particularly among adolescents, change a great deal. This alone insures that adolescents will be much more exposed to the political views of their parents than those of their peers. [51]

Another issue which is of great importance to adolescents is school performance. This too is influenced both by parents and by peers. The sociologists Gary Natriello and Edward McDill found that peers, and teachers, set higher standards for students with good scholastic ability than do parents. This is true because peers, and teachers, can choose to associate only with students who are successful in their school performance. Parents have no such choice. Therefore, the reverse is true of students with only average or poor scholastic competence. Parents must deal with poor academic performance by their children and therefore parents, according to the Natriello and McDill study, set higher standards for students with less scholastic ability, with low educational expectations and who are not enrolled in a college preparatory track than is true of peers and teachers. [52]

---

51. Kent L. Tedin, "Assessing Peer and Parent Influence on Adolescent Political Attitudes," *American Journal of Political Science*, 24, no.1 (February 1980):142.

Parents who have high expectations of their children find that mostly such children perform better than those of whom little is expected. That is also true of peer expectations. Evidently, adolescents and no doubt all of us are more likely to "rise to the occasion" than not. Hence, high expectations from any source and under any circumstances are most likely to promote greater effort and better outcomes.

Adolescents in the US live in two different worlds at once. One world is the school and its related activities and the other is the family and parental demands. Adolescents are therefore forced to participate in the culture of their peers, a culture which has its own dress, its own music, its own manners of speech and its own expectations of behavior.

PARENTS, PEERS AND DELINQUENCY

The behavior of young people has been the subject of endless discussion for centuries. It can easily be shown that the earliest available documents among the most ancient of civilizations were concerned with the conduct of the young. This is still true in present day American culture.

Some of the behavior of adolescents is called delinquency because it has been so defined and adjudicated. Those who study delinquency have made considerable efforts to discover its causes and have developed numerous theories concerning the origin of delinquency. Among these students was Edwin Sutherland (1883-1950), who proposed his theory of differential association as a means of explaining delinquent and criminal behavior. Sutherland's explanation of delinquency is in part based on time and the intensity with which any reference group can influence the behavior of adolescents.

Sutherland begins by showing that delinquent behavior is learned in a process of interaction with other persons and in a process of communication. Evidently then, parents who communicate well with children can hope to have more influence than street gangs or school friends. He goes on to argue that the principal part of the learning process goes on within intimate personal groups. This again favors parents over peers under normal circumstances. That intimacy, which is normally only available within the family, allows the family or peer

---

52. Gary Natriello and Edward L. McDill, " Preformance Standards, Student Effort on Homework and Academic Achievement, *Sociology of Education*, 59, no. 1, (January 1986): 28.

group to manipulate the younger family members. Learning either criminal or non-criminal behavior, according to Sutherland, requires rationalizations and attitudes which are first learned in the family. Finally, the family can introduce the child to attitudes favorable or unfavorable to delinquent behavior. Of course, Sutherland's theory can be applied to all behavior and explains how parents are most vital in influencing the conduct of the young. Sutherland's theory of differential association has yet additional facets. Suffice it to show here that the influence parents or peers have on adolescents can well be explained by differential association.[53]

Differential association teaches us then that parents who spend a great deal of time with their children influence their behavior considerably. This influence is limited by the considerable amount of time spent in school where peers predominate. The relationship between peer influence and behavior can be just as great or greater than the influence of the parents. Nevertheless, we need to remember that parents are first in the life of a child and that therefore we can hold with Hirschi that: "The child attached to his parents may be less likely to get into situations in which delinquent acts are possible simply because he spends more of his time in their presence." [54]

In addition it is likely that children who are attached to their parents are less likely to seek the approval of their peers than children with little or no attachment to parents. Such children are also less likely to acquire delinquent friends because they seek to avoid parental criticism. Evidently, then, it is when adolescents are immediately associated with delinquent friends they met in school or elsewhere that parental attachment will undergo its most vital test. That test consists of the level or internalization of parental values that the adolescent may need to resist the temptation of becoming delinquent, because such adolescents will feel that their parents are always "psychologically present," as Hirschi has written.[55]

There is, however, another dimension to this relationship. While the evidence supports the view that adolescents not yet delinquent are more likely to refrain from future delinquent attachments if they are well attached to parents, it is also true that those already delinquent do not relinquish such delinquent behavior because of parental attachments. In short, once an adolescent has delin-

---

53. Sue Titus Reid, *Criminology, Seventh Edition,* (Orlando, Fla. Harcourt Brace & Co. 1994) p. 232.
54. Travis Hirschi, *Causes of Delinquency,* (New Brunswick, N.J. 2002) p. 88.
55. Ibid. p. 89.

quent friends, parental attachment is not sufficient to reduce or even eliminate such friendships.[56]

Lyle Larson made a major effort to discover the influence of parents and peers during adolescence. His findings were that the majority of adolescents chose to accept the wishes of their parents in three of four situations he studied. One of his conclusions is that despite pressure from peers to join a club or go to a party, the majority of adolescents were "parent compliant" and did not do what their parents opposed, even in the face of considerable peer pressure. Larson also found that adolescents who are willing to be parent compliant in one situation are likely to also comply to parental wishes in other situations.[57]

Several other findings by Larson are important. First, Larson found that parent oriented youth seldom comply with the wishes of their friends. Second, Larson found that adolescents who are equally interested in their parents and friends are less parent compliant than those who are parents oriented. Finally, Larson found that neither pressure by parents or peers have a mitigating influence on the choices adolescents will make.[58]

Among the many choices adolescents can make are the many consumer choices available to American adolescents. In fact, it is one of the marks of the youth culture in America that goods and services exclusively aimed at adolescent youths exist here. There are few countries which have segregated adolescents as much as we have, so that a special youth market does exist in the US. Therefore, children and adolescent youths are consumers like adults. Even young children between the ages of 4-12 spend over $24 billion in direct purchases. As children get older and reach adolescence they begin to spend money on alcohol, tobacco and illegal drugs. Of course it should be remembered that for those under 21, alcohol and tobacco are both illegal, ipso facto.[59]

Robert Merton has been more influential in the study of juvenile delinquency than any other sociologist. His contribution has been that delinquency results from a state of "anomie" in American society. "Anomie" is viewed as a

56. Anastasios Marcos, Stephen J. Bahr and Richard E. Johnson, "Test of a Bonding/ Association Theory of Adolescent Drug Use," *Social Forces*, 65, no.1 (1986):135-161.
57. Lyle E. Larson, "The Influence of Parents and Peers during Adolescence: The Situation Hypothesis Revisited," *Journal of Marriage and the Family*, 34, no.1(February 1972):67.
58. Ibid: p. 73.
59. Deborah R. John, "Consumer Socialization of Children: A Retrospective Look at Twenty-five Years of Research, *The Journal of Consumer Research*, 26, no. 3 (December 1999): 297.

breakdown in the cultural norms or expectations of any society so that some people cannot achieve the goals taught them in American society because the means for achieving them are not available to them. This gap between goals and means creates a rejection of the goals. The examples are delinquent children from poor families. They, like all American children, are taught success and achievement goals. However, for the poor there are no means to achieving such goals. Therefore, children from lower socio-economic backgrounds perceive few if any opportunities for gaining success by conformist means and hence turn to delinquent behavior such as auto theft or drug dealing as a means of achieving money, recognition and security. In sum, this means that the lower the opportunity the higher the delinquency.[60]

Although the media sometimes portray American young people as a vast collection of delinquents, sex fiends, drunks and dangerous deviates, the facts are quite different. The fact is that a considerable majority of teens are far more worried about their homework and their parents than their teen friends or their stylish clothes. This was revealed by a recent Unilever/Girl Scout Self-esteem Study, conducted by Roper ASW.

That study also shows that most, i.e. 75% of teen age girls are highly satisfied with the academic and social aspects of their lives, including their intelligence and the number of friends they have. The same study also reveals that the relationship teens have with adults are major confidence boosters. This means that the relationship they have with adults has a great deal to do with whether or not teens feel good about themselves.

Pre-teens and teens are concerned with their achievements in school and with the reaction of their parents to their accomplishments.[61]

Peer Pressure and Deviant Behavior

We have so far seen that a majority of adolescents are parent compliant. Nevertheless, there is a large adolescent minority who exhibit conduct which is either not approved by parents or is not viewed kindly by the adult community in general. Among these are violence and bullying in school, teen pregnancy, and poor school performance as well as drinking and drug use.

---

60. Robert K. Merton, "Social Structure and Anomie," Robert K. Merton, Social Theory and Social Structure, (Glencoe, Ill. The Free Press, (1957)p. 135.
61. Kaitlyn Troy, "Worries About Academics and Making Parents Proud are Top Concerns as "Tweens Start a New School Year," *Market Wire*, (September 17, 2003):1.

Two examples of peer pressure leading to violence and self destruction occurred in New York City in 2003. Both cases reflect an effort by youngsters to be noticed, to gain recognition and to "be somebody" even if only visible to their own peer reference group.

The first example concerns Eric Alvarez, who sought attention by climbing on top of a subway car near the 14th Street station. Accompanied by classmates from Chelsea High School, Alvarez meant to gain attention and did in fact do so when he "surfed" atop the car. He had hardly reaped the attention when he was smashed by a beam and fell to his death. Such stunts had given Alvarez the reputation of a clown. He had achieved many laughs and enhanced his standing among his peers by numerous such performances in the past.[62]

Seeking to be noticed, some youngsters engage in "dare-devil" stunts while others seek attention by bullying other children. Most children who see a bully attack another child in school fail to defend the victim for fear of becoming victims themselves.

The Youth Culture of Hostility

There is now, in some American schools and neighborhoods, a "youth culture of hostility." This hostility is seen both in the impoverished urban neighborhoods of many American cities but also in wealthy suburbs and small towns.

This "youth culture of hostility" appears to be a counter-culture, seeking to deny the values of the majority and seeking to distinguish themselves for fighting, obscenities and drinking. Both white and black gangs of youths are engaged in this form of conduct designed to reduce the pain of living on the bottom of the social order.

Annette Hemmings, an education professor at the University of Cincinnati, explored the "youth culture of hostility" in several American high schools and found that numerous inner city high school students engage in crime, fighting, verbal disrespect, sexual harassment, drug use and violence. Hemmings wrote that there is a continuum of such conduct ranging from considerable involvement in deviant conduct to conformity to middle-class norms. Many of the students she studied felt that no one cared about them, and that the

---

62. Joe McGurk, "Tears for Tragic Teen Train Surfer," *The New York Post*, (October 26, 2003) online edition.

society in which they live has adopted a hostile stance toward them which in turn leads to reciprocity on the part of adolescents.[63]

In October of 2003, The New York Daily News reported that a grandmother came home from work and found that her 15-year-old grandson participated in kicking a boy in the face as the boy lay on the pavement, having been assaulted by a gang of teenagers. Asked to explain this horrendous behavior, the boy explained that "everybody else was doing it and I didn't want to seem weak."[64]

The bullying problem is one of the most troubling aspects of American education today. Every day 160,000 students skip school for fear of being attacked. Students goad each other to smoke "weed," have sex and engage in fights. Even wearing last year's clothes can lead to trouble for some students in American schools. Those who want to be viewed as important must present the latest styles.[65]

One of the most notorious examples of bullying in high school were the events surrounding the Glen Ridge, N.J. rape of a retarded high school girl by fellow students. This event became notorious because it occurred in an upper-class small town among an almost entirely white or Euro-American population.

In 1997, Bernard Lefkowitz, a Columbia University professor, published a book concerning the crime committed by an athletic clique of football players in 1989. The book is called Our Guys: The Glen Ridge rape and the secret life of a perfect suburb. Here Lefkowitz reveals that it took eight years to finally convict four of the felons who assaulted a helpless victim. Even then, the penalty given the defendants was minimal compared to the punishment for similar crimes given other defendants. In fact, the judge let the convicted defendants go free after the verdicts were announced by the jury and until their appeals could be decided. Lefkowitz shows that adults refused to do anything about the atrocities committed by their football players even before the rape accusations became known. Parents who knew that their sons were involved in predatory or plundering sexual behavior did nothing about this. The football players stole money, masturbated in class, and treated girls like acolytes, i.e. followers or servants. Because football players are regarded as "supermen" in many American high

63. Annette Hemmings, "Youth culture of hostility: discourses of money, respect and difference," *Qualitative Studies in Education*, 15, no. 3, (2002):305.

64. Carrie Melago and Alison Gendar, "Peer pressure: saving kids from themselves," *Daily News*, (October 26, 2003):6.

65. Ibid. 6.

schools there are innumerable schools in which football players and basketball players and others "lord it over" the other students and are seldom challenged if they take advantage of the adulation they receive for their football prowess. There is little doubt that academics mean little to most American students and their parents but that sports, and particularly football, is everything.[66]

TEEN PREGNANCY, ALCOHOL AND DRUGS

Because many high school girls are pressured to have sex, teen pregnancy rates are high (although the declining US birth rate includes a 17% decline in teen-age pregnancy during the decade ending in 2002, mainly because of increased use of dependable contraceptives). Nevertheless, each year one million teen-age girls become pregnant. Four out of ten of these girls are not yet 18 years old. Of births to teenagers 78% occur to single girls, so that 31% of all non-marital births involve teenagers. Seventy-eight percent of these births are unplanned and involve youngsters who come from low income families. It is noteworthy that the United States has twice as many teenage unmarried mothers as Canada, England or Wales and nine times the rate of Japan or the Netherlands.[67]

It is commonly believed that teen pregnancy is principally related to a lack of parental influence of teen sexual behavior. Yet, a recent press conference held by the National Campaign to Prevent Teen Pregnancy announced that teens say their parents have the biggest influence on their sexual decisions. In fact, only one third of teens claim that friends have the most influence on their sexual decisions. Therefore it is evident that parents overestimate the influence of peers and underestimate their own influence. Furthermore, 69% of teens surveyed by the National Campaign to Prevent Teen Pregnancy say that it would be much easier for them to avoid pregnancy if they had better opportunities to discuss sex with their parents.[68]

---

66. Bernard Lefkowitz, *Our guys: the Glen Ridge rape and the secret life of the perfect suburb.* (Berkeley, Cal. University of California Press, 1997).
67. Stanley K. Henshaw, "Unintended Pregnancy in the United States," *Family Planning Perspcectives*, 30, no.1, (1998):24
68. Susan Reimer, "Parents must realize it is important to speak up. Family Matters," *The Baltimore Sun*, (October 19, 2003):1N.

Drinking alcoholic beverages and other drug use by adolescents is viewed as a serious delinquency in this country and elsewhere. Excessive drinking involves many dangers which are either ignored or downplayed by adolescents because the use of alcohol has a special meaning in the subculture of delinquency.

Adolescents and young adults, particularly those of high school and college age, engage in social situations which pressure participants to drink far more alcohol than they would ever choose without that pressure.

This is only one of the conclusions reached by the National Research Council and the Institute of Medicine in a report entitled Reducing Underage Drinking: A Collective Responsibility. That report reveals that alcohol is the most commonly used drug among American youth and that more young people drink alcohol than smoke tobacco or use marijuana. The report also shows that despite laws prohibiting alcohol use by those under age 21, almost all American youths drink alcohol before that age. In fact, 48.6% of twelfth grade students, i.e., those age 17, report using alcohol. Furthermore, those adolescents who drink drink a good deal more than adults.

This report also shows that more than one fourth of children aged 12-20 have used alcohol more than once and that underage drinkers spent $22.5 billion on alcohol a year across the United States. Underage drinkers consume about 20% of all drinks. Children as young as 14 report that alcohol is easy to find.

A further finding concerning adolescent drinking is that more than a quarter of all high school students in the US consume more than five drinks in a row. [69]

Among college students, 44% engage in binge drinking, as do about 30% of high school seniors. Binge drinking is responsible for some 1,400 student deaths per year. Examples of such deaths are frequently published in the media, including the Illinois fraternity member who died of an overdose of alcohol during a weekend of drinking at that university. Then there is the intoxicated Cornell student who fell down a gorge and died and the Pennsylvania State University student who barely survived after her blood-alcohol level reached seven times the Pennsylvania limit allowed drivers.

Several universities have made considerable efforts to reduce the drinking on their campuses but so far achieved nothing.[70]

---

69. Richard J. Bonnie, *Reducing Underage drinking: A collective Responsibility*, (Washington, D.C., The National Academy of Sciences, 2003) p. 35.
70. Buddy T. "College Binge Drinking Kills," *Health and Fitness*, (November 25, 2003):1.

There are also 70,000 American students who are sexually assaulted each year. Such sexual assaults are facilitated by the use of Rohypnol, also called "the date rape drug." Attackers can slip this drug into the drink of a woman they intend to rape. The drug leads to dizziness, disorientation, difficulty in speaking and finally, unconsciousness. Victims do not remember what happened to them while under the influence of that or other "date rape" drugs. A recent survey revealed that 13% of students said that they had been assaulted by another student who had been drinking or had used drugs.[71]

Among adolescents who are members of gangs, illicit drugs are generally used. This is not as true of girls as of boys, although both sexes use such drugs. The reason for the lesser involvement of girls in drugs than is true of boys is the belief, still quite common, that girls and women must not behave in an uncontrolled manner. This belief is related to the need women have to prevent sexual predators from using them, thereby gaining a "bad" reputation.

The use of illegal drugs by adolescents has a symbolic meaning. There are many youths who define themselves in terms of which drugs they use and which method of drug administration they employ.[72]

BODY PIERCING AND OTHER RISKS

The use of signs, insignias and labels as marks of distinction is an ancient one. Body piercing and tattooing have been part of human culture for thousands of years. Archeological evidence from ancient Egyptian, Mayan and other societies indicates that body piercing and tattooing was and is widespread and can be found in cultures which are otherwise totally distinct and which flourished in widely separated parts of the world, including the Polynesian. The British explorer Captain James Cook introduced the word tattoo to English speakers after his return from a voyage around the world between 1768 and 1771. He found the word in use in Samoa and Tahiti, two islands which also gave us the word taboo. A tattoo is a permanent mark made on the skin by a process of pricking

71. No author, "Drinking Kills 1,400 College Students Each Year," (CNN Tuesday, April 6, 2002).
72. Robert Room and Hanako Sato, "Drinking and drug use in youth cultures," *Contemporary Drug Problems*, (Summer 2002):249.

the skin and then ingraining an indelible pigment into the scar. Tattoos consist of designs and words and are installed by tattoo artists.[73]

In recent years, American adolescents have engaged in so much body piercing and tattooing that in 2002 more than 13% of adolescents surveyed said they had a tattoo and nearly 30% had pierced a part of their body other than the ear lobes.

Some had their tattoos and body piercing done by a professional and some had it done by an amateur. Carroll et al. found that those whose tattoos were made by an amateur were more often dissatisfied with their status-role and were exceptionally involved in problem behavior and also exhibited poor school performance. they also found that tattooing and body piercing is found more often in females than males, 16.6% versus 8.1%. Almost any body part may be subject to piercing or tattooing. Excluding the earlobe, ear cartilage was pierced by 13.6% of the sample studied by Carroll et al., the mouth and the tongue were pierced by 11.2%, 10.7 % pierced their navel, and 1.2% pierced their nipples. Even the genitals do not escape piercing by 0.8% of those studied.

Tattooing and piercing of the body is evidently associated with other risk taking behavior. Carroll et al. found that drug use, sexual activity, suicide and disordered eating behavior are all positively associated with piercing and tattooing. Furthermore, those adolescents who engage in tattooing and piercing are at greater risk of using marijuana, alcohol and tobacco than is usual among adolescents.

Violence is found to a greater degree among males with tattoos and piercings than among other males and, finally, the use of hard drugs such as amphetamines, cocaine and Ecstasy increases as the use of piercing and tattooing increases. In sum, clear differences were found between adolescents with or without tattoos and/or body piercing.[74]

The psychologists Christina Frederick and Kristy Bradley studied the psychological and motivational characteristics of young adult tattooers and body piercers. They found several motivations led young adults to engage in these practices. One of these motivations is peer pressure related to an effort to maintain group affiliation. The need to conform is of course particularly strong among adolescents, although it is found in all age strata.

73. The American Heritage College Dictionary, (Boston: Houghton Mifflin 2002).
74. Sean T. Carroll, Robert H. Riffenburgh, Timothy A. Roberts and Elizabeth B. Myhre, "Tattoos and Body Piercing as Indicators of Adolescent Risk-taking Behavior," *Pediatics,*(, 109, no. 6, June 2000):1021.

Among adolescents, tattooing and piercing are also seen as acts of rebellion against adults or the "establishment." Tattooing and/or piercing have shock value and are also considered by some adolescents as a method of becoming a unique individual.

There are also some adolescent and older couples who use shared tattoos as indications of loyalty and trust or as signs that the tattooed individual is a member of a religious group or has undergone a spiritual experience.[75]

Among college students studied by Frederick and Bradley, 21% reported having tattoos and/or piercings. They also found that body piercing in particular fosters a sense of self-identity and is also often conducted in order to "fit in" with a gang of violent boys. Many tattooers and body piercers see this as autonomous behavior. Frederick and Bradley also found that piercers often believe that this will lead to a permanent means of enhancing one's body and receiving social approval at the same time.

Frederick and Bradley also found that younger people who engaged in piercing had a higher psychopathology score than older people who did this. Nevertheless, their overall conclusion is that body piercing is generally the outcome of a short-lived symbolic act of rebellion and has no major psychological implications.[76]

BULLYING AND THE AMERICAN YOUTH CULTURE

Bullying is a common form of deviant behavior related to the youth culture. Much of this behavior by boys targets girls, who are seen by many "jocks" as undifferentiated "sex objects." Such bullying may include derogatory language and even assault, with those who played the school bully in their younger years sometimes becoming rapists as older men. Sports also define masculinity and femininity in America. Thus, "real men" bear pain in silence, do not cry, do not complain and show no emotion.[77]

Because football is the most highly regarded of the sports promoted in American high schools and colleges, it has been argued that the schools teach

---

75. Christina M. Frederick and Kristy A. Bradley, "A Different Kind of Normal? Psychological and Motivational Characteristics of Young Adult Tattooers and Body Piercers." *North American Journal of Psychology*, (2000, 2, no. 2):380.
76. Ibid. p.388.
77. Steven Schact, "Mysogeny on and off the 'pitch'," *Gender and Society*, 10, no. 5, (1996):550.

that the infliction of pain and the acceptance of physical violence are commendable. This attitude is augmented by the will to win by dominating others. That too is taught directly or indirectly in school. Sociological research has shown that aggression breeds aggression, so that the combative attitude which football provokes has a number of consequences for all children —who, by law, must attend school.

Bullying is perhaps the most egregious of these consequences. Bullying has been defined as "aggression in which the behavior is intended to harm or disturb; the behavior occurs repeatedly over time, and there is an imbalance of power, with a more powerful person or group attacking a less powerful one."[78]

Bullying affects safety, academics and self-esteem. It consists of spreading rumors, excluding the victim from conversation and activities, making threats and using physical violence. The impact on the victims can be severe. At the very least, victims of bullying will pretend to be sick so that they can avoid school. Other indications of victimization by bullies may be withdrawal, passivity and self-destruction. Some children who are so victimized cry a good deal, while others show signs of fear in normal situations. Many victims of bullies develop learning problems and/or show physical symptoms such as stomach pains and fatigue.[79]

An additional consequence of bullying can be that the victims will arm themselves and carry out violent actions in response to the bullying they have suffered. The most publicized of such actions was the slaughter of 13 people at the Columbine High School in Colorado on April 20, 1999. Two students, Eric Harris and Dylan Klebold, indiscriminately murdered fellow students and teachers and were then killed by the police. Evidently, these students had been the victims of bullying for some time and saw these killings as justified revenge.

In July of 2003, Oaklyn, N.J. police arrested three suspects, ages 18, 15 and 14, who were armed with handguns, machetes and 2000 rounds of ammunition. These students were apparently plotting to kill school bullies.[80]

Bullying may also take place in the context of "hazing." An example of this kind of sadistic behavior by high school students occurred at Woodridge High School in Peninsula, Ohio in December of 2003, where soccer players had their

---

78. Brian Pace, "Bullying," *Journal of the American Medical Association* 285, (April 25, 2001):2156.

79. Ibid. 2156.

80. Terry Bitman, "Schools teaching students not to tolerate bullies," *The Philadelphia Inquirer,* (November 23,2003):8.

heads forced into toilets. At the Mepham High School in Bellmore, NY, football players were sodomized with broomsticks, pinecones and golf balls. As a consequence the football season was canceled, the coaching staff was fired and three students faced criminal charges.

In suburban Chicago, a girls' football game between seniors and juniors at Glenbrook North High School led to a fight requiring five girls to seek medical treatment. In May of 2003, the district attorney filed charges against 33 seniors and 20 juniors who participated in a brutal hazing. Sixteen teens were convicted of misdemeanor battery and alcohol charges.[81]

Similar conduct has been alleged all over the United States. In South Dakota students were sodomized and others were showered with vomit and urine. Elsewhere brutal paddling was reported. These incidents and many more led a team of investigators at Alfred University to conduct a national survey of Initiation Rites in American High Schools. This survey led to several findings. One of these findings is that students often felt that adults condone hazing. Furthermore, students often do not see hazing as a problem. It was also found that hazing is quite common in church groups. In addition, students often see hazing as "fun" and exciting. The study also discovered that hazing begins young and may continue throughout life.[82]

Whether bullying or hazing, a good part of this kind of aggression is related to the tremendous pressure placed on American youngsters to succeed in sports.

SPORTS AND THE AMERICAN YOUTH CULTURE

Sports define the American adolescent. This refers mainly to boys but can also be viewed among some girls in our schools. Sports defines masculinity in a direct and aggressive manner. Adolescence implies numerous physical, emotional and social difficulties in a world controlled by adults. Adolescents suffer from a lack of power, and they have a sense it will be conferred on them if they succeed in sports. Sports offer an escape from homework, "teacher's ugly looks," sexual problems, failure to understand one's identity, and parental control.

---

81. Tom Weir, "Hazing issue rears ugly head across USA" *USA Today*, (December 9, 2003):1.
82. Nadine C. Hoover and Norman J. Pollard, *Initiation Rites in American High Schools*, (Alfred, N.Y. Alfred University Press, 2002).

Sports contribute a great deal to the construction of a sense of self for those who participate. Sports allow adolescents to compete with one another, free from parental supervision. Sports therefore become a key experience for those who engage in it. Sports, unlike scholastic effort, bring immediate gratification to the participants. This is especially true of football and basketball but also of the "minor" sports such as track and field and swimming. Sports compensates the physically mature for their exclusion from the rewards of the adult world. Adults can engage in "conspicuous consumption," as Thorsten Veblen called it. Adults have power and control all the social institutions as well as the home and the school in which adolescents must live.[83]

The sports field is the territory of the adolescent himself. There he rules while parents, teachers and others sit on the sidelines. It is on the sports field, and particularly in football, that boys can earn the adulation of others, including girls and their families. Sports also permits boys and girls to bond with their fathers and mothers, who are much more likely to give their sports competent children far more attention for sports achievements than for academics.

Every society has culture heroes. In some cultures military achievements are most important. In others, business ability is most honored, while yet others concentrate on religious perfection or political acumen. All of these characteristics are viewed with favor in this country. However, sports achievements, particularly in football, furnish the greatest heroes in American life.

This adulation of football players and other athletes spills into the schools and poses a real danger for some athletes. That danger is the possibility of becoming all absorbed by the sports subculture to the detriment of reality. Indeed there are high school athletes who later become professional basketball or football players and earn a great deal. The truth is, however, that failure to earn a high school diploma or college degree because of an all absorbing interest in sports can have disastrous consequences. In sum, sports ability in an adolescent's younger years can lead to an "albatross around the neck" when he gets older.

The dilemma concerning high school sports lies in the contradictory message which the most popular sports send to high school students. Football and basketball prowess permit the few with outstanding athletic ability to earn immediate gratification in the form of popularity and prestige. Yet, this very absorption in the sports subculture often leads to failure to achieve academic

---

83. Lawrence B. Angus, "Women in a male domain: gender and organizational culture in a Christian Brothers college," in: Lawrence B. Angus, editor, *Inequality and Social Identity*, (Washington D.C. Palmer Press, 1993).

success, with the consequence that the greatest high school sports heroes become unemployable in their adult years or have to work at the most menial jobs for lack of education. Most children know at age nine whether or not they excel at sports or even have an interest in sports. Therefore there are a good number of school children who don't fit into the prestige hierarchy in our school system because that hierarchy is almost entirely dominated by sports achievement. Consequently there are many boys and girls in our schools who are regarded as losers and who may therefore become the targets of bullies who are exempt from criticism because of their sports ability. This does not mean that sports ability is the only means of gaining recognition in our schools. There are alternative status systems available to American high school students and other adolescents. One of these is the ability to perform youth culture music.

MUSIC AND THE AMERICAN YOUTH CULTURE

Music has been associated with youthful rebellion for some time. The waltz (German for "turning") was first introduced to Viennese society in the 18th century and was promptly termed "immoral" because the dancers faced one another and embraced. It took nearly a hundred years for the waltz to be viewed as acceptable in polite society, since all previous dancing, such as the minuet, allowed only minimal contact between the sexes.

Likewise, the dances of the 20th century were seen as immoral and pernicious when first introduced. In fact, in 1985 a group of well-connected Washington wives calling themselves the Parents' Music Resource Center testified before a US Senate Committee concerning the dangers of "rock" music; the women testified that the lyrics can lead to corruption of youth, meaning violence, rebellion, substance abuse, sexual promiscuity and perversion and Satanism.

Five years later, in 1990, a US district court judge in Fort Lauderdale, FL, found an album produced by a "rap" band called "2 Live Crew" to be obscene. This ruling was followed by the arrest of several "heavy metal" and "rap" musicians in the Florida area at the time.

"Rock" music was also held responsible for "corruption" in the popular media. The author of an article appearing in the Reader's Digest claimed in 1988 that the lyrics associated with rock music "glamorize drug and alcohol use, glorify death and lead to violent rebellion." [84] Even the *New York Times* participated in the assault when columnist William Safire wrote that "Kids get special protection in law...and deserve protection from porn-rock profiteers."[85]

It is tempting to note that parents have always suspected youthful enter-tainment, including music, of harmful influence. The Parents' Music Resource Center must have been driven in part by the perennial generation gap. As Russell Baker wrote in the *New York Times* in 1985, at the height of the controversy about "rock" music, "Stirred by the PMRC alarmed mothers, my mind began playing back the full repertory of bawdy, off color and just downright dirty songs it had gathered during years when my mother would have cringed if I let on that I knew a more emphatic way of saying 'gosh darn it all to the dickens.'"[86]

Still, nearly 300 studies have concluded that violent media does indeed foster violence (see the section on electronic media, below). Sometimes, the fears are justified. The titles alone may be viewed as pornographic, obscene and rebel-lious, as in these songs from an album called OU812: "Let's put the X in sex"; "Suicide Solution," "Necrophobic," "Fuck the Police"; "Me So Horny," "The Fuck Shop." An analysis of the contents of the lyrics of these songs show that many show a strong distrust of the older generation, others include swear words, many are graphic depictions of sexual activity while others refer to the use of drugs and alcohol.[87]

The arguments against the lyrics associated with youth culture music run into the issue of First Amendment rights and freedom of speech. Some of the "rap" songs and "heavy metal" songs which some consider offensive could perhaps be outlawed as a form of pornography as defined by the Roth Decision of the US Supreme Court. (That decision held that pornography is not protected by the First Amendment. Attempts to define pornography by using "community standards" and "social value" has led to a great deal of confusion, so that numerous additional decisions concerning pornography have been made since. None has satisfied everyone, so that today a good deal of so called "X-rated" material may be seen and heard on the Internet, in video stores and on the music scene.[88])

When Elvis Presley achieved super-stardom in the 1950s, the Jesuit mag-azine America warned its readers to "Beware Elvis" and the communist boss of East Germany, Walter Ulbricht, ordered the arrest of fifteen teenagers who had

---

84. Amy Binder, "Constructing Racial Rhetoric: Media Depictions of Harm in Heavy Metal and Rap Music," *The American Sociological Review*, 58, No. 6 (December 1993):754.
85. William Safire, "Porn-Rock" *The New York Times*, (October 10, 1985):Sec.1, p. 31.
86. Russell Baker, *The New York Times*, (October 13, 1985) Sec, 6, p. 22.
87. Amy Binder, "Constructing Radical Rhetoric," p.764.
88. Gerhard Falk, "The Roth Decision in the Light of Sociological Knowledge," *American Bar Association Jurnal*, 54, (March 1968):288.

marched through the streets of Leipzig, shouting "Long live Elvis Presley."[89] Television had also come of age and now the gyrations of Elvis Presley were visible in every living room in America. This led to the accusation that juvenile delinquency was caused by television viewing and that Elvis and others like him were heavy contributors to all that was and is wrong with young people. Some people think today's controversy is no more than a re-run of earlier ones. Others point out that, in fact, the popularization of such entertainment did undermine the teachings of the Church, and did promote individualism at the expense of society.

Elvis Presley appealed to young people all over. His success was enjoyed by many who identified with his poor origins and his ability to confront the "establishment." Born to poor sharecroppers in Tupelo, Mississippi in 1935, Presley continued the tradition of Southern folk music, which merged the music of African slaves with that of cowboy tunes of the West, Latin music and the Delta blues. This American music blend then gave rise to "rock and roll" as produced by Buddy Holly, Bill Haley, Carl Perkins and Jerry Lewis. Elvis exemplified the revolt of the teenagers of his day against the conformity of the 1950s older generation. Elvis Presley was the generation gap personified. While television depicted middle-class conformity with such shows as *Father Knows Best* and *Ozzie and Harriet* or *The Donna Reed Show*, teenagers rejected all of that as well as the music of Perry Como, Bing Crosby and Frank Sinatra. Instead, young girls screamed with excitement as Elvis Presley, a white man, sang like a black man and swiveled his hips in what appeared to have sexual overtones. Frank Sinatra, formerly the beneficiary of the screaming girls of his generation, called Presley's songs "the most brutal, ugly, desperate, vicious form of expression it has been my misfortune to hear." Parents smashed Presley records and church groups denounced him, but teenagers followed him and made sure that rock and roll was here to stay.[90]

In 2004, the Presley phenomenon continues in the person of Marshall Bruce Mathers III. Using his initials, he calls himself Eminem and sings "rap" music. Like Elvis before him, he is a white man singing black songs. He is the 2005 "teen dream" but is also seen as a menace by church groups and the "older generation," i.e. those who were enthralled by Elvis the Pelvis.[91]

---

89. Peter Guralnick, *Last train to Memphis: the rise of Elvis Presley*, (Boston: Little Brown &Co.1994) p.196.
90. Mitch Yamasaki, "Using Rock 'n Roll To Teach the History of Post-World War II America," *The History Teacher*, 29, no. 2 (February 1996):188.

Music is of course not the only source of teenage rebellion against the older generation. The generation gap is driven even further apart by teen movies and television shows. In the 1950s Marlon Brando appeared in *The Wild One* and James Dean portrayed a troubled teen in *Rebel Without a Cause*. Elvis Presley then appeared in a number of movies such as *Jailhouse Rock*, which depicts him as a convict who defended a woman against an assault by a would-be rapist. That and other hip gyrations were now visible in every living room.

In the new century, Eminem continues the angry rebel tradition with such movies as *The Slim Shady Show, Da Hip Hop Witch* and *8 Mile*. These movies include foul language, gross gestures and a plot not worthy of a demented clown. Nevertheless, these movies sell records and produce high revenues. Their message, if any, is that poverty is great, that urban warfare has merit and that "music" consists of loud drumbeats.

All this confirms the existence of a permanent "generation gap" visible in every generation, although not the experience of everyone. There are those who follow in the footsteps of their parents to such an extent that no generation gap really exists for them. Others distance themselves from the older generation as if the generation gap was as wide as the ocean and as deep as the sea. We shall therefore next examine the generation gap in more detail and do so from both sides of the age barrier.

SUMMARY

Two views of the youth culture and the generation gap have been explored by social scientists. One holds that parents are more important, the other that peers are more decisive, in the conduct of the younger generation.

Peers influence behavior that is adjudicated as delinquent. Such conduct includes the use of alcohol and other drugs, body piercing and tattooing and teen pregnancy. Sports are an essential aspect of American adolescent culture, and this seems to encourage widespread bullying with sometimes violent consequences. Violence and the subculture of hostility are also expressed in adolescent music, which is one aspect of the generation gap to be explored in the next chapter.

---

91. Renee Graham, "Whatever You Say I Am: The Life and Times of Eminem," *The Boston Globe*, (November 5, 2003):E1.

Chapter 3. The Generation Gap

The phrase "the generation gap" implies a deep chasm which opens up between parents and children, between the old and the young, and which is somehow insurmountable. This view was first promoted by the sociologist Kingsley Davis, who claimed in an influential article in 1940 that rapid social change made parent-child youth conflict ubiquitous and inevitable. This article led to a massive amount of research concerning "the generation gap" with various results.[92]

There are of course those who have rejected the older or the younger generation entirely and whose values, attitudes and lifestyle differ so immensely from the earlier or later generation that they have nothing in common and no relationship whatever. Such conditions exist but are uncommon. We have already seen that parents and grandparents greatly influence the subsequent generations despite the differences between them and despite the experiences of the old and the young which do not seem to mean much to the preceding or subsequent generation. Nevertheless, we need to view the "generation gap" as far more shallow than the phrase implies and a good deal less confrontational than the media like to portray. In fact, there is a good deal of reciprocity between the generations. Without full realization, parents and grandparents pass on a part of themselves to children and grandchildren. Parents, especially mothers, will, for instance sing

---

92. Kingsley Davis, "The sociology of parent-youth conflict," *American Sociological Review*, 5 (August 1940):523-535.

songs to a child which are remembered from one generation to another and thus be retained and repeated to those that follow. They may pass on phrases and peculiarities that belong to their particular and unique family. Millie Kunde, an eighty-five-year-old widow, used a German word "Schlapperhans" (slob) that had been passed on by her father, who was an immigrant from Europe. He in turn had learned this from his father, Mrs. Kunde's grandfather. The word continued for generations and was used by the elderly woman's middle aged niece.

Still, it cannot be overlooked that there are differences between generations which revolve around such issues as power, status and responsibilities. Evidently, the older generation has more control over how any issue will be handled and how resources will be spent. The younger generation usually has no say in such decisions at all. Therefore, the benefits of any decision made by those presently in power will most likely benefit them. An example is how money is saved or not for the next generation; it is not the decision of the eventual recipients of such funds.

Of course, the opportunity to dominate changes as time goes on. Each generation gets older and older and is finally forced by time to give up control and hand it to the next generation. Therein lies much anxiety and conflict, because the old are slow to give up power and the young are in a hurry to dominate and to exercise power.[93] Linda's parents were determined that she remain in their home town and attend college there to become a teacher. They had great hopes for her since both parents were educated people and they felt that their daughter would be an excellent pedagogue who could always earn a living by this means. At 19 Linda rebelled, exercised her power, left school and moved to a warm climate where she could work and become "independent" of the older generation's control, even though it was potentially to her detriment.

Every generation believes that it is making sacrifices for the younger generation and that the young do not appreciate these sacrifices. This may be a matter of money in that parents and grandparents finance the education of the young or buy them a car or give them spending money. This of course raises the question as to why one generation would do anything for the next generation.[94]

One answer to that question lies in the fact that all were at one time children and were therefore subject to either good or bad treatment by their

93. Kimberly A. Wade-Benzoni, "A Golden Rule Over Time: Reciprocity in Intergenerational Allocation Decisions," *Academy of Management Journal*, 45(October 2002):1011.

94. Norman S. Care, "Future generations, public policy and the motivation problem," *Environmental Ethics*, 4 no.3, (1982):195-213.

parental generation. There are those who treat their own children in a manner that reflects how they were treated by their parents. Randall Kramer was the adult son of a very strict upbringing. His parents believed in the old adage: "Spare the rod and spoil the child." He was frequently treated to the proverbial strap for fairly minor infractions. As an adult he adored his father and attributed his work ethic and his success to his father's actions toward him. Randall in turn treated his children in the same autocratic and punitive fashion. However, we may also deal with our young in a fashion that reflects how we would have liked to be treated but were not.

The philosopher John Rawls has dealt with this issue at length in his famous volume, A Theory of Justice. In that book Rawls seeks to substitute the idea of the social contract for the utilitarianism which now dominates American and Western thought in general. Rawls believes that the social contract possesses an inviolability founded on justice, which includes the basic rights anchored in the American constitution.[95]

It is of course unusual that a younger person can reciprocate what has been done for him by parents and others. Therefore, anthropologists have identified "generalized exchange," which differs from "restricted exchange" in that those who cannot directly reciprocate have the option of benefiting the next generation when they are ready to do so. In short, grandparents help children and children help their children in an unending chain of intergenerational exchange.[96]

This means that the older generation seeks to "repay the debt" owed the previous generation who have died and cannot be reached. Of course, there is also the possibility that members of any generation may not feel obligated to help anyone because they received no help themselves. Furthermore, the younger generation may be the beneficiary of a "free ride" in that they can and must accept what is done for them by the older generation without having to necessarily repay anyone later. In fact, there are adult children who abandon their parents in their old age despite the benefits they gained from them.[97]

---

95. Jon Rawls, *A Theory of Justice*, (Cambridge, Mass. Belknap Press of Harvard University Press),1999.

96. Peter P. Ekeh, *Social Exchange Theory*, (Cambridge, Mass. Harvard University Press), 1974..

97. Toshio Yamagishi and Karen S. Cook, "Generalized exchange and social dilemmas," *Social Science Quarterly*, 56,(1993):235-248.

Some Earlier and Some Recent Research

In 1975 the sociologists Jacobsen, Berry and Olson made an empirical test of the generation gap leading to the conclusion that older and younger generations are neither entirely in agreement nor entirely in disagreement on a number of issues the researchers presented. In fact, Jacobsen et al. found that there is within families a range of shared values over and above various disagreements. The conclusion that parents and children share many values has been well documented for young children and for college students.

College students are likely to disagree with their parents concerning sex and a number of social issues. Such disagreement increases with age and advancement in college. As college socialization continues, the number of disagreements with parents also increase. This is particularly true of families whose parents are "working class" and whose children are college students.[98] John Courtney, a welder, came for counseling because he was depressed over his son's attitude toward him and his profession. The son (Jack) refused to follow in his father's "footsteps" in spite of the fact that John had built up his welding business so that his boy could take over and "make an excellent living." He felt that Jack was denigrating him because he had two years of college so far and he flaunted this, insisting that he will complete his education and that he, Dad, "knows nothing." Jack could not understand how his father was able to be proud of his occupation and be able to enjoy the "monotony" of the welding occupation.

More recently, management professor Kimberly Wade-Benzoni published four studies dealing with the generation gap and found that the behavior of a previous generation influences the behavior of a subsequent generation toward future generations. Her most important finding is that the majority of her respondents acted on behalf of future generations even though they knew they would never benefit from them. This finding contradicts the cynics and pessimists who view all younger folks with disdain. These findings also contradict game theory, which holds that there must always be a zero sum outcome to every exchange.[99] Mrs. Rendit, a retiree with a less than average income, saved a meager portion of her monthly pension check so that her grandchildren would

---

98. R. Brooke Jacobsen, Kenneth J. Berry and Keith P. Olson, "An Empirical Test of the Generation Gap: A Comparative Intrafamily Study," *Journal of Marriage and the Family*, 37, no. 4, (November 1975):841-852.
99. Kimberly Wade-Benzoni, "A Golden Rule,"p.1022.

have a better start in life than she had. She took great pride in enabling them to be and have what they wanted for their future.

In an extensive study of the possible polarization of social attitudes among Americans in the 1970s and the 1990s, the sociologists DiMaggio et al. found no major differences between the attitudes of the young and their parental generation with respect to such issues as gender roles, racial integration, crime and poverty. Polarization among all Americans occurs only with respect to abortion. Yet that issue is divisive not on the basis of age, but on the basis of religious belief. Moreover, DiMaggio et al found that the celebrated 1960s generation, with their revolutionary attitudes on all social issues, did not influence their children or the subsequent generation to be "liberal" in the Sixties sense. Instead, the researchers found a declining age polarization between those under age 35 and older Americans on all social issues tested.[100] Grace and Charles were a couple with innumerable prejudices. Their two young children heard their negative remarks, especially about Afro-Americans, almost daily. They were close replicas of the Archie Bunkers of a television situation comedy. Unlike Archie Bunker, they succeeded in imbuing their prejudices into their children who repeated their unacceptable behavior and retained their parents' attitude.

In August of 2003 researchers at the University of Texas issued a report entitled "Focus Group Study of Youth and Politics." This study was carried out in five American cities and sought to test some popular views of young Americans. These views are that youth care only for themselves and are utter hedonists who seek the maximum pleasures of the moment and are therefore immune to any appeal to make social life better. A second popular idea concerning young people is that the young constitute a culture totally removed from adult society. In this view young people have their own language, tastes, values and interests, leading to their total lack of interest in politics. Thirdly, it is believed by many adult Americans that "today's youth" have no serious concerns and no moral obligations but will regain "their senses" when they reach maturity. Finally it is common knowledge among American adults that the young cannot be trusted with democracy because the young are reputed to have bizarre political opinions and are usually attracted to the most extreme point of view.

---

100. Paul DiMaggio, John Evans and Bethany Bryson, "Have Americans' Social Attitudes Become More Polarized? *American Journal of Sociology*, 102 no.3 (November 1996) 690-755.

The results of the Texas study vary considerably from these assumptions. These results show that the present generation of young Americans care a good deal about politics but view themselves as observers of politics and not as actors. This "observer" status is mainly connected to the enormous amount of political publicity engulfing anyone who so much as drives down a street, turns on television, listens to the radio or reads a newspaper. In short, neither the young nor the old can escape being an observer of the US political system.

A large majority of young Americans believe that "all politicians are alike" and that politicians tell people what they want to hear. They believe in common stereotypes about politics but are unable to explain what politicians do for a living. Generally uninformed, young Americans have few solutions to social problems and are also unconvinced that the political process is aimed at finding the best solutions.

The Texas study also found that young Americans are much more interested in local or community issues than in national or international politics. Furthermore, those surveyed showed an understanding of the importance of elections and the consequences of voting for one or another politician.[101]

The Institute of Politics at Harvard University agreed with the Texas study that the attitudes of young Americans toward the political process is positive. In a survey conducted in April of '03 it was discovered that almost 10 million college-age Americans could have become the "swing vote" in the November 2004 election. This is particularly true of the 9.5 million 18-24 year olds who attend college, of whom 41% are unaffiliated voters so that neither party can count on their support. Among all young people the economy is their first priority, as it is with all other potential voters.[102] Historical data show that today's unemployed have concerns very similar to those of the folks who lived through the Great Depression of the late 1920s and early 1930s. Anthony, a laborer who was terminated by the Nabisco plant in Niagara Falls, along with all of his colleagues, felt depressed and hopeless. He had been searching for a job since the closing of that factory and was at the end of any benefits accrued him. Waves of desperation were experienced by him as well as by his family.

---

101. Jay Childers and Roderick P. Hart, *Focus Group Study of Youth and Politics*, (Austin, Tex. The University of Texas Press)2003.
102. Alvin Powell, "IOP survey find college youth engaged," *Harvard University Gazette*, (May 29, 2003):1-2.

We turn now to some other issues of concern to young Americans as well as everyone else. One of these is religion. Here a generation gap really exists, according to the Survey Research Center at the University of California at Berkeley. A study of attitudes towards religion based on nationwide interviews with Americans aged 15-92 led to some surprising conclusions. For example, 59% of adults aged 27-59 favor school prayer. Among teenagers, 69% favor prayer as part of school activities. Similarly, the youngest Americans are more in favor of federal aid to faith-based charities. While 40% of adults aged 27-59 support such funding, 59% of college aged Americans were willing to support such expenditures. Among young teens, 67% said they favored federal aid to faith-based charities. Even Christian fundamentalists received a more positive response from the young than from their elders. Despite the rather low support fundamentalists enjoy in any age group, 33% of those 15-26 favored fundamentalists while only 26% of those over age 26 held such views.

Perhaps there is no more divisive issue in American religion than abortion. Here again the young are more willing to accept government restrictions on abortion than is true of their elders. Only 34% of adults over 26 are willing to have government restrict abortion, but 44% of those aged 15-22 support it. These findings are particularly surprising because the young are less likely than older Americans to attend religious services or to consider religion a guide in their lives.[103]

No generation gap also exists with reference to the issues of social security. The young are evidently just as supportive of government spending on health care for seniors as their elders. However, when it comes to spending on education, which benefits youth, only 52% over 60 favor increased spending on schools while 70% of the young and middle aged support such expenditures. Charlie and Jane are a childless senior citizen couple. They are not happy about spending taxes on school programs from which they feel they gain nothing. They resent requests for expansion of school curricula or building repairs. They seem to have little concern for the young and their needs. This despite the fact that their nieces and nephews are students in the school system and that two of the older nieces are very active in politics, fighting to get better health care and cost free pharmaceuticals for the elderly.

---

103. Janet Gilmore, "Youth more conservative than their elders on issues involving religion and abortion," *Campus News*, Berkeley, Cal. University of California (September 24, 2002):1.

The young also want the government to do more to protect women and racial minorities from job discrimination and also consider discrimination against gay and lesbian people a serious problem. Older Americans do not support these notions much, nor are older people nearly as concerned with the environment or the needs of the poor as are younger Americans.

THE EXPECTED AND THE UNEXPECTED

Real differences in generational attitudes also exist with reference to the broadcasting of sex and violence on television. Among those aged 27-59, 67% think sex and violence are serious problems while only 47% of those of college age think so.[104]

There are of course teenagers who have so little in common with their parents and others among the older generation that they do not fit in with the homework-doing, sports-playing average teenagers in America. It is this minority, however, who are consistently featured in the media because stories about their pain and their problems sell far better than any discussion of the normal, the expected and the usual. Teenage drug users are highlighted in the media. That includes sons and daughters of famous actors and important political figures. In the recent past the eighteen-year-old freshman who was hazed by his fraternity was featured, as an example. This young man was an excellent student. He was directed by his fraternity brothers to drink uncounted amounts of alcohol. He died. The public reading this item believed that the majority of college students behave in the manner described.

At a forum entitled "Teenagers In A Changing America," journalists and others were shown a documentary entitled "Girls Like Us." Clips from this film and three others were shown the forum consisting of retired people, middle-aged working people and teenagers. The films depicted teen delinquency ranging from homosexuality to smoking, partying and drinking. The films included the life of a 13-year-old girl who drinks so much at parties she can't remember the next morning what happened to her the night before. Another film showed a 15-year-old living alone in an apartment house in an empty room because she lost all contact with her family after a fight about her boyfriend. The forum discussed

---

104. Ibid. p. 1.

these films and sought to discover the causes of deviant behavior as depicted in them. No dispute between the generations concerning blame for such deviance developed. Instead, members of the forum listened to one another and respected each other's views, no matter the age of the participant. Here was another sign that the "generation gap" is far smaller than the media or public have commonly assumed.[105]

There are some social service organizations which have attempted to bring old and young people together so as to lessen the "generation gap," if it exists at all. One such example is the effort by the Long Island, NY Children's Association. They have developed an "Intergenerational Mentoring Program" designed to improve school performance, develop interpersonal relationships and increase positive social behavior. In this program each child is paired with a senior who is over 55 years old. The old take the young on field trips to museums, sporting events, family picnics and the "Getting to Know You" event sponsored by the association. According to the Family and Children's Association, children and adults both gain a good deal emotionally and psychologically from these encounters.[106] In a number of nursing homes throughout the United States, including in a Buffalo, New York nursing facility, children visit the elderly on a regular basis. Some very close ties have developed. After a few visits a number of children "adopted" one of the residents. Mary, age 12, is one of many such children. She first saw eighty-year-old Ernestine when her public school class went to the nursing facility to entertain and sing as a group. It wasn't long before she came alone to spend two hours every week with her newly adopted friend. Ernestine and she take time reminiscing about the "olden" days. They exchange stories and talk about each other's feelings. They discovered each other's similarities, which include hobbies which they both enjoy.

In 1978, Marion H. McQuade founded National Grandparents Day for the prime purpose of championing the cause of lonely old nursing home patients. This effort led then President Jimmy Carter to announce that Grandparents Day would be celebrated every year on the first Sunday after Labor Day. Although that designation has been given little attention by the public, the J.F. Smucker Co., which manufactures peanut butter and jelly spreads, has donated these spreads to events honoring grandparents and sponsored by the Boy and Girl

105. Ashley Kemper, "Teen Weekend," Start bridging the generation gap now: focus on the positive," *Lancaster New Era*, (September 25, 2003):5.
106. Lisa Josefak, "Long Island's Family and Children's Association works to bridge the generation gap," *Long Island Business News*, (October 31, 2003):NA.

Scouts of America across the country. This effort is by no means small because the Boy and Girl Scouts of America serve 3.5 million children.[107]

Despite this and other evidence that the generation gap is by no means an unbridgeable chasm, there are indeed differences in perception and demeanor exhibited by those who come of age at different times. At any time those who represent the older generation may be called traditionalists. If this label is applied to those who were born or matured during the Great Depression and who participated one way or another in the Second World War, then we can distinguish between that generation and those who came after them.

One distinguishing characteristic of the Depression-World War generation is that that generation was modeled by the military. The military is of course a command and control environment with a distinct vertical approach to human relations. Furthermore, the traditionalists here considered are patriotic, hard working and fiscally conservative. These people are appalled by the conduct of those younger than themselves. Authority struck, they find it obnoxious that younger people call the boss by his first name and send a "thank you" note via email.

Three generations have been born in the US since the traditionalists came of age. The first of these generations was born between 1946 and 1964 and are often called "the boomers" because that period in our history saw a baby boom or increase in the population. These "boomers" experienced a long economic expansion after World War II. Raised in an era of optimism, this generation believed they could do anything including changing the world.

The generation of Americans called "boomers" include 80 million people. Highly competitive, they have a great deal of interest in "getting ahead" by means of education and job advancement. They are annoyed by the so-called "60s generation, also called "Generation X" who are far less anxious and much more relaxed in their attitude towards careers, families or the treatment of bosses sometimes called "superiors." These "boomers" have been willing and able to change careers long before retirement. At the beginning of the 21st century, many "boomers" are seeking to retire within the next decade, i.e. between 2014 and 2024.

The "boomer" generation has been succeeded by a far smaller generation of only 46 million, born between 1965 and 1981. Because they were so few, the so-called "Generation X" has always been employed. In their experience there were

---

107. Hannah Baysden, "Bridging the Generation Gap with Peanut Butter and Jelly," *Financial News*, (September 2, 2003):1.

always jobs and not enough people to fill them. Accustomed to rapid change, the members of this generation have been very independent and very much involved in starting their own businesses. Those of this generation expect that no employer will keep them for a lifetime but that they must make changes in their expectations at all times.

By 2005, the "millennials" were entering the workforce. Born after 1981, this is the cyberspace generation. Raised on the computer, taking the Internet for granted, they are highly concerned with the environment. Even more illiterate than previous generations, the "millennials" know only what they see on a screen. They have rarely held a book in hand. "Millennials" are most likely to have several careers and will therefore be involved in lifetime learning by means of technology, of course. Most of the "millennials" are still in college and are interested in work which has "meaning." This attitude comes from their "boomer" parents.[108]

Taking a look at the attitudes of "millennials" towards the issues of the day, we find that here again, the young appear more ready to support conservative views than the older generation. In November of 2003 the Gallup poll asked a number of Americans several questions concerning these issues. The poll divided "the young" from the "older" by using 18- to 29-year-old respondents as compared to those more than 30 years old. The poll then reported that 62% of young adults said they approved of the job President Bush was doing, while among older adults only 53% approved. Young adults also were more inclined to think that the war in Iraq was worth fighting. In the same poll 61% of the young supported the war while only 53% of older Americans did so.

Fifty-eight percent of the young at that time thought the economy was improving while only forty-eight percent of the older group thought so.

It was only on the issue of homosexual marriage that the young at that time were more "liberal" than their parents. More than half, 53%, of the young were then willing that homosexuals marry while only 32% of older adults found it acceptable.[109] In the years prior to 1950, homosexuals were considered an "abomination" and an abnormal "aberration." Their acts and behavior were considered a crime against God and society. They were described as deviants in the psychiatric literature and were to be avoided at all costs.

---

108. Lynne C. Lancaster, "The Click and Clash of Generations," *Library Journal*, 128, no.7, (October 2003)
109. Deborah I. Acomb, "Generation Gap," *National Journal*, 35, no.45 (November 8, 2003).

THE ELECTRONIC GENERATION

Because ageism is so entrenched in the American psyche, many "older" people depict the ignorance of the "young" as a shortcoming of the "old." This reminds us of the stupid statement by the first Henry Ford that "history is bunk."[110]

That view was by no means limited to Henry Ford. In his day as in 2005, many Americans viewed history as nonsense, having no importance or meaning. Of course, the definition of history plays a part in such an assessment. There are those who seek to produce "instant history" by analyzing events which occurred within a decade or a lifetime. This appears to be more like journalism than history, as the consequences of current events cannot be analyzed without the passage of time.

The vast majority of people are of course not historians. For them, the past is likely to be of no importance because it is generally unknown. This is no doubt true of all generations. However, the defining events of anyone's lifetime are seldom forgotten. It is in this area that the youth culture and the generation gap became most visible. Surely, a veteran of the Second World War who fought at Anzio or participated in the invasion of Iwo Jima or remembers "D Day" finds it astounding that people born after 1960 — much less 1980 — may be quite ignorant of these events or consider them unimportant.

A number of surveys have revealed that ignorance of American history is widespread. In April of 2003 the Washington Times reported that David McCullough, a prize-winning historian, actually told the US Senate that ignorance of American history is a security threat. It is astounding that more than half of high school students in a survey thought that Ulysses Grant commanded the American forces at Yorktown during the Revolutionary War and that six percent thought it was Douglas MacArthur. One half of high school students surveyed believed that Japan and Germany were US allies during the Second World War and only 60% could identify the decade during which the Civil War occurred.

This and many other examples of historical ignorance reveals that the youth culture holds anything they themselves did not experience in contempt, even as the "older generation," equally ignorant of what preceded them, finds it

---

110. E.D. Hirsch, Ed. *The New Dictionary of Cultural Literacy, 3rd Edition,* (New York: Houghton Mifflin Co.,) 2002 p.18.

astounding that the most crucial events of their own lifetime are not known to their children.[111]

At Beloit College, professors have attempted to alter their teaching to conform to the ignorance of their students. University of Wisconsin faculty have evidently succumbed to this method as well. Even so-called "personalities," i.e. entertainers such as the actor Paul Newman, were not known to students in the Wisconsin freshman class of 2003, and the Soviet Union never existed (at least for them). Adults therefore "look upon 18-year-olds as if they are from Borneo or outer Mongolia." Eighteen-year-olds know little if anything about "adults" who are now 20 years old.

Professors who must teach those who have so little knowledge of the past may seek to use examples which are derived from current experiences or current events. However, such teaching cannot contribute to knowledge of American history nor to an understanding of American democracy.[112] It takes an extra effort to break into the closed world of such students; when a student mentioned that certain a certain German drug company "carries ethical baggage for their action in some war," professor Marianne Jennings at Arizona State University had to interrupt to clarify to the class that it was World War II, the "dominant conflict of the 20th century."

Today (2005), about 36% of professors are more than 55 years old. This may be regarded as an obstacle to communication between professors and students, although age differences cannot be considered an automatic obstacle to learning. There are those who believe that students born in 1985 or later cannot learn anything unless it is presented in Internet chat rooms, so-called electronic bulletin boards or by means of email. Yet, the means used to communicate are hardly as important as the subject matter, i.e. the message. The issue should not be whether the professor uses the latest technology to reach students but whether students make every effort to learn the subject matter even if presented in a book and not an "e" book readable on a computer. Says professor Virginia Vaughn of Clark University in Worcester, Mass., "It's phony for professors to immerse themselves in youth culture — sitting through novels they don't like or music they can't stand." Such an approach may be called "pandering," a term derived from Chaucer and related to prostituting oneself. Told by a student that

111. Geroge Archibald, "Ignorance of US history called threat to security," *The Washington Times,* (April 11, 2003):1.
112. Mark Fisher, "Mind-set list really a challenge," *Dayton Daily News,* (September 4, 2003):A1.

he was "lecturing above [his] head," the professor answered: "I lecture where your head ought to be."[113]

Those members of the youth culture who graduated from college after 2000 are of course much more computer literate than earlier generations. That generation and those who follow have been called "digital natives" because they grew up in an electronic world allowing them skills at parallel processing, multi-tasking and hyperlinking. Those involved in recent electronic developments have access to worldwide information. They have become used to the idea that all experiences have an immediate payoff. These considerations affect not only schools but also corporate trainers who seek to bridge the "generation gap" by using such relatively new technologies, such as cell phone models which threaten to supplant personal computers.[114]

THE SOCIOLOGY OF THE GENERATION GAP

It is commonly assumed that age is a chronological condition which is unalterable and therefore "only natural." This assumption implies that someone ten or forty or eighty resembles all others of the same age because nature dictates that resemblance. It is also assumed that all who belong to the same age cohort will act the same, i.e. according to their age. In fact, we are constantly enjoined to "act your age" and therefore we do just that. Children therefore are frequently trained to act in unacceptable ways since they are "only young once." In years of experience as a psychotherapist, the author found that youngsters who were trained to misbehave take this behavior into their adult lives. Jimmy was the only boy among three sisters. He was allowed to take their toys, help himself to whatever he could find in their rooms and in their possessions. He was also not expected to help with the household chores and informed that it is the girls' job to do the dishes and the in-home chores. As a teen he became just what the parents had created. They complained about him in my session with them but conveniently forgot what they so aptly taught him. Yet, age, like race and gender, is a social construct and is therefore a great deal more than the years that have

---

113. Mark Clayton, "'Talkin' 'bout my generation," *Christian Scinece Monitor*, (September 16, 2003):13.
114. Jennifer J. Salpek, "Going Native: Cross the generation gap by leaning to speak game," *T + D*, 57, no. 6 (June 2003):1.

passed since birth. Age is a performance based on whatever is normative or expected in various cultures. Therefore age is interactive so that we act our age in accordance with the expectations of others concerning our behavior as related to our perceived age. Age, then, has meaning. That meaning is expressed by the manner in which we interact with others, the ambitions we promote, our expression of beliefs and feelings and our social policies. The sociologists Blumer and Garfinkel have labeled this approach to our understanding of our status-role "symbolic interactionism" or social constructionism. Blumer has summarized this approach in three central premises. These are that human beings act on the basis of the meaning that things have for them; that meaning is derived from social interaction and that meaning is interpreted by every person based on experience.[115]

Assumptions about age and the life-course shape a person's self-image. Culture and meaning derived from culture determine largely how one relates age to self-image. Usually, studies of aging refer to "old age" but seldom to ages not called "old." A study of age, unlike a study of aging, refers to an analysis of all ages and the relationship between them. Age as a concept is created by the culture which assesses it, so that beliefs concerning various age categories are dictated by the culture in which one lives.[116]

The widespread view that age is an objective chronological fact is true only if we overlook that people of the same age may not display the same age-related looks or behavior. Age is to some extent determined by inheritance, so that some who have reached a rather advanced age look no older than others who are far younger. Such differences in appearance have social meaning because those who appear younger than their years will be treated as younger than chronology would dictate, while those appearing older will be treated like someone who is older. Therefore, an "objective fact" such as age begins to lose its meaning as the number of years a person has lived is no longer a guarantee that his actions will have one or another consequence. Cultures other than our own give age a different interpretation so that number of years is not a determining factor to age analysis in all cultures.[117]

---

115. Robert J. Brym and John Lie, *Sociology*, (New York, Wadsworth) 2003 p. 124.

116. Matilda W. Riley, "On the significance of age in sociology," *American Sociological Review*, 52 (1987):1-14.

117. Jennie Keith, "Age in social and cultural context: Anthropological perspectives," In: Robert Binstock and Linda George, eds. *Handbook of Aging and Social Sciences*, (Boston, Academic Press)p. 91-111.

Chronology, then, is not an objective fact but is made important by cultural dictates. Therefore it is by no means "natural" that American adolescents listen to loud rock music and reject out-of-hand all Italian operas and German symphonies. Such bigotry is learned. Likewise, it is not at all necessary that the young view the old with disdain and/or contempt. Such attitudes are learned and are based on several assumptions known in Western culture. While we do not demand to see a birth certificate before treating others as a child, an adolescent, an adult or a "senior citizen," we use visible signs as well as dress and/or actions. Nevertheless, there are contexts in which we do indeed ask for age identification, including obtaining a driver's license or gaining access to alcoholic beverages. Age then has an "objective" dimension and a "social" dimension and these are not always the same.[118]

Age is a status-role. This sociological concept refers to the sum of our privileges, called statuses, and the sum of our obligations, called roles. Every culture determines the status available to people of different ages and the roles that we are to play in each status. In the United States almost all power is in the hands of the middle aged. Therefore, the role of the middle aged is one of activity, involvement and action. It is expected that the young follow the demands of the middle aged and that the old do likewise. These categories highlight and exaggerate differences and minimize similarities between age groups. The method used to exaggerate differences between age categories is the tendency to view age as an individual attribute. Hence correlation is viewed as causation, so that age is used to explain all phenomena whether voting behavior or television viewing preferences. In the US, age is usually seen as the exclusive attribute of old people but not of younger people. Theses expectations or norms concerning age are forced upon all of us, so that we act in accordance with the pressure to conform in our behavior and our actions to the age related expectations of the society in which we live. This pertains especially to the "old," as everything they do or fail to do is related to their age. This phenomenon is quite common in that there are many men who attribute everything a woman does to her gender and not her individuality. Sociologists refer to the perception that one attribute exceeds in importance all other attributes of a person as his "master status." Anyone may be many things, such as a son, a businessman, a Republican, a "born-again Christian" and a lawyer and will yet be seen by those so socialized as

---

118. Candace West and Don H Zimmerman, "Doing gender," *Gender and Society*, 1, (1987):125-151.

"the old man." Age is here the master status and all other attributes of a person disappear in favor of that "master status." The same holds true for the young. There are many Americans who see only the age of a young person and conclude that this "master status" determines all his beliefs, actions and attributes.[119]

Evidently, the view that age is the only attribute visible leads to a generation gap of considerable proportions. It is certain that many "young" people have a lot more in common with people older than themselves. However, it is also a matter of experience to know that common interests between the old and the young far outweigh age if given a chance.

Some sociologists have suggested that age be seen as accomplishment rather than as a social problem. Such a view alleviates the stigma associated with old age in American culture and promotes the view that as age progresses, one's achievements increase.[120]

This would mean that the generation gap could be easily closed by promoting common interests between the young and the old and the middle aged. That is difficult to do in a society in which the young spend their time in school, the middle aged spend their time at work and the old are often relegated to a nursing home.[121]

THE SECOND GENERATION GAP

Because life expectancy increased considerably during the century ending in 2003, a generation gap can exist not only between the young and the "old" but also between the not-so-old middle aged and their truly old parents. This great change is seen by looking at past life expectancy tables. Such a view shows that in 1900 males born that year could expect to live only 48.2 years and females born that year expected to live 51.1 years. By 2000, males born that year could expect to live 73 years and females born that year could expect to live to age 79. Therefore, there are many more "old" folks in America and providing a "second" generation gap between middle aged adults and their truly old parents.

---

119. Ross L. Matsueda, "The Current State of Differential Association Theory," *Crime and Delinquency*, 34, (1988):277.

120. Gerhard Falk, *Stigma: How We Treat Outsiders*, (Amherst, N.Y., Prometheus Books, 2001)p. 129.

121. Ursula Adler, *A Critical Study of the American Nursing Home*, (Lewiston, N.Y , 1991).

The old have many needs which they may not be able to fulfill, and social services and government agencies have attempted to meet some of these needs, including health care, financial assistance that may include "retirement jobs," and adequate housing. Most important to the elderly is the need to have intimate and affectionate contacts with children, grandchildren and others (whom sociologists regard as the primary group). Of course, old age is not the only stage in life in which primary contacts are important. Infants need their mothers, young adults need their "significant others" of the opposite sex, children need their parents and everyone needs friends. The need for primary group contacts is universal and life long, but can be particularly difficult to fulfill when one is old.

Many an old person loses the spouse who supplied affection for years. One third of all women and 9% of all men over 55 are widowed. In 2000, those over 75 were even more isolated. At that age 21% of men and 49% of women were living alone because their spouse had died. Since only 29% of women age 75 or more were still living with their spouse, 22% were living with children or other relatives or were incarcerated in nursing homes. Men fared better at that age since 67% of men 75 years old or older were living with their spouse and only 21% were living alone. Hence only 12% of men were living with children, other relatives or in a nursing home.[122]

These numbers increase with age, so that the oldest are most likely to be alone and without the love and physical affection they have enjoyed for over half a century or more. In addition, those among the old, whether widowed or not, who are in ill health, are very much in need of sympathy and the protective care of a spouse or child. This is particularly true because the American medical establishment insults, humiliates and rejects the old precisely when they need help the most. Robert Butler, M.D. writes: "Medical ageism is contracted in medical school. There medical students learn to use such vocabulary as "gomer," which is an acronym for "get out of my emergency room," and "gork," which means that "God only really knows [what ails the old complainer]." Most common among the labels attached to old patients by the medical establishment is "vegetable.""[123]

A comprehensive review of ageism in the medical profession and in other institutions reveals that ageism is normative in America and that the old expe-

---

122. US Department of Commerce, Bureau of the Census, *Current Population Survey*, (Washington, D.C. United States Government Printing Office, 2000)p.12.
123. Robert Butler, M.D. *Why Survive? Being Old in America*. (New York, Harper and Row,1975)p.13.

rience its sting in the economy, in religion, in education and on the part of government. Even in the family ageism can play an ugly part despite the fact that the principle function of the family is to supply love.[124]

When old people live with children and other relatives the relationship is not always a happy one. Even old parents and adult children who live separately can have difficulties and antagonisms. Here the generation gap becomes most visible as the needs, interests and wants of the middle aged and old diverge. Some middle aged children are so incensed by the demands of their parents that they make such comments as: "You ought to take every person over sixty-five out and shoot him" or "Why don't the old fools die?"

Although such ugly comments exist, the International Linkages Survey conducted by the American Association of Retired Persons reflects a positive attitude by the American population towards the old. That survey showed that 69% of adult children have weekly contact with their mothers and 20% have daily contact with their mothers. Other surveys have shown that 40% of adult children have face-to-face contact with their parents once a week.[125]

The 2004 National Survey of Families and Households shows that 78% of adults view their relationship with their mother and father as excellent. Only 0.03% of those surveyed viewed that relationship as "bad." The remainder were ambivalent in their perception of their parents. In short, the overwhelming majority of adult children report close relationships with their parents. This finding is confirmed by much older studies of the same phenomenon also conducted by the National Survey of Families and Households.

Of those surveyed, 66% contacted their parents once a week or more and only 10% did not deal with their parents at all. In part, this is a product of the distance at which adult children live from their parents. The 2004 survey showed that 67% of adult children live within 100 miles of their parents and that 38% live within ten miles of their parents. However, a full 20% of those surveyed live 1000 miles or more away from their parents. This latter situation is almost always a function of vertical mobility.[126]

124. Ursula Adler Falk and Gerhard Falk, *Ageism, the Aged and Aging in America*, (Springfield, Ill. Charles C. Thomas, Publisher, 1997).
125. Dianne N. Lye and et.al. "Childhood living arrangements and adult children's relations with their parents," *Demography*, 32, (1995):261-280.
126. James A. Sweet and Larry L. Bumpass, *The National Survey of Families and Households*, (Madison, Wis. University of Wisconsin Center for Demography and Ecology, Working Paper #1 2004).

Because close relationships between old parents and adult children are the rule, economic support of adult children by old parents is by no means uncommon. For most American families finances are most strained during the period when dependent children are still in the house. It is at this stage that many families need financial assistance, which is frequently forthcoming from "old" parents, i.e. grandmothers and grandfathers.[127]

In part, that financial assistance is produced by the normal events of the life cycle such as births, confirmations (or Bar Mitzvahs), graduations, weddings and funerals. Both grandmothers and grandfathers are likely to make contributions to the welfare of the next generation although the contributions of grandfathers are commonly overlooked. Because "the old" at the beginning of the 21st century are usually far better educated than was true only 20 years ago, the "old" are in a position to give a good deal more than was the case heretofore. It is a facet of American culture to expect grandmothers to be giving and solicitous of their adult children and their grandchildren.[128]

Grandparents support the families of their children in a number of ways. Most common is the support of grandchildren. About 76% of parents over 55 have grandchildren who are frequently the recipients of help from grandparents. The "Commonwealth Fund Productive Aging Study" has analyzed the value of the help grandparents give grandchildren, and ipso facto adult children, and found that typically grandparents give grandchildren assistance for seven hours a week. The same study discovered that nine percent of grandparents assist grandchildren 20 hours per week or more.[129]

These numbers translate into 14.1 million grandparents helping grandchildren every week. The average of 13 hours of help received from grandparents each week represents the equivalent of 4.2 million full time workers each year.

Assuming that child care costs at least $2 per hour, and rises to $3 or $3.25 in some regions of the country, the number of hours provided by grandparents equates to between $17.4 billion and 29.1 billion a year.[130]

---

127. Ursula Adler Falk and Gerhard Falk, *Grandparents: A New Look at the Supporting Generation,* (Amherst, N.Y. Prometheus Books, 2002)p.172.

128. Gail Wilson, "Women's Work: The Role of Grandparents in Inter-generational transfer,"*Sociological Review,* 5, no. 4 (1987):703.

129. Kenneth A. Coleman, " The Value of Productive Activities of Older Americans," in: *Older and Active: How Americans Over 55 Are Contributing to Society,* Scott A. Bass, ed. (New Haven, Conn.: Yale University Press, 1955)pp. 169-203.

130. Ibid. p.31.

RACE, ETHNICITY AND GENDER

Race and ethnicity insure considerable differences between whites and blacks and their family relationships. Principal among research findings concerning these relationships is that blacks have more frequent contacts with their parents and adult children than whites and that these relationships are of a higher quality and involve more exchange of assistance. The National Survey of Black Americans confirms that black adults tend to live closer to the majority of their kin and that most have at least weekly contact with members of their extended family. This is also true of Mexican immigrants to the United States. The National Survey of Hispanic Elderly shows that 80% of old Mexican immigrants live within a few minutes of an adult child and that even among those who did not live with an adult child, nearly half had daily face-to-face contact with an adult child.[131]

Immigrants whose origins are overseas are less likely to be living in proximity to their relatives. Evidently, Mexicans can enter the United States illegally at any time. This is not possible for those who come from far away and must arrive by plane or boat. Furthermore, there are in the US immigrants who came because their entire family was murdered in the holocaust or the Cambodian mass slaughters so that these immigrants have no relatives.

Gender also influences adult-child relationships with their "old" parents. The relationship between mothers and daughters has traditionally been closer than the relationship between sons and either parent. In part this closer mother-daughter connection is promoted by the "kin keeper" role which almost always accrues to women. "The kin keeper attempts to maintain and perpetuate the family network, by passing on the history of the family, living by a family theme or ethos, promoting family unity, and helping with family responsibilities."[132]

Aging mothers are more likely to choose daughters rather than sons as confidants. Mothers also receive more emotional support from daughters or sons than fathers. Therefore, mothers and daughters both are more likely to make an issue of disagreements between themselves than is true of sons. Adult daughters are also more likely to provide routine help to their parents than is true of sons and mothers are more likely to provide assistance to their adult children than is

---

131. Tracy L. Dietz, "Patterns of Intergenerational Assistance within the Mexican-American family: Is the family taking care of the older generation's needs?" *Journal of Family Issues*, 16, no.3, (1995)pp.344-356.
132. Ursula Adler Falk and Gerhard Falk, *Grandparents*, p.142.

true of fathers. Mothers are also more likely to receive assistance from adult children because women live longer than men. Parents with only one daughter are more likely to receive both emotional support and other assistance than those who only have sons.[133]

The sociologists Merril Silverstein and Vern L. Bengtson have studied intergenerational solidarity between adult children and their parents by using a survey undertaken by the American Association of Retired Persons in collaboration with a research team from Harvard University and the University of Southern California. The survey involved a sample of 1,500 adults aged 18-90 years from randomly selected households in 48 contiguous states. The survey questionnaire and the telephone interviews dealt only with adult children living away from their parents and focused on the relationship between these generations. This study supports the findings already discussed in this chapter. First, Silverstein and Bengtson found that the belief that the family is in decline is a gross exaggeration. The researchers found in fact that there are five "underlying types of intergenerational relationships." None of these "types," however, are dominant so that there is no "model" type of intergenerational family.

The researchers also found that, although many American families are geographically dispersed, they are not necessarily emotionally distant. Assistance to other family members is rendered even when there are great physical distances involved. The researchers also found a considerable difference in the relationship of adult children with their mothers and their fathers. They found that almost four times as many children are detached from their fathers than their mothers. Where divorce is a factor, this phenomenon can only be exacerbated by the custom of divorce courts to favor mothers over fathers in allocating child custody. The study also supports the findings of almost all students of adult-child and "old" parents relationships that daughters are closer to mothers than to fathers, while sons are equally distant to both parents.

Divorce, of course, affects the relationship of divorced parents to their adult children. The magnitude of the effects of marital disruption are greater with respect to fathers than mothers. Finally, and certainly not surprisingly, Silverstein and Bengtson found that young adults depend on their parents more

---

133. Paul Amato, S.J. Rezac and A.J. Booth, "Helping between adult parents and young adult offspring: the role of parental marital quality, divorce and remarriage," *Journal of Marriage and the Family*, 57, (1995):363-374.

than middle-aged adults do, and that parents in their old age are also more likely to ask for and receive help from their middle-aged children.[134]

THE YOUTH CULTURE

There is an aspect of the "generation gap" which is involuntary and the product of age alone. That is the young person's belief that he is invincible. This belief is expressed in the music, language, sexual mores and hours of sleep of those in their teens and their willingness to take risks. In the case of an accident, or the death of parents and friends, the "older" generation is cautioned and considers age and physical condition as very important, even as the "young" view these events as distant from themselves and of no great threat to their power and self-assurance. The young are often unable to recognize the eventual consequences of their present actions. This assessment is perhaps even more true in America than in some other cultures throughout the world.[135]

One aspect of the youth culture in the US is the low credibility which adolescents, and sometimes even older children, afford their parents. In part this refusal to listen to any advice or opinion of parents is needed by the young because each generation has to become independent so as to reach maturity. In most children this "credibility gap" occurs between the ages of 12 and 18 although some develop a hostile attitude towards the older generation at an older age.[136]

One means of discerning the existence of the youth culture in American life is to analyze the television viewing habits of 12 to 17 year olds. The Houston Chronicle reports that 14 of the top 25 shows among 11 to 17 year olds "are nowhere to be found" among the top 25 shows for all viewers. Teens evidently favor humorous shows or those which that age group considers humorous. In fact, comedies account for more than half of their top 25 shows.

One aspect of the youth culture as it exists at the beginning of the 21st century is the extensive electronic entertainment environment that was never

134. Merril Silverstein and Vern L. Bengtson, " Intergenerational Solidarity and the Structure of Adult-Parent Relationships in American Families," *American Journal of Sociology*, 103, no. 2, (September 199):429-460.
135. Paula Voell, If ignorance is bliss, wisdom has its price," *The Buffalo News*, (January 19, 1996):C6
136. Ann Taylor, "Credibility Gap: It's only a temporary condition," *50 Plus Lifestyles*, July 1, 2003):A6

available to previous generations. These electronic devices, such as television, the Internet and video games, allow for so many choices that almost all tastes can be satisfied. Included are such favorite entertainment for teen age children as reality shows revolving around dating and rejection, i.e. relationship issues. Advertisers are of course aware of the teenage market, which centers around movies, soda and cosmetics.[137]

Television is not the only concern of the participants in the youth culture. Very important to young Americans is the need to gain independence, autonomy and the respect of others. In the Euro-American community this is often achieved by earning money or achieving in school. In minority communities these goals are not as often attainable and therefore a "macho" culture may take the place of more conventional achievements. Those who work in poorly paid jobs such as fast food restaurants, those whose earnings are small and whose work prospects are poor, learn early in their lives that the most important criterion of social prestige in America is occupation.[138]

The youth culture centers around adolescents who may be defined as "marginal people" in that they must live in both the world of the dependent child and the world of the beginning adult. That marginality is caused by the gap between biological maturity, which we define as the ability to reproduce oneself, and economic maturity which we define as the ability to support oneself. As the next section of this book describes, adolescents seek to establish their identity, a process made more difficult for those who have come to this country as immigrants or who have the status of migrants within the United States. All young people are in addition faced with the problems which American society has created by the immense confusion concerning sex roles and sex at all ages and social strata. This confusion impacts most severely on those involved in the youth culture and that too will be explored in the next section of this book.

---

137. David Hiltbrand, "Teens living in their own TV universe," *The Houston Chronicle*, (May 28, 2003):1.
138. John J. Macionis, *Society: The Basics*, (Upper Saddle River, N.J., Prentice Hall, 2004)p.203.

SUMMARY

The generation gap is not as wide as popularly assumed. Nevertheless, it is inevitable that the middle aged have most of the power and decision making opportunities.

As each generation passes from youth to middle age and reproduces itself, it passes on to the younger generation the benefits it received from the previous generation. These benefits include the contributions made by the "old" to the young, particularly grandchildren. Therefore, there are many shared values between the generations. Numerous research studies have shown that there is a great deal of sympathy between parents and children despite some differences in opinion and attitude. Presently, we call the new generation the "millennials," who have been raised on electronics, so that the youth culture centers upon television, the Internet and video games. Adolescents seek to discover their own identity by using their peers as a "looking glass." This issue will be explored in the next chapter.

Part II. Age Peers

Chapter 4. Identity and Self Concept Among Adolescents

The Study of Identity

A century ago, the sociologists James Horton Cooley (1864-1929) and George Herbert Mead (1863-1931) introduced the idea of the "looking glass self" and the notion of seeing oneself objectively. Cooley showed that when we interact with others they interact with us in a fashion which reflects, like a mirror, our own words and actions. We therefore interpret who we are by how we see ourselves judged by others.[139] Our appearance is validated by others.

Social psychology, and particularly symbolic interactionism, is the perspective which has led to a great deal of research concerning identity with particular emphasis on the "me" concept as it molds every individual's sense of self. This view was introduced to philosophy by Martin Buber (1878-1965) in his famous book Ich und Du, or, I and Thou.

When symbolic interactionism is applied to the identity development among adolescents, then it becomes at once evident that that age group must first confront the need for relating gender to sex. Sex is our biological inheritance. Gender is our social position as derived from sex differences. Because women and men are differentially equipped by nature, the differences are translated into differences in meaning and hence differences in social facts. Social psychologists have shown that the differences in interpretation as to what is

---

139. Charles Horton Cooley, *Human Nature and the Social Order*, (New York: Scribner's 1902):3.

feminine and what is masculine severely restricts social behavior. Subjective social interpretations of what is feminine and what is masculine force upon us prescribed actions and expectations. We enforce upon the sexes manners of speaking, thinking, writing and dressing and then treat this learned behavior as if it were "only natural." [140]

In a study of adolescent sexuality, the social psychologist Janice Irving identifies nine areas that contribute to identity building during the adolescent years. These are gender relations; sexual identities; reproductive strategies; sexual language; the role of the family; non-reproductive sexuality; the purpose of sex; meaning of the body and sexual violence. Irving shows that cultural differences color each of these categories even as culture creates differences in understanding and behavior everywhere. [141]

Identity is, of course, also related to race. Yet, race and ethnicity are not certain categories but cultural constructs. For example, ethnicity may be defined differently as the demographic make-up of a society shifts. The changing needs of those empowered to define ethnicity can be seen in the changing ways that Euro-Americans look at the ancestry of certain ethnic groups. Prior to the influx of large numbers of South American and Asian immigrants to the United States, Americans of European ancestry emphasized differences among themselves; now, however, a broadly defined "Euro-American" ethnic group sees itself as relatively coherent, and stands with a larger, unified cultural base to oppose the other ethnic groups. [142]

The most recent development in the establishment of identity is new communication technology, especially television and the world wide web. These electronic media have reorganized the world and created new forms of social interaction. People previously isolated and powerless, such as the disabled but also children and adolescents, are empowered by the Internet to send out messages and receive them and unite with others facing similar problems. The differences which divide children from adults are now the differences that divide those who are computer literate from those who are computer illiterate. At the

---

140. Dorothy Smith, *The Conceptual Practice of Power*, (Boston: Northeastern University Press, 1990)p.199.

141. Janice M. Irving, "Cultural differences and adolescent sexualities," In Janice M. Irving, Ed.: *Sexual Cultures and the Construction of Adolescent Identities*, (Philadelphia: Temple University Press, 1994)p.11.

142. Richard D. Alba, *Ethnic Identity: The Transformation of White America*, (New Have, CT., Yale University Press, 1990)p.306.

same time, adults who are computer literate, like their children, now find that the play world of the child is directly linked to the work world of the adult. The keyboard thereby becomes the door to interaction.[143]

IDENTITY AND THE ADOLESCENT

Identity in America depends on several socio-psychological factors, of which social class is foremost. The most important feature of social prestige in America is occupation, and occupation in turn is strongly related to social class.[144]

It is evident that social class is always ascribed for children but may be either achieved or ascribed for adults. The distinction between achieved and ascribed class and status was first developed in the influential book by Blau and Duncan, The American Occupational Structure. Blau and Duncan observe that physical traits (such as gender, race or bodily appearance) as well as the family into which one is born are ascribed to a person and cannot be altered. Achieved status is therefore that aspect of social standing which is attained by such efforts as education, the accumulation of wealth and, above all, occupation.[145]

It has long been assumed that the self-esteem of children, and in particular the self-esteem of adolescents, is strongly related to the social class of their parents and in particular the occupation of the child's father. In American society, unemployment, welfare and "bad neighborhood" are all stigmatized; this is a society which measures its members' worth by what they have and what they do.

Jay MacLeod described the impact of parental poverty on children in his book Ain't No Makin' It and gives this example: "When my kids go with me to the grocery store shopping, and we go through the checkout line, my kids usually take off. They told me they are embarrassed when I use my food stamps. They don't want to be seen with me."[146] Here is a situation in which social class has been directly translated into self-esteem.

---

143. Joshua Meyrowitz, "Shifting worlds of strangers: medium theory and changes in 'them' vs. 'us'." *Sociological Inquiry*, 67, no. 1 (1997):59-71.
144. Robert J. Brym and John Lie, *Sociology*, (New York: Wadsworth, 2003)p.188.
145. Peter M. Blau and Otis Duncan, *The American Occupational Structur*, (New York: Wiley, 1967).
146. Jay MacLeod, *Ain't No Makin' It: Leveled Aspirations in a Low Income Neighborhood*, (Boulder, Co.. Westwood, 1987) p.5.

It is of course true that the father's or mother's occupation and income are related to the self-esteem of their children. Nevertheless, what affects children and adolescents more directly are the consequences of parental education and wealth. If a billionaire was a high school drop-out at age sixteen, it is unlikely that his children would suffer very much from their father's lack of education.

The psychologists Carolyn Sartor and James Youniss discovered four major aspects of the relationship between parenting and adolescent identity development. First is parental knowledge of the daily activities of adolescent children. This is strongly associated with higher identity achievement. Second, emotional support from parents is positively related to identity achievement. Third, there is no gender difference for identity achievement; and fourth, there is evidence that identity achievement and parental support changes with age.[147]

There is also some doubt as to the impact of parental social position on the self-esteem of children. This doubt is related to the fact that children have their own occupation, i.e. student, and that therefore children can gain an achieved status by doing well in school. Such achieved statuses, academic prowess or scholarly attainment, can give some children a sense of achievement of their own, unrelated to the successes or failures of their parents. The work of the sociologists Rosenberg and Perlin concludes that: "Our self-regard depends primarily on what we have done....Children's self-esteem..is probably just as dependent as adult self-esteem on achievement; but this achievement is their own, not their parents'."[148]

The reason for the greater importance relative to the self-esteem of adolescent achievement than parental achievement or ascribed status lies in the fact that adolescents, in our culture, live in an adolescent subculture. This was adequately described by the sociologist Coleman. Says Coleman: "cut off from the rest of society...with his fellows he comes to constitute a small society, one that has most of its important interactions within itself and maintains only a few threads of connection with the outside adult society."[149]

Human identity is of course not related to only one kind of experience. Identity will be related to occupation, in the case of adolescents that is student,

147. Carolyn E. Sartor and James Youniss, "The relationship between positive parental involvement and identity achievement during adolescence," *Adolescence*, 37, no.146 (Summer 2002):221.

148. Morris Rosenberg, *Society and the Adolescent Self Image*, (Princeton, N.J., Princeton University Press, 1965)p.66.

149. James S. Coleman, *The Adolescent Society*, (New York, Free Press, 1961)p.73.

and to family and to income etc. In fact, some people will hold as more important factors of role identity and self-esteem which others may not value very much. Therefore, role identity becomes hierarchical in that some factors will be deemed more important and other less important by each person. Some people are very much identified with their occupation while others place family first. Therefore, role identity is a link between the self and others. Role identities for adolescents and for adults define the self as demanded by the culture in which the individual lives. The culture determines in advance that one kind of occupation is more prestigious than another, that one address is worth more than another or that membership in a club or organization carries great prestige. The individual then measures himself against these cultural assumptions and determines whether he is a success or failure. Therefore, each person develops self-esteem by reflecting on his self-definition. Positive self-esteem rests on a positive role identity. Putting this into adolescent terms we can say that a child who discharges his obligations in a positive manner (role) will develop a positive self-esteem. This then influences his relationship to others. Each individual then selectively perceives those relationships that are important to him. As McCall and Simmons put it: "A hungry man driving down the street will perceive a 'Restaurant' sign; a man with a headache will notice the 'Drugs' sign.'" This means that social relationships will be perceived in terms of their importance to each person's role-identity. Role-identities announce to others who we are. Therefore, in an occupation-driven society it is more important to be an insurance salesman, account executive, carpenter or dentist than a stamp collector — even if the salesman, the stockbroker, the carpenter and the dentist all collect stamps. It is the master status of an individual, generally derived from occupation, that determines the expectations we have of each other.[150]

Children in school all have the same occupation. Therefore, role identity and self-esteem within the school setting will relate to one or several aspects of school life as perceived by each child. It is unlikely that a 5'6" boy will find it possible to assume the role of football player. Yet, the same boy may be capable of being identified as the best actor in the school play.

A girl with musical ability can become identified with playing in the school orchestra even if she cannot do well in algebra. In short, the school offers

---

150. Sheldon Stryker, "Identity salience and role performance: the importance of symbolic interaction theory for family research," *Journal of Marriage and the Family*, 30, (1968):558-664.

numerous possible routes to success and positive role-identification. That, however, is not true for everyone.

Generally, people seek self-identities which are congruent with their own self meaning. This has a direct bearing on gender identity because grade schools in particular, but also junior high schools or middle schools, are predominantly taught by women. This means that feminine behavior is prized and that boys are often viewed as disruptive, too aggressive and even "delinquent" because their conduct reflects male hormones.

When observing a class of fourth graders in an urban public school it was noted that the young boys had difficulty sitting quietly. They shuffled their feet, stretched their arms and legs, and made many more physical responses and noise moving around in their seats than did the girls, who sat comparatively still at their desks. This invites speculation that a child's gender identity may have an impact on his success in school and will therefore be reflected in gender differences on scholastic performance tests. Numerous researchers have reported again and again that girls perform better throughout their scholastic careers in areas requiring verbal skills and that this difference becomes visible at age eleven and continues in high school and college.[151]

Up to a certain age, performance in so-called "analytic" subjects such as mathematics and science are evidently not gender linked because all studies show mixed results, so that boys and girls have an equal expectation of succeeding in these areas. In an attempt to understand the reasons for such differences in scholastic achievement which do exist, researchers have tried to link these differences to gender identity.[152]

The almost unanimous outcome of these studies is that gender identity is related to grades received in school. Boys and girls with more feminine gender identities earn higher grades than boys and girls with more masculine gender identities. This is true for blacks and whites, for female or male teachers and across all subject matter, including mathematics, science, social studies, arts and foreign languages. The principal reason for this unanimity in the findings is what has been called semantic congruence, which refers to the evidence that people

---

151. Harold W. Stevenson and Richard S. Newman, "Long Tem Predictions of Achievement and Attitudes in Mathematics and Reading," *Child Development*, 57, (1986):646-659.

152. Cindy L. Raymond and Camilla Benbow, "Gender Differences in Mathematics: A Function of Parental Support and Student Sex Typing?" *Developmental Psychology*, 22, (1986):808-819.

with particular role identities choose role behavior which has meaning similar to the meaning of their identity.[153]

It is of course possible that some behavior such as sitting still and paying attention is viewed as feminine by male students and is therefore avoided by boys. Conversely, it is possible that some behavior identified as "masculine" is avoided by some students and is avoided by children with feminine identities.

Plainly, children recognize what it means to be a boy or girl because boy or girl behavior is tied to gender identity. That meaning is conveyed to everyone by the treatment they receive from others. In school, treatment by teachers is undoubtedly related to gender, as documented by the social psychologists Rosenthal and Jacobsen.[154]

The school and numerous recreational facilities in America are used to help adolescents in forming their identity. Therefore, voluntary participation in discretionary activities can lead to finding one's place in the social structure. Structured school activities are less likely to have an impact on identity formation than voluntary activities because the imposition of academic requirements on all children in school leaves little opportunity for identity options. The opposite is true of discretionary or voluntary activities such as sports, which are more likely to lead a young person to consider "who I am."[155]

Several different studies show that involvement in constructive but non-academic activities are associated with academic achievement during adolescence and into adult years. These studies also indicate that the peer group with whom one associates in voluntary activities can have an either positive or negative effect on adolescents in our culture. It is possible that some programs are so designed that they attract only a limited number of adolescents who share the values a specific program promotes. It may therefore be that some programs will select out of the adolescent population those who already have a negative or positive attitude as defined by present American culture.

The school can have either a positive or negative impact on the identity formation of an adolescent. Evidently there are those who receive the adulation of others, such as football players and basketball heroes. Because our schools

---

153. Peter J. Burke and Donald C. Reitzes, "The Link between Identity and Role Performance." *Social Psychology Quarterly*, 44, (1991):83-92.

154. Robert Rosenthal and L. Jacobson, *Pygmalion in the Classroom*, (New York: Holt, Rinehart and Winston, (1968).

155. Hansen, D.M., Larson, R.W. and Dworkin, J.B. "What adolescents learn in organized youth activities," *Journal of Research on Adolescence*, 13, no.1, (2003):25-55.

value sports highly but discount academic achievement, it is far more likely that a 15-year-old sports hero will develop positively than someone perceived as bookish and academically superior. Nevertheless, there are of course alternative status systems in the schools just as there are alternative status systems in all American communities. Those, however, who differ most distinctly from expected behavior or expected social position are most likely to be damaged by their encounters with other high school children in our schools.

STIGMA AND THE ADOLESCENT

Stigma originally referred to the branding of slaves in ancient Greece. In American usage it has come to mean the rejection of numerous individuals, and often entire groups of people, on various grounds. These include the physically disabled, mentally impaired, homosexuals, ex-convicts and a host of others who are also labeled deviant from the expectations of any group.[156]

This definition has a direct impact on any adolescents in our schools who deviate in any fashion from the conformist expectations demanded there. Because school attendance is the full time occupation of adolescent children, the school is most influential in promoting self-esteem or causing devaluation of the self by others. Devaluation is defined as "the lessening or discounting of one's status through their beliefs, that are, in turn, reflected in their actions."[157]

Such devaluation of adolescents occurs first in institutional settings such as so-called "Homes for Children" or "Group Homes" or "Reformatories." In such institutions adolescents are subject to excessive restrictiveness, arbitrary rules, lack of individual consideration, insult, and a constant turnover of so-called caregivers. The level of prestige of the institutional child is most often the reverse of the child who lives in a normal home environment. The youngster who creates the greatest havoc is frequently the one with the greatest institutional prestige:

Johnny, a fourteen-year-old institutionalized boy, was considered a hero and the most popular in his cottage. He had managed to steal three cars successfully and his latest adventure included the theft of a bright red convertible, the

---

156. Gerhard Falk, *Stigma:How we treat outsiders,* (Amherst, N.Y., Prometheus Books, 2001)p. 32.

157. Susan M. Kools, "Adolescent Identity Development in Foster Care," *Family Relations,* 46, no. 3 (July 19997):263-271.

property of the town's high school principal. A number of the boys wanted to emulate him and his prowess.

Maria, in one of the girls' cottages, took pride in boasting about the number of sexual encounters she had with the boys "on campus" as well as with a house parent. She was the envy of a number of the other females and they looked up to her and enjoyed her thrilling recitations.

Children who are placed in foster homes face similar status changes as children in institutions. Sociologists define a status as any position in any social relationship, such as husband or wife. In addition, sociologists also view status as the sum of one's rights and privileges. Status then refers to a recognized social position that an individual can occupy.[158]

The status of a child in an institution or in a foster home is decidedly negative, abnormal and damaged. The reason for this negative evaluation of a child in an institution or in foster care is the prompt assumption that the child, or adolescent, must be delinquent or a psychiatric "case." The adolescents who are incarcerated or placed in foster care are indeed depressed and often unreasonable because of the circumstances in which they must live. We therefore have a form of circular interaction bearing down on the adolescent who is caught in the grip of the state and of social agencies. He is incarcerated because he is viewed as "bad" and he is "bad" because he is incarcerated.

The self image and identity of such an adolescent is of course severely damaged. Having an "abnormal" status, such children are subject to intense scrutiny by other children and teachers in our schools. Adolescents who do not live with their parents are asked intrusive and embarrassing questions about their families, their past experiences and their "delinquencies." Children who are under scrutiny find that everything they do or do not do is attributed to their diminished status as "foster" children or "institutionalized" adolescents.

Bullying, teasing and ridicule is a regular feature in the life of foster children and institutionalized children. Adolescents who live in this environment are particularly pained by such aggression because they are at an age when conformity and sameness and peer approval are more important than at any other time in their lives. All of these encounters lead to the self-devaluation of those who, through no fault of their own, are forced to suffer these indignities in school.

---

158. John C.. Macionis, *Sociology*, Upper Saddle River, N.J., Prentice Hall, (2001)p. 140.

Added to this process as initiated by other adolescents is the lack of respect and the impersonal treatment which devolves upon such children from teachers and "caregivers." Foster children and institutionalized children are a category and not individuals.[159]

We have already discussed the work of Mead and Cooley to the effect that a negative "feedback" from others results in a stigmatized self identity. Those who are rejected, those who are bullied, those who are excluded, adopt these experiences and harbor them in their psyche so that their personality reveals a negative self image which invites additional rejection, bullying and exclusion. The adolescent so treated is stigmatized.

Stigmatization has an impact on independence, which is so highly prized in American life. A negative self-identity resulting in low self confidence also has a direct influence on a future career because, as adolescents contemplate what they want to become, stigmatized adolescents are likely to focus on what they cannot do rather than on what they can do. Furthermore, stigmatized adolescents, and stigmatized adults, tend to focus only on the present; they view the future in a negative light since they believe they cannot succeed.[160]

Stigma can also relate to gender identity in adolescents. As a consequence of severe emotional distress leading to "behavioral disorders," adolescents will become targets of negative attention in school, both from teachers and bullies among other children. In a few adolescents this results in a wish to be the other sex, leading to conduct that is incongruous with the expectations of each sex. One phenomenon which this disorder can produce is cross-dressing. Here, the adolescent literally wears the clothes of the opposite sex. Boys will wear girls' clothing and girls prefer to dress as boys. Of course, since it has become normal for girls to wear pants, it may not be apparent what constitutes cross-dressing on the part of a girl. However, it is absolutely unacceptable for an adolescent boy to wear heels or a skirt (although the Scottish costume permits this on some ceremonial occasions).

A second indication of a gender identity disorder in an adolescent is a need to play with objects for games normally associated with the other sex, or to avoid play or games associated with the same sex. An adolescent girl seeking to play football might be an example; then again, since the schools have established

---

159. Ibid. p. 266.
160. Susan Harter, "Self and identity development," In: S. Shirley Feldman and Glen R. Elliott, *At the threshold: the developing adolescent.* (Cambridge, Mass. Harvard University Press, 1990) pp. 352-387.

soccer and rugby teams for girls, it is difficult to say just who it is that is confused.

Thirdly, an indication of a gender identity disorder is a persistent preference for friends of the opposite gender — not out of romantic inclination, but because that is the cohort with which the adolescent identifies. There are boys who seek the company of girls exclusively. There are girls who seek the exclusive company of boys. Finally, those adolescents who suffer from a gender identity disorder of the type who have a dislike of their own sexual characteristics dislike themselves, their physical identity and their bodily functions.[161]

Obviously, evidence of such a gender identity disorder will lead to the stigmatization of any adolescent. Psychiatrists who have studied this phenomenon conclude that gender identity disorders in adolescents do not usually continue into adulthood.[162]

ADOLESCENT SELF CONCEPT

In December of 2003, Jungwee Park published the results of a study of adolescent self concept. This study revealed that in middle childhood both sexes seem to feel equally good about their appearance. With the onset of puberty, however, physical development for girls is generally negative while physical development for boys is generally regarded as positive. The reason for this difference is associated with menstruation and a gain in body fat among girls.

This does not mean that boys are not affected by accelerated hormone production, growth spurts and voice changes. In addition to these physical changes adolescents also face numerous social changes. These include the transition from elementary school to junior high school or middle school, causing some children considerable disturbances and upheavals in self concepts.

Another influence on self concept among adolescents is household income of their parents. This affects those age 16 to 19 much more than it affects younger children. The reason for this difference is that in younger children social class is ascribed. Among older adolescents social class becomes associated with achieve-

---

161. Domenico Di Ceglie, Claire Sturge and Adrian Sutton, "Gender identity disorders in children and adolescents," *Council report C. R. 63*, (London, Royal College of Psychiatrists, 1998):3.
162. Ibid. p.4.

ments and therefore has a far greater influence on the older adolescent's standing in school than is true of young children.

It is remarkable that the Park study found no association between living arrangements and adolescent self concept. In other words, Park's work did not show that it made any difference to an adolescent's self concept whether he was living with both parents, one parent or no parent.[163]

Nonetheless, Park found that emotional support provided by family members is always positively associated with a good self concept for both boys and girls. A good self concept based on such support has been found to protect against stress. Depression stems from stress; people whose self concept is weak are far more likely to suffer depression than those whose self concept is strong.

Park also found that a strong self concept is associated with physical activity. It is of course possible that a strong self concept is required before physical activity can take place. Depression is commonly associated with the inability to do anything while physical activity is associated with a decrease of depression, if not its elimination altogether.

People with a strong self concept are more likely to be active and to avoid risky behavior. Park therefore concluded that a strong self concept is a key factor in developing good mental and physical health.[164]

Those adolescents who lack a good self concept can therefore be expected to exhibit the conduct that is generally called delinquent behavior. This should not be interpreted to mean that all adolescents with a poor self concept must be delinquent or that all delinquency is the product of a poor self concept.

One such delinquency, which has received little attention, is pathological gambling by adolescents. Gambling has of course been recognized as a major adult difficulty, but little has been said about this obsession on the part of adolescents. No doubt gambling among adolescents is related to the general impulsiveness of young people whose need for immediate gratification can sometimes be satisfied by winning at gambling. It has also been found that pathological gambling is associated with alcohol abuse and that both phenomena exhibit many similarities. These similarities are both related to social risk.[165]

---

163. Jungwee Park, "Adolescent Self Concept and Health into Adulthood," *Canadian Business and Current Affairs*, 14, (December 2003):41.

164. Ibid. p.50.

165. David S. Husted, Nathan A. Shapira and Martin Lazaritz, "Adolescent Gambling, Substance Abuse and Other Delinquent Behavior," *Child and Adolescent* Pychiatry, (September 2003):52.

Social risk refers to the frequently observed characteristic of adolescents relating to instant gratification without concern for its long term consequences. These behaviors include, tobacco use, alcohol and drug use, risky sexual behavior and gambling.[166]

Gambling evidently increases substance abuse among adolescents, just as it does among adults. The reverse is also true. Substance abuse can lead and does lead to gambling because of decreased inhibitions. The reasons are evident. Both gambling and substance abuse are caused by impulsivity, delinquent peers and, among some adolescents, lack of parental supervision. There are of course numerous parents who gamble, who drink to excess, who bring a number of sex partners into their houses, so that parental conduct actually induces deviant adolescent behavior in some youngsters. [167]

Those who follow the media will be surprised to discover that gambling is a much more common adolescent vice than drug and alcohol use, cigarette smoking and sexual activity. The psychiatrist Kaminer et al. reports that 70% to 80% of adolescents are involved in gambling and that the average age of onset of gambling behavior is age nine. The popularity of gambling is driven by the opportunities to gamble at home, at the home of friends and in school. Boys are more likely to gamble than girls.[168]

Gambling is only one of many forms of risk taking conduct by adolescents. Gambling is correlated with drunken driving, sexual promiscuity, drug use, truancy, stealing, prostitution and aggression. All of these forms of behavior depend on a delinquent self concept which makes it possible for some adolescents to carry on activities which are utterly foreign to millions of other adolescents.

There is a good deal of evidence that risk-taking behavior is strongly related to low self-esteem. This means that the risk takers seek to compensate their poor self image by playing "hero" before an audience of their peers. Since self concept consists of self-esteem and the ability to control one's own life, adolescents are faced with the need to maintain some control over their own being in defiance of adults. For boys this need is best met, as discussed in Chapter 2, in sports. Outstanding among these sports is football, which is the very epitome of

---

166. Frank Vitaro, M. Brendgen, R. Ladouceur, R.E. Tremblay, "Gambling, delinquency and drug use during adolescence," *Gambling Studies,* 17,no.3, (2001):171-190.

167. Ibid. p. 180.

168. Yifra Kaminer, J.A. Burleson, A. Jadamec, "Gambling behavior in adolescent substance abuse," *Substance Abuse,* 23, no.3, (2002):191-198.

masculinity in America. Suffering from a lack of power over their own lives, adolescent boys can play football or other sports and escape parental control, sexual anxiety and homework. Football and other spectator sports bring immediate recognition to the participants. These sports also relegate adults to mere spectators while adolescents are in the limelight. This gives the adolescent athlete a sense of importance and self-esteem hardly available through academic success.[169]

Although there are, of course, girl's sports, and non-gender-specific theatrical presentations, band concerts and other activities in the typical American high school, it is the boys' sports that draw crowds of spectators. Therefore, it should not be surprising that boys and girls differ in their self-concepts and their understanding of their identity. Boys are less likely to be depressed than girls, usually have a higher self-esteem and, if depressed, can let out their depression through sanctioned aggression against others. Girls are more often depressed and have far less opportunity to participate in prestigious activities than boys, and they exhibit a low self-esteem far more often than is true of boys.[170]

Whether the differences between the sexes are hormonal or learned may never be settled to the satisfaction of everyone. It is however certain that girls and boys feel and do things differently. Adolescent girls are more likely to internalize their feelings while boys, and men, are more comfortable than girls and women to exhibit hostility. There is, however, common ground between the sexes relative to depression and low self-esteem. That is obesity. Obesity, according to a study conducted by the psychologist David Wolfe, is strongly correlated with depression in both sexes. Therefore, to the extent that parental pressure can contribute to teen depression, Wolfe advises that adults should not try to force adolescents to become what the parents want but should let each adolescent decide for himself how to proceed with his life.[171]

Bullying can also be linked to self concept. In the course of adolescent turmoil, some girls and boys develop into bullies, exhibiting cruel behavior towards their peers. Usually this kind of conduct begins at age eleven or twelve and seeks to shun, if not harass, students not viewed as "cool" or popular. Girls are more likely than boys to develop their identity through relationships rather

---

169. Lawrence B. Angus, "Women in a male domain," in; Lawrence B. Angus, Editor, *Inequlity and Social Idendity*, (Washington, D.C., Palmer Press, 1993).

170. No author, "Teen girls stay more depressed as adults," *The Canadian press*, (November 20, 2003,):D 9.

171. Ibid. p. D9.

than autonomy. Therefore, girls in particular find it in their interest to exclude some girls from the "in" crowd so as to segregate those who live by the norms or expectations of the group and those whose exclusion delimits the group. In short, all groups must indicate who is out so as to discover and know who is in.

The "in-and-out syndrome" is of course also the function of the criminal law. By designating some people offenders, everyone else learns the limits of acceptable conduct in the group at hand.

IDENTITY AND WORK

Work or occupation is the principal criterion of social prestige in the United States. In fact, occupations are commonly ranked by the American public, as has been documented by the National Opinion Research Center. That research organization has shown that, over many years, the physician is the most prestigious American occupation, while shoe shiner ranks at the bottom.[172]

Working for money is of course not limited to adults. In fact, between one quarter and one half of all 8th, 9th and 10th graders hold part time jobs during the school year and three-quarters of 12th graders do so. Many high school students work 20 or more hours per week.[173]

Researchers have found that there is a positive correlation between long hours of work and drug, tobacco and alcohol use. Psychiatrist Erik Erikson calls adolescence a "psychological moratorium" in which adolescents are given a chance to answer the question "Who am I?" in order to determine their identity. Those adolescents who work many hours have little or no time to engage in extracurricular activities such as sports or hobbies, and they can hardly complete their schoolwork. The school teams, performing arts and school clubs that allow adolescents to improve their self-esteem as they do well in one or more activity are out of reach for those who work long hours. Health maintenance is also related to self-esteem and is associated with long-term health habits reaching all the way to adult life; evidently, students who go to work are prevented from exercising and often from sleeping or even eating well.[174]

---

172. Macionis, *Sociology*, p.274,
173. Deborah J. Safron, John E. Schulenberg and Jerald G. Bachman, "Part –Time Work and Hurried Adolescence," *Journal of Health and Social Behavior*, 42 (December 2001):425-449.

At the same time, work can enhance self-image. With reference to adolescent identity, work for money is of course associated with adult life. Therefore, work allows the adolescent an opportunity to shed his role of child and enter into the adult world almost simultaneously. Therefore, working teenagers can view themselves as adults, and many do. This view has been called "pseudo-adulthood" or "pseudo-maturity" and refers to adolescents who want to enjoy the freedoms of adulthood without experiencing its responsibilities. Indeed, the adolescent who works long hours resembles an adult who does the same. However, adolescents seldom have to pay the rent and utilities or support a family. They can therefore spend their earnings on consumer items, which can easily include alcohol and drugs as well as the symbols of adolescent status such as hairstyles, clothes, music and other technological toys which are "in."[175]

The majority of adolescents participate in the youth culture. This is important to each adolescent because it allows the development of a distinct identity without rejecting all adult values. There are, however, those whose participation in the youth culture is extreme and excludes all adults. Such adolescents are in danger of acting an adult role too soon; such "pseudo-adults" may become pregnant at a very young age or may become involved in substance abuse.

The kinds of jobs which adolescents usually do are almost always poorly paid and are of the least skill type of work. Working adolescents cannot commit to activities which meet at the same time each week such as sports practice or drama clubs. Hence, working adolescents are more likely to engage in unstructured activities with peers and are therefore more prone to have opportunities to use alcohol and other drugs. It is often proved by research that one of the most important reasons for abusing any substance is association with friends who do the same.[176]

Working in various kind of employment can mean that adolescents gain an "adult" identity earlier than those who do not work, but this may come at the expense of grades, opportunities to enter higher education and chances to participate in structured after-school activities.

---

174. Mihaly Czikszentmihalyi and Barbara Schneider, *Becoming Adult: How Teenagers Prepare for the World of Work*, (New York: Basic Books, 2000).
175. Jerald G. Bachman and John E. Schulenberg, " How Part -time Work Intensity Relates to Drug Use," *Developmental Psychology*, 29(1993):220.
176. Judith S. Brook, Martin Whiteman, Lisa J. Czeisler and Joseph Shapiro, "Cigarette Smoking in Young Adults," *Journal of Genetic Psychology*, 158, (1997):172-198.

Clearly, the poor are more likely to work and go to school than the wealthy. Furthermore, the need to work creates for the poor an environment much more conducive to substance abuse and other "deviant" forms of behavior, which in turn serve to block the opportunities which conformity confers on those who do not (or need not) work while going to school.

One of the most visible kinds of work performed by adults and children is housework. Paid work outside the home is far less visible because few family members ever gain an opportunity to visit each others' place of work. Housework, however, is done face-to-face and has traditionally been identified with women. In fact, despite the "gender revolution" of the 1980s, many jobs remain more or less categorized as women's work and men's work, although there are now male flight attendants and male nurses, and female CEOs of large corporations and university presidents.

There is still a gendered division of household labor in most families. In fact, when women marry they usually increase the amount of time they spend on housework while men, at marriage, reduce the time they spend on housework. This division of labor has a direct effect on the identity of adolescents of both genders. Furthermore, parents usually assign different tasks to boys and girls and praise or criticize performance of housework based on gender expectations. This may be called "household modeling."[177]

It needs no particular insight to understand that children learn about gender-appropriate behavior by imitating their parents. This should mean that adult men who routinely participate in housework come from homes where their own father also routinely engaged in doing household chores. By the same token, mothers who work a great deal outside the home will foster an understanding among their children that this is normal. Children of employed mothers are of course more likely to perform numerous chores in the house that would otherwise be done by stay-at-home mothers. If parents display a gender-neutral attitude and treat children of both sexes fairly and equally, then it can be expected that children will share housework equally.[178]

The presence and number of children in any household increases the amount of household work that must be done. In large families, greater segre-

---

177. Sampson L. Blair, "The Sex -Typing of Children's Household Labor: Parental Influence of Daughter's and Son's Housework." *Youth and Society*, 24, (1992):178-203.

178. Mick Cunningham, "The Influence of Parental Attitudes and Behaviors on Children's attitudes towards Gender and Household Labor in Early Adulhood," *Journal of Marriage and the Fmily*, 63, (2001):111-122.

gation of household tasks by gender is possible. In such families men are more likely to participate at least in part in some of the household tasks. The influence of parental attitudes towards housework, and everything else, is of course more important in developing attitudes in young children than in older children. There can be little doubt that young children who see their father participate in housework will almost always pitch in when they become adults. Furthermore, daughters of working mothers are less likely to be willing to do all the housework themselves, assuming they are working when they marry. In short, the traditional stereotype of women's work and men's work is weakened by the manner in which parents demonstrate the efficacy of work equality.[179]

The formation of a personal identity is vastly influenced by the observations children make of the division of labor demonstrated for them in their parental home.

ADOLESCENT SELF-ESTEEM

The identity of adolescents, and the identity of all Americans, is most dependent on the self-esteem derived from Cooley's "Looking Glass Self." It is therefore appropriate to discuss some strategies for the self enhancement of adolescents. In 1965, the psychologist Morris Rosenberg defined self-esteem as "evaluation which an individual makes and customarily maintains with regard to himself or herself."[180]

It is during early adolescence that an intense effort is made to discover one's self-identity. During this time, many adolescents experience numerous obstacles to establishing an identity based on a sense of self worth.

It is argued here that low self-esteem is not the only reason for limited academic achievement or adolescent drinking or other forms of deviance. It is entirely possible for an adolescent to have an excellent opinion of himself and to engage in aggression because of it. This has occurred among high school athletes and those who "bully" other students. Therefore, some have advocated youth self-esteem programs both for adolescents who have a poor self image and for

179. Theodore N. Greenstein, "Husbands' Participation in Domestic Labor." *Journal of Marriage and the Family*, 58, (1996):585-595.
180. Morris Rosenberg, *Society and Adolescent Self Image*, (Princteon, N.J., Princeton University Press, 1965)p.5.

those who are so "cocky" and self assured that they presume they have a right to mistreat fellow students.[181]

Students of adolescent behavior have shown that bullying and excessive conformity to the dominant group among adolescent school children are generally associated with group pressure derived from older peers. Comparison with other and/or inflated self views are seen as dysfunctional by many observers of adolescent conduct. Such dysfunctional feelings can be observed in the form of adolescent depression and self-doubt or in the form of externalized emotions such as frustration and anger. Evidently, family, school, peers and sports are usually seen as positive influences, although all four can also have negative outcomes for adolescents.

Adolescents and their observers agree that the most important influence of self identity and self-esteem for almost all adolescents are friendship, popularity/ cliques and victimization. An example is the excessive emphasis by school cliques on clothes derived from a particular store or exhibiting a specific name brand.

Since the cost of such clothing may be prohibitive for poor children, relative wealth becomes an asset even among the young, just as it is among all Americans. Therefore, adolescent identity may well depend on the financial resources of an adolescent's family and not only on the individual's ability to manipulate others.[182]

It is common knowledge that adolescence is that part of the life course in which problems of adjustment are more evident than at any other stage of life. This is a time when physiological changes associated with puberty occur even as relations with parents and peers are changing as well. Therefore, self-esteem is also at stake at that time.

Research on self–esteem among high school students have shown that it is possible to predict high school grade point averages on the basis of characteristics of children measured in middle school. Such research reveals that early appearing personality characteristics and aspects of the self in children are related to how well they adapt later to high school. The manner in which personality characteristics such as self-esteem lead to ways of dealing with other

---

181. Susan Harter, *The Construction of the Self: A developmental perspective*, (New York: Guilford Press, 1999).

182. David L. DuBois, Erika M. Lockerd, Kelle Reach and Gilbert R. Parra, "Effective Strategies for Estaeem Enhancement," *Journal of Early Adolescence*, 23, no.4, (November 2003):419.

people and with new information as taught in school has a direct effect on succeeding in high school.[183]

Of course, self-esteem is not global. That means that adolescents, and
people at other life stages, may have a good deal of self-esteem in one situation
and not in another situation. Such fluctuations in self-esteem depend on the role
one is playing at any one time. The psychologists Harter, Waters and Whitesell
have demonstrated this in a study of adolescent self-worth carried out in 1998.
They found different levels of self-worth among adolescents depending on the
context of their interaction with parents, with teachers, with male classmates or
with female classmates. This study demonstrates that adolescents do judge their
worth as a person differently across these four contexts. As Mead recognized
seventy years ago, the opinions of significant others are incorporated into one's
sense of self worth. Yet not all adolescents rely only on the perceived opinions of
others. There are those who understand that if one likes oneself as a person then
others will agree and also like or support the self. That much insight is not
available to small children, who are almost entirely dependent on the "looking-
glass" self. However, adolescents can achieve that much insight, although there
are adults who can never divorce their sense of self worth from the opinions of
others.[184]

Self-esteem is also related to bodily appearance. In the US that means that
those who appear overweight at any age will be the subject of overt or implied
criticism. Among school children, and adolescents in particular, overweight
leads to teasing and other types of confrontation. Adolescent girls, even more
than boys, develop a considerable sense of "body dissatisfaction" from such
rejection in a culture which pressures everyone to be thin. The gender difference
in "body dissatisfaction" is no doubt due to the greater investment girls have
made in the appearance of their body than is true for boys.[185]

Because there is so much emphasis on body weight among adolescents,
those who are teased about their weight have low self-esteem, are dissatisfied
with their bodies and are much more likely to contemplate suicide than other

183. Susan Harter, "The development of self representations," In N. Eisenberg, Ed. *Handbook of child psychology: Social and personality development*, (5th Ed. Vol.4, New York, Wiley)
p..553.
184. Susan Harter, Patricia Waters and Nancy R. Whitesell, "Relational Self-worth" *Child
Development*, 69, no.3, (June 1998):756.
185. Marika Tiggemann, "Person X situation interactions in body dissatisfaction." *International Journal of Eating Disorders*, 29, (2001): 65.

adolescents. Overweight teens also have smaller social networks than normal weight adolescents. Richard Strauss, MD and Harold A. Pollack Ph.D. investigated the social networks of overweight and normal weight adolescents. Their study found that overweight adolescents were more socially isolated and were usually only peripheral to the social networks common in high schools. The overweight were seldom listed as friends by other children except that those who did list them as friends were themselves usually less popular than other high school students. Furthermore, Strauss and Pollack found that overweight adolescents were 70% more likely to receive no friendship nominations from other students in their classes than was true of normal weight students.[186]

RACE AND ADOLESCENT IDENTITY

Identity formation among adolescents includes recognition of the individual's place in society. Included in the social process of identity formation is social class, gender, family, community and ethnicity. Of course, positive racial or physical identity results in a positive self image among adolescents and adults. The imposition of a negative community attitude towards anyone leads to a negative self image. This means that Afro-American children who face negative stereotyping every day are most likely to internalize a negative self image which can be accompanied by mental health problems.[187]

The most influential study of Afro-American identity was conducted by Cross in 1991. Cross calls the identity development of Afro-Americans "negrescence." According to Cross, Afro-Americans undergo five stages of racial identity development. In the first stage, race is not viewed as an important aspect of adolescent identity. At this stage, some blacks have a positive opinion of white society and/or are so involved with religion or politics that they hardly notice the racial factor. In the second stage of identity development, black American adolescents have encountered events in their lives which have racial components and which are directly related to their race. Such experiences lead black adolescents to re-examine their identity and to produce either a positive or negative

---

186. Richard S. Strauss and Harold A. Pollack, "Social marginalization of overweight children," *Archives of Pediatrics & Adolescent Medicine*, 157 (August 2003):746.

187. Howard C. Stevenson, "Raising safe villages: Cultural-ecological factors that influence emotional adjustment of adolescents." *Journal of Black Psychology*, 22 (1998):498-508.

black identity. The third stage of black adolescent identity development, according to Cross, results in immersion in the black community and the development of anti-white attitudes. Obsessed with identifying with black culture, they attempt to internally endorse all values and all traditions within black culture. Then, in the fourth stage, black youths gain satisfaction and inner security about being black, so that in the fifth stage of identity development black adolescents can translate acceptance of being black into action.[188]

How one feels about his racial identity affects one's mental health. This has been consistently found by numerous studies conducted over two decades. The variable in this relationship is stress. Stress, of course, is negatively associated with mental health (as found in the Rosenberg Self-esteem Scale, and the investigations of the psychologists Zimmerman, Ramirez-Valles and the work of Alva and Reyes). These investigators show that there is a direct relationship between stressful events and internalized symptoms of depression and anxiety leading to excessive use of alcohol, marijuana and other drugs.[189]

No doubt, the most common source of stress among Afro-American adolescents is the experience of discrimination. A recently developed discrimination inventory found that 98% of black respondents reported racial discrimination events within one year. Such events are reportedly related to anxiety, depression, obsessive-compulsive behavior and a host of other psychiatric symptoms.[190]

These difficulties must of course have consequences for the academic performance of Afro-American children. One of these outcomes is the oft-encountered belief among black Americans that academic achievement is the province of whites and not of blacks. This results in the view of many Afro-Americans that academics are to be devalued because they are a white domain and because education is not viewed as a route to social mobility.

Similar problems are encountered by homeless adolescents and by immigrant and migrant youths. That will be the content of our next chapter.

---

188. William E. Cross, *Shades of Black: diversity in Afro-American identity.* (Philadelphia: Temple Univesityr Press, 1991).

189. Marvin A. Zimmerman, J. Ramirez-Valles, and K. I. Maton, "A longitudinal study of stress-buffering effects for urban African-American male adolescent problem behaviors and mental health," *Journal of Contemporary Psychology,* 28, (2002):17-33.

190. C.L. Broman, "Race related factors and life satisfaction among African-Americans," *Journal of Black Psychology,* 23, (1997):36-49.

SUMMARY

The concept of the "looking-glass" self as developed by Cooley and Mead relates to gender identity among adolescents as sex becomes gender according to the dictates of every culture. Ethnic identity also bears on the identity development of adolescents as does social class. Adolescents will take many risks because they seek to exhibit themselves before their peers and gain approval by such risk taking behavior.

Included in identity development is the concept of self-esteem. This is heavily influenced by the experiences of adolescents in school, where several alternative status systems are available. Some children, however, cannot take advantage of any of these status systems either because they are devalued by reason of their physical appearance or because they are institutionalized. Adolescents, like all Americans, derive status from work based on both traditional and non-traditional divisions of labor by gender.

Racial minorities face a special need to learn their own identity, a need which is also visible among the homeless and immigrants. These adolescents are the focus of our next chapter.

CHAPTER 5. HOMELESS, MIGRANT AND IMMIGRANT YOUTHS

HOMELESSNESS

Some 700,000 Americans are homeless on any one night of the year and have been homeless for some time. In addition, 2 million Americans have been homeless one night during the year past on any one day. Children are among these homeless people. The US Conference of Mayors reported that in 2002, families with children accounted for 41% of the homeless and that this proportion was then even higher in rural areas than in cities.[191]

There were only 500,000 homeless on American streets in 1989. The more than doubling of the homeless in the 15 years from then to 2004 is not the product of population increase, but the result of a number of contributing conditions. The survey of cities included in the Conference of Mayors report concluded that the lack of affordable housing, mental illness (23%), a lack of needed services, substance abuse (32%) and low paying jobs (22%) all contributed to this disaster.

People remained homeless an average of six months in the cities surveyed. Single men constituted 41% of the homeless population, families with children 41% and single women 13%. Seventy-three percent of homeless families are headed by a single parent, mostly the mother.

---

191. National Coalition for the Homeless, *Homeless Families with Children*, (Washington, D.C. 2001).

"Unaccompanied youths" amount to 5% in the survey. Forty-three percent of children living on American streets and homeless are male and 57% are female. Of these, 2-5% have children of their own. (The number of children included in the survey by the US Conference of Mayors includes only those 17 years old and younger.[192])

Children who live in America's streets are generally labeled either "runaways" or "throwaways." A "runaway" is a child who has left home because of conditions which the child views as intolerable. Of course, such children face the judgment of those more fortunate who cannot understand why any child would leave his home. Several reasons can be cited here. Some have been beaten and assaulted over and over again by fathers or mothers, or both. Ninety percent of the children in the streets have been sexually or physically abused by both or one of their own parents. Some have been abused by the second husband or wife of their natural parent.

Few "normal" people can understand how a child can take care of himself in a homeless situation. Indeed, such children have immense disadvantages and terrible difficulties. Homeless children cannot usually go to school since they don't even have an address, so that no school district is responsible for them. Such children are also without the support of their parents or other adults and usually must earn a living by prostitution or theft or other forms of "hustling." A few do have "decent" jobs such as waitress or "short order" cook. Yet, others live by stealing, drug dealing and a number of other "dishonest" means.[193]

It is commonly believed that homeless children could go home if they wished. This is not true; a large number of homeless children have been turned away by their parents. They may have been locked out of their houses or sent to nonexistent or non-welcoming relatives. Others have been abandoned on the road.

Among the many children who are "runaways" there are few who have any idea what faces them. Some of these children were adopted and therefore seek their biological mother in the hope of a warm welcome. This seldom succeeds. There are also children who seek to escape parental authority even if it is not cruel or physical.

---

192. US Conference of Mayors, *Hunger, Homelessness on the Rise in Major USCities*, (Washington, D.C. Conference of American Mayors, December 18,2002).

193. Paul G. Shane, *What About America's Homeless Children?* (Thousand Oaks, Cal. Sage Publications)p.15.

Margaret O. Hyde, in her book *Missing and Murdered Children*, tells the story of "Sarah," who had run away from home and then found work in a diner. She could not tolerate the long hours and hard work demanded there, but could not find any other work because she had no proof of age. After only two days on the job she met some "street smart" children in the diner with whom she began living in a "crash pad." There she was required to have sex with male members of the group and to earn money by doing sex with strangers. She also stole food, dealt drugs and lived in filth and misery until she learned of "Covenant House," which helped her.[194]

Covenant House provides shelter for homeless children. It was begun in New York City in 1972 and from there expanded to fourteen other cities from coast to coast. It is also found in Canada and four Latin American countries. Principally, Covenant House is concerned with providing immediate food, shelter and clothing to children who arrive in an emergency situation. The largest privately funded agency to deal with homeless children, Covenant House also helps those who have been involved in drug abuse. Covenant House has a mother/child program, education and vocational training, legal services and health care. In one year, Covenant House services over 76,000 children nationwide, including 35,000 children who were reached on the street by "out-reach" workers.[195]

Drop-in centers like Covenant House have two advantages. First, they can be established at relatively low cost and with little assistance from volunteers and religious groups. In addition drop-in centers allow social service agencies to contact adolescents who are homeless. Nevertheless, some shelters have turned away homeless adolescents not accompanied by an adult because of "liability" issues, meaning they could be sued by parents or other adults. Drop-in shelter employees and volunteers are required to report the presence of a "runaway" child to the state Department of Children and Family Services, as it is called in Illinois. These departments exist in all states. Therefore, many adolescents avoid these shelters because they fear the bureaucracy of the state more than the street. This despite the evidence that many adolescents and younger children who live in the street are abused by adults, both sexually and otherwise.[196]

---

194. Margaret O. Hyde, *Missing and Murdered Children*, (New York: Franklin Watts, 1998)p.35.

195. www. Covenanthouse.org/about.html

196. Editorial, "Reaching out to homeless teens," *Chicago Daily Herald*, (March 24, 2004):14.

There are other agencies designed to help homeless children. These agencies proliferated after Congress passed the Runaway and Homeless Youth Act of 1972. That law led to the funding of 169 centers for runaways throughout the country. These centers seek to provide emergency help and family mediation, particularly those who are "thrown away" by their parents.[197]

Despite this effort to give limited and temporary help to homeless children, it is self-evident that homeless children have no rights. Teens usually are too old to get help from child protection agencies but are too young to receive legal standing. Homeless children do not qualify for welfare because parents and not children receive money under the Aid to Families with Dependant Children Act. In addition to all these difficulties, homeless children are normally unable to go to school as they do not even have an address, let alone the money to buy school supplies. This means that homeless children cannot lead a normal life in their youth and are destined to a low income amidst innumerable occupations which require more and more education.[198]

In 1987 Congress passed the Stewart B. McKinney Homeless Assistance Act, which was signed into law by President Ronald Reagan. Included in that law is a provision that funnels federal money to states for the education of homeless children. The purpose of this provision was to give homeless children the same access to education as available to other children.

One example of the manner in which this Federal mandate has been carried out is the Pennsylvania plan. This plan eliminates the residency and guardianship requirements which school districts normally use and which keep homeless children out of school. Transportation to and from school is another barrier a homeless child must overcome. The homeless have no address. Therefore they need to have an agreement with a school concerning a place of departure for school and a place of return after school. Homeless children seldom have school records. Yet, schools usually require such records before enrolling anyone. Similar problems exist for many immigrant children.

Homeless children also have emotional problems not imaginable to the child who has never known anything but a home to which to return after school.

---

197. US Congress. Subcommittee on Human Resources of the Committee on Education and Labor. House of Representatives, Ninety-Seventh Congress, Second Session. (1982).
198. *Commonwealth of Pennsylvania*, Pennsylvania Homeless Student Initiative, (Harrisburg, Pa, Pennsylvania Department of Education,1989).

Adolescents and younger children face numerous obstacles in any effort to gain an education. Homelessness is associated with developmental delays, with emotional problems and with poor school attendance resulting in low academic performance. Several studies of homeless schoolchildren have confirmed that such children easily dropped out of school, that many were truant and that others were expelled. In addition, homeless children score a good deal below average on achievement tests in both mathematics and reading.[199]

Homeless children cannot perform "homework" after school because there is no place where they can do this. Homeless children seldom have parents who can visit the teacher on behalf of the child nor is there anyone in their life who can or will admire their work in school nor is there anyone around who supports them when they fail. Furthermore, the stress of survival alone keeps most homeless children from even attempting to go to school.

Homeless children are not given school supplies or clothes by their parents, as is normally assumed in the families of schoolchildren. Homeless children therefore are without good clothes and are rejected by other children who have the means of being accepted in the school environment. Homeless children can seldom pay attention to classroom procedures.

Because homelessness is associated with drug and alcohol abuse, many children of homeless parents have been beaten and otherwise abused by their parents. All this leads to the alienation of homeless children from other children in school and therefore results in yet another generation of poverty, if not homelessness and delinquency.[200]

Although there are numerous explanations for delinquent behavior among American youths, such as Sutherland's differential association theory and the numerous developmental theories put forward by sociologists and psychologists alike, there is little doubt that living "in the streets" creates much delinquency because of the absence of informal social controls and the lessening of social bonds homeless children have experienced. This means that homeless children experience neglect by their families and have few if any attachments to anyone else. Delinquency can certainly be a response to living in a painful environment. Homeless youths are usually caught up in two painful environments in that they

199. Paul G. Shane, *What about America's homeless children?* p.109.
200. Crystal Mills and Hiro Ota, "Homeless Women with Minor Children," *Social Work*, 34,no.6 (1989):435.

have fled from an abusive home and conflict in school only to face the truly dreadful difficulties of living in the streets.[201]

Like adults, adolescents who live in the streets are confronted with poverty, unemployment, hunger and lack of shelter. Added to these threats is the high rate of arrest of homeless people. For example, the sociologist David Snow and his colleagues found that the homeless have a significant greater arrest record than citizens who have homes. This does not prove that the homeless are more criminal or more delinquent than homeowners, as it is entirely possible that the higher arrest records stem from the greater visibility of the homeless and their greater vulnerability vis-à-vis the police.[202]

Several studies of runaway adolescents have shown that the longer an adolescent stays away from home the greater the possibility of his becoming involved in stealing. Such delinquencies come about because the runaways are encouraged by others to steal and/or use drugs. Those with extensive street careers are most likely to become involved in criminal conduct. These studies suggest that although homeless youths are a small proportion of all adolescents, they are involved in a substantial and disproportionate share of crime.[203]

Therefore it can be confirmed that the conditions of the streets are such that the problems of sustenance and security create the delinquencies endemic there and that street life is directly associated with crime and delinquency. Runaway youths are also at a high risk for drug use and unsafe sexual conduct.

In a recent study of homeless youths, the sociologists Ennett, Bailey and Federman found that a relative large number of runaway youths said they had no social relationships. Such youths are also at great risk of illicit drug use, having numerous sex partners and trading sex for subsistence. Sexual relationships among homeless youths are casual. Sex partners were seldom listed as belonging to a clique or network of friends.[204]

---

201. Robert Agnew, "A Revised Strain Theory of Delinquency," *Social Forces*, 61, (1985):151-167..

202. David Snow, Susan Baker and Leon Anderson, "Criminality and Homeless Men: An Empirical Assessment," *Social Problems*, 36, (1989):532-549.

203. John Hagan and Bill McCarthy, "Mean Streets: The Theoretical Significance of Destitution and Desperation among Homeless Youths," *American Journal of Sociology*, 98(1992):597-627.

204. Susan T. Ennett, Susan L. Bailey and E. Belle Friedman, "Social Network Characteristics Associated with risky Behaviors among Runaway and Homeless Youth," *Journal of Health and Social Behavior*, 40, no. 1 (March 1999): 63-78.

Homeless children also face more health risks than other children. It has been estimated that 40% of homeless children with or without a family have breathing diseases, including asthma. That is more than six times the rate for all children nationwide. Since the number of the homeless has increased between 1998 and 2004, there has also been an increase of the number of medically unserved children among them. Many of these homeless children go untreated since homeless adults and children are usually without medical care, alone because they have no insurance and cannot afford to visit doctors and hospitals. In New York City there were 9,400 homeless children with families in 1998. In 2004, this had increased to 16,000 children living with their families in homeless shelters or without any shelter at all.[205]

THE YOUTH CULTURE AMONG MIGRANTS

A migrant differs from an immigrant in that the migrant is generally a native of the country in which he now lives. Natives of Puerto Rico who work in the States are therefore migrants and not immigrants, because Puerto Rico is part of the United States and the population, although predominantly Spanish speaking, are acquainted with English and enjoy American citizenship.

The manner in which the children of migrant workers become involved in the youth culture and possibly the generation gap bears special consideration.

Although all children are at risk of becoming the victims of abuse and neglect on the part of parents, the risk of victimization of migrant farm workers' children is disproportionately high. This is true in the first place because the children of migrant farm workers are subject to the same hazards as the adult workers themselves. These hazards include poor sanitary conditions, accidents, chronic exposure to health hazards, poor nutrition, chemicals and other dangerous substances together with circumstances associated with working or playing in the fields.[206]

Many migrant workers were themselves mistreated as children. These adults are likely to continue the kind of aggression against children which they themselves experienced. Further, one feature of the traditional Hispanic culture

---

205. John J. Goldman, "Asthma takes toll on homeless kids," *Los Angeles Times*, (March 4, 2004):A8.

206. S.A. Young and M. Kaufman, "Promoting breast feeding at a migrant health center," *American Journal of Public Health*, 78, (1988):523-535.

is the concept of "machismo," which refers to the respect, honor and pride of fathers and males in general. Farm workers are frequently exploited by owners and bosses and are often unable to provide adequately for their families, and many a Hispanic man becomes abusive towards his own family and children as a consequence of losing self-respect.[207]

It is no secret that success in school is most likely when there is agreement between parents and school officials and fellow students concerning values, experiences, objects, language and behavior. The opposite is also true. Children whose families differ from the majority because of their families' expectations frequently suffer from a loss of self-esteem. Neither teachers nor administrators are usually aware (or able to do much about) the conflict a child may suffer because his family is so different from the others. And migrant workers have little understanding of academic success; as a result, their children are at high risk of becoming the victims of educational neglect.[208]

Health care is also less available to the children of migrant workers than to those with a permanent address. Low income and lack of health insurance coverage guarantee that migrant workers and their children will not receive adequate health care. Neither physicians nor hospitals are likely to treat anyone who cannot pay; and, often, these families are unable to speak English and do not always observe the rules of cleanliness.[209] Furthermore, migrant workers are constantly new to the area in which they work and are therefore seldom acquainted with the medical establishment in their surroundings. This leaves children and adolescents particularly vulnerable to health hazards and accidents in the unsanitary environment in which they must live.

In a major study of the health condition of migrant farm workers, Professor Edgar Leon of Michigan Sate University showed that malnutrition is one of the causes of abnormally high rates of chronic illness among migrant children and adolescents. In addition, migrant farm workers also suffer a high rate of HIV infection, which is related to a lack of education. This leads many farm workers

---

207. William F. Alvarez , John Doris and Oscar Larson III, "Children of migrant farm work families are at high risk for maltreatment," *American Journal of Public Health*, 78, no.8, (1988): 934-936.

208. B. McConnell, "Education as a cultural process," in: JoBeth Allen and Jana M. Mason, *Risk makers, Risk takers risk breakers*, Portsmouth, NH , Heinemann Educational Books, (1989)pp. 201-222.

209. Charles Sakala, "Migrant and seasonal farm workers in the United States," *International Migration Review*, 21, (1987):659-687.

to believe that the AIDS virus can be self-treated by using vitamins or self-administered intravenous medicine.

According to Leon, tuberculosis is also a high risk among migrant farm workers. It is twenty times as common among them than in the general American population. This risk is in turn related to the inability of most migrant farm workers to visit clinics because the hours of the clinics fall within the workday. In many clinics there is so little room that farm workers have to wait outside or in their cars. Many of the migrant farm workers in the United States are here illegally and therefore fear deportation if they visit a hospital or clinic.

Drug use and alcohol abuse are common among migrant farm workers. These in turn result in a good deal of domestic violence, with the consequence that children so treated rear another generation who continue the violence and abuse in which they were reared.[210]

Adolescent children of migrant workers are also at risk because the social institutions which usually serve the stable community do not help migrants. For many years, migrant workers have been exempt from safety and health laws on the job. Even when these laws include migrant workers, they are seldom enforced on their behalf.

Because the family needs the income, both parents are usually employed among farm migrant workers. This leaves older children in charge of younger children, leading to physical as well as emotional damage among young children and their adolescent caregivers.[211]

Weight is also a health hazard for immigrant children and the children of migrants, as it is for all American adolescents. A recent study conducted by the Health Resources and Service Administration of the US government in Europe, Israel and the US concluded that teenagers in all three locations were frequently overweight but that this problem was far worse in the US than anywhere else. Most important is that the study revealed that teenagers from immigrant families who speak a foreign language at home were at far greater risk of overweight than other teens. The study showed that 12.6% of adolescent boys were overweight and that 10.8% of adolescent girls were also overweight. At age fifteen,

---

210. Edgar Leon, "The Health Condition of Migrant Farm Workers," *Occasional Paper #71 Julian Samora Research Institute*, (Lansing, Michigan, The University of Michigan Press 2000.)

211. Oscar Larson III, John Doris and William F. Alvarez, "Migrants and maltreatment," *Child Abuse and Neglect*, 14, (1990):375-385.

14% of boys and 15% of girls were overweight. Further it was found that the majority of overweight adolescents become overweight adults.[212]

The Convention on Migrant Rights

Migrants are found in all parts of the world, not only in the United States. A number of countries, but not including the US, have agreed to a treaty called the United Nations Convention on Migrant Rights. According to that convention the United States had nearly 35 million migrant workers in 2000, constituting 12.4% of the entire population.

The announced purpose of the convention is to prevent inhuman living conditions, physical abuse and degrading treatment. Also included are guarantees that the signatory states will allow migrants freedom of expression, access to information concerning their rights, access to legal equality, access to educational and social services and the right to participate in trade unions.

The Convention nevertheless recognizes that many migrants are victimized by those who use misleading information and incitement to migrate illegally, with most unfortunate consequences for the undocumented aliens. Therefore, the convention seeks to sanction smugglers and employers of such migrants.[213]

These rights are of course already included in American law and guaranteed by the US Constitution. Therefore the Convention, even if the US joined, would not alter the position of migrant workers. The problem for migrant workers is the enforcement of these rights for a population whose political "clout" is almost nonexistent and who are largely invisible.

The Great Migration

The migration of southern Afro-Americans to the North began in the decades after 1910. This movement ended around 1970 and has been called The Great Migration. During this time the percentage of Afro-Americans who lived in rural areas decreased from 73% to 19%; the vast majority of Afro-American families moved to urban areas between 1910 and 1970.[214] This means that a complete transformation of the Afro-American culture took place during those years.

---

212. Mary Overpeck, " Research finds US teens most likely to be overweight-immigrant teens face social problems." *States News Service*, (January 6, 2004).
213. Jeanette Blom, *Information Kit on the United Nations Convention on Migrants Rights*, (New York, United Nations High Commissioner for Refugees 2003).

The Great Migration favored young men. Labor agents, sent by Northern employers, traveled throughout the South and promised the Afro-American workers high pay and steady employment. These workers were mainly uneducated adolescents. The labor agents were also helped by the black press, which advertised the need for laborers and semi-skilled workers. Many of the migrants took work which paid wages well below the existing scale in the North. Black adolescents took these "dead-end" jobs because they were excluded from the mainstream of society and had few realistic options.[215]

One of the reasons for the recruitment of black Southern workers during the 1940s was the need to fight the Second World War, which also interrupted the flow of poor European laborers to the United States.

The best example of the migration of Blacks to northern cities is the experience of Chicago. Here black families were forced to move into extremely cramped housing among the most used, most worn out and most derelict shelters in the city. Most of the new arrivals from the South were unskilled and many received some kind of governmental "relief." Chicago, as well as other northern cities, all developed highly dense "black neighborhoods" by "red lining," by restrictive zoning, by racial steering and by violence. This then led to the physical and social removal of Afro-Americans from American society.[216]

In the 1980s, upon the assumption of the presidency by Ronald Reagan, a great shift in labor activity occurred in the United States. Beginning at about that time, there was a considerable decline in the demand for unskilled labor in this country, with large employment losses in the manufacturing and construction industries. Since blacks were highly concentrated in central city manufacturing jobs in the Midwest during the 1970s, they suffered the most from these employment losses.[217]

In November of 2003, the US Department of Labor reported that joblessness among Afro-Americans was at an all-time high. This was true despite the reduction in unemployment beginning to be felt in the US economy that

214. Townsand Price-Spratlen, "Gendered Ethnogenesis and the Great Migration," *Race, Gender and Class: An Interdisciplinary and Multicultural Journal*, 6, no.2 (1999):147-170.

215. Carole Marks, "Black Workers and the Great Miogration North," *Phylon*, 46, no.2, ((1985):148-161.

216. Douglas Massey and Nancy A. Denton, "Spatial Assimilation as a Socioeconomic Outcome," *American Sociological Review*, 50, (1985):94-105.

217. John Bound and Henry J. Holzer, "Demand Shifts, Population Adjustments and Labor Market Outcomes during the 1980s" *Journal of Labor Economics*, 18, n0.1 (January 2000):20-54.

month. In fact, unemployment in the US was 6.0% in October of 2003 and fell to 5.5% by February of 2004. That means that there were about 8 million people out of work in 2003. For blacks, however, unemployment rose to 11.5% in October of 2003 and remained there into 2004. The prime reason for the discrepancy between black unemployment and the general unemployment trends was and is the lack of educational attainment in the black population. That in turn is the product of the migratory black experience between 1910 and 1970 as well as the tendency of black job applicants to be younger than the average American. Younger people have less experience than older workers and therefore may have more difficulty finding a job. Nevertheless, education is the most important criterion for economic success in the twenty first century and it is educational deficiency which is most responsible for the unemployment of black youths. The manufacturing sector of the US economy was at one time the main source of income for the black and white community. It is however the manufacturing sector of the economy which has contributed most to unemployment in America during the years since 1990, as good jobs and adequate wages are now the product of education and training.[218]

One consequence of this gloomy economic picture is the exceptional rate of violent crime committed by Afro-American young men. For example, in 2000, 48.7% of all murder reported in the US was committed by blacks. That same year the Sourcebook of Criminal Justice Statistics showed that 34.8% of all rapes, 53.8% of all robberies and 33.7% of all assaults were committed by young Afro-American men. Since only 12% of the population of the US is of African descent, the disproportionate involvement of blacks in American violence is evident.[219]

Crime is of course not the only measure of disrupted lives and a culture of despair. Welfare and its concomitant disabilities is even more indicative of the consequences of migration in the US than criminal activities. Welfare in the US is designed to relieve economic need. That need is in turn related to family size and to work opportunities. We have already seen that lack of education can be a serious handicap in becoming self-supporting. The other handicap could be welfare itself.

In a wide ranging study, three financiers, Michael Tanner, Stephen Moore and David Hartman, found that for some Americans welfare can create a

218. Kathy A. Gambrell, "Minorities unaffected by economic recovery," *United Press International*, (Washington, D.C. November 12lk 2003).
219. *Sourcebook of Criminal Justice Statistics*, (Washington D.C. The US Government Printing Office, 2001)p.356.

dependent lifestyle which prevents those on welfare from gaining a better education or elevating their income by advancing at work.

For example, Tanner et al. found that in Hawaii the value of all welfare benefits for a mother with two children was worth $36,400 and in Mississippi earnings of $11,500 would match all welfare benefits for a family of three. The study further found that in seven states, including New York, welfare pays $12 an hour, which is much more than the minimum wage. In 40 states welfare pays more than an $8.00-an-hour job and in 17 states welfare exceeds a $10-an-hour job. In large cities, welfare is even more generous. In New York City welfare paid $14.75 an hour, in Philadelphia $12.45 an hour, in Baltimore welfare paid $11.35 and in Detroit $10.90 an hour.

Additional findings of this study were that in nine states welfare paid more than the average salary of a teacher. In 29 states it paid more than the average salary for a secretary and in 47 states welfare paid more than the average salary of a janitor. Even a computer programmer earned less in 6 states than could be collected by remaining on welfare.[220]

This study was conducted in 1995 and is now a decade old. Nevertheless, the implications of that study remain the same. Evidently, welfare can reduce the interest of a recipient to work for a minimum or entry-level wage, thereby preventing the possibility of advancing financially later. Welfare can even void an interest in gaining enough education to earn more money later, as some entry-level jobs pay less than welfare.

All of this means that the children and grandchildren of southern migrants who came north between 1910 and 1970 were greatly helped by generous welfare laws even as some were defeated by these same laws as they became permanent welfare recipients over several generations. These handicaps are then the hurdles that adolescent blacks and some whites must overcome in order to be productive members of American society. This is of course also true of the immigrants who have come to the United States in the past decade (1995-2005) and before.

---

220. Michael Tanner, Stephen Moore and David Hartman, "The Work Versus Welfare Trade-off: An Analysis of the Total Level of Welfare Benefits by State," *Cato Policy Anaylisis No.240*, (September 19, 1995).

Immigrant Youths

Immigration and emigration are common all over the world. During the first half of the 20th century over 100 million people migrated voluntarily or forcibly from one country to another.[221]

Immigrant children make up a large proportion of American schoolchildren. The Bureau of the Census estimated that the percentage of schoolchildren who therefore have difficulty speaking English represents about 5% of American schoolchildren. This varies by region in the country, from 11% of children living in the West to 2% of children living in the Midwest.[222]

There is no lack of literature concerning the consequences of emigration and immigration on children. That literature clearly indicates that immigration has an adverse effect on both the social adjustment and emotional well being of children and adolescents. In fact, migration between nations involving significant cultural changes create grave psychological risks for children. This means that more immigrant adolescents than native adolescents were rated poorly by their teachers on measures of anxiety, aggression, frustration tolerance, low self-esteem, dependency and poor relations with peers.[223]

The areas of self-concept and identity conflicts with parents are most pronounced among adolescent immigrants. This phenomenon has been widely observed by sociologists. Immigrant adolescents and adolescent children of immigrants have been called marginal men, a concept first developed by the sociologist Everett Stonequist in 1937. A marginal man was there described as someone whose personality is in conflict because he lives in two cultures at once. That is precisely the condition of immigrant children and the children of immigrants because these children are confronted with one culture at home and a different culture in school and on the street. This culture conflict refers not only to language, in that most immigrant children come from homes which do not use the English language. It also refers to value conflict. An example is the position of a dominant father in the world of the immigrant, who may demand that his adolescent children give him the money they earn at after-school jobs. Such a practice is unheard of in the American culture. Likewise, immigrant parents may

221. Charles Zwingmann and Maria Pfister-Amende, *Uprooting and after...*(New York, Springer Verlag 1973)p.23.
222. US Census Bureauk *Current Population Surve,* (Washington, D.C. US Printing Office, 2000).
223. A.R. Nicol, "Psychiatric Disorders in the Children of Caribbean Immigrants," *Journal of Child Psychology and Psychiatry,* (1971) 12:273.

be most intrusive concerning adolescents' dating behavior. Such a practice is seldom known among Americans. Innumerable other differences in personality and culture concern the immigrant child and the children of immigrants, all of which create real conflict among them.[224]

These cultural differences frequently lead to intense conflict between parents and children and provoke a serious generation gap. The transition into adolescence introduces a good deal of disruption into the relationship between parents and childrenm, a disruption indicative of the need of children to assert their independence and proclaim their maturity. Adolescent children want to rid themselves of parental authority as their orientation to their peers increases. Although these events are common they do not mean, as we have already seen, that very many disregard their parents altogether. All this is thought to be a healthy and necessary development in Euro-American families. This is believed because individualism is a core value in Western civilization.[225]

This raises the question of whether adolescents from non-European immigrant backgrounds are also interested in separating from their parents and gaining the measure of autonomy considered "only natural" among Euro-Americans. This question comes to mind because Asian and other non-European rooted families are far less likely to teach their children the importance of autonomy and are therefore much more likely to value family unity and paternalism than is true in American families born in this country.

The psychologist Andrew Fuligni studied adolescents from Mexican, Chinese, Filipino and European backgrounds to see whether adolescents having different cultural origins and holding different beliefs about parental authority than Euro-Americans would report similar conflicts with the older generation.

His first finding was that adolescents from various ethnic backgrounds reported "strikingly similar relationships with their parents." This was interpreted to mean that foreign values, not supported by the host culture, play only a minor role in parent-child relationships. Instead these relationships gradually change to resemble the attitudes of the dominant group.

A second finding is that Filipino as well as Mexican children were less willing to argue with their mothers and fathers than is common among American born children. Nevertheless, these adolescents expect to be given

---

224. Everett V. Stonequist, *Marginal Man: A Study in personality and culture conflict*, (New York: Russell and Russell, 1937) p.1

225. Brett Laursen and W. Andrew Collins, "Interpersonal conflict during adolescenmce," *Psychological Bulletin*, 115 (1994):197-209.

autonomy at a fairly early age. This is more pronounced among native born children of foreign born parents, although the foreign born recognize the advantages accruing to their native born peers and demand them for themselves.[226]

In addition, such a value conflict contributes a great deal to juvenile delinquency, as first outlined by Thorsten Sellin in his epochal research on culture conflict and crime.[227]

Sellin argued in that monograph that ethological rather than legal norms should be used to study criminal conduct. Such studies have been made in abundance since Sellin wrote his monograph in 1938. Since then sociologists have shown that culture conflict can be a major contributor to delinquency. This was also the conclusion reached by Edwin Sutherland, the father of American criminology, in his important work Criminology. Sutherland held that delinquency can arise when the norms of one culture come into conflict with the norms of another culture. A norm is here defined as expected behavior. Evidently this kind of conflict arises when the children of immigrants are faced with the demands of the "old world" culture at home and the demands of American culture on the street and in school.[228]

This was also the argument of Clifford Shaw and Henry McKay in their influential study Juvenile Delinquency in Urban Areas published in 1942. Here these authors show that the same area in Chicago continued to have high rates of delinquency decade after decade as different ethnic groups occupied the housing in this area. These different ethnic groups were immigrants from various cultures whose children exhibited high rates of delinquency because of the culture conflict they encountered each day.[229]

Adolescence is itself a condition of culture conflict as we have already seen. Therefore a comparison of adult crime statistics with juvenile delinquency statistics will illustrate the excess of crime committed by the young as compared to crime committed by adults. This has been placed on an index basis so that comparison is possible.

---

226. Andrew J. Fuligni, "Authority, Autonomy, and Parent-Adolescent Conflict and Cohesion: A Study of Adolescents from Mexican, Chinese, Filipino and European Backgrounds," *Developmental Psychology*, 34,no.4 (1998):782-792.

227. Thorsten Sellin, *Culture Conflict and Crime*, (New York: The Social Science Research Council, 1938).

228. Edwin H. Sutherland and Donald R. Cressey, *Crimilology*, (Philadelphia, J.B. Lippincott Co., 1978)p.114.

229. Clifford R. Shaw and Henry D.McKay, *Juvenile Delinquencyin Urban Areas*, (Chicago: University of Chicago Press, 1942).

For example, in 1980 the index offense rate for adults in the US was 5,950. For juveniles, however, the index rate that years was 7,414. This means that the number of reported crimes divided by the population of the US (225,349,264) that year yielded a far higher rate of offenses committed by the young than all age groups combined. Looking now at several other years, we find that juvenile crime rates always exceed the crime rate of the total America population. Here are some examples:

Adult and Juvenile Crime Rates in the United States by Selected Year

Year	Population	General Index offense rate	Juvenile Index offense rate
1980	225,349,264	5,950.0	7,414.3
1983	233,981,000	5,175.0	6,750.8
1986	241,077,000	5,480.4	7,505.0
1989	248,239,000	5,741.0	7,730.9
1992	255,082,000	5,060.2	8,232.1
1998	270,248,000	4,620.1	8,525.9
2001	284,796,887	4,160.5	6,889.8.[a]

a. National Center for Juvenile Justice,(May 31, 2003) *Juvenile Arrest Rates by Offense. See also: Bureau of Justice Statistics, Reported Crime in the United States-total,* (Washington D.C. 2002).

This table shows that juvenile crime exceeds the adult crime rate by about 30% in any one year. The reason for the high juvenile crime rates, then, is that adolescence is in itself a time of marginality and stress. In addition, great stress is placed upon adolescents by the pressure caused by immigrant status. Therefore we can expect that the children of immigrants will have a higher delinquency rate than the children of natives and that adolescents associated with newly arrived members of any ethnic group will have a higher rate of delinquency than the native born. The members of racial and ethnic minorities are clearly marginalized in American society. So are immigrants and their children; and those whose opportunities are blocked by their minority status, their immigrant condition and/or their migratory past are more likely to engage in delinquency than those belonging to the majority culture.

The following table illustrates the difference in juvenile arrest rates:

Juvenile Arrest Rates by Race and Selected Year

Year	White Violent Crime Index	Black Violent Crime Index
1980	189.4	1,190.4
1985	172.3	1,096.3
1990	253.7	1,435.3
1995	312.7	1,708.6
2000	222.5	787.9[a]

a. Ibid..

These statistics clearly demonstrate one of the consequences of "The Great Migration."

The children and grandchildren of those who moved from the South to the North are adolescents living in two cultures at once, feeling nowhere at home, and exhibiting all those attributes of marginality first explored by Stonequist.

The effect of the labor market on immigrants and the children of immigrants has been particularly severe during the first years of the 21st century.

All criminological literature and all studies of adolescents have shown that an adolescent's attachment to family, school and peers are important correlates of delinquency. Diminishing local employment has had a particularly devastating effect on the American family. The de-industrialization of the United States during the decades since 1980 together with the flight of many industrial jobs to foreign soil has led to a good deal of family turmoil among those who have been unemployed or employed part-time.[230]

The years 1980 to 2004 have seen a phenomenal increase in immigration to the United States. In fact, the children of immigrants and immigrant children have become the fastest growing segment of the American population during those years. 15% of all children in the United States are immigrant children or the children of immigrants.[231]

These children, unlike their elders, usually have no connection to "the old country" and therefore use the current American culture as their reference group. They therefore evaluate themselves and are evaluated according to the

---

230. Robert D. Crutchfield and Susan R. Pitchford, "Work and Crime: The Effects of Labor Market Stratification," *Social Forces*, (1997) 76, :93-118.
231. Robert S. Landale and N.S. Oropesa, *Immigrant children and the children of immigrants.* (Lansing, Michigan, Population Research Group of Michigan State University, 1996).

standards of the United States. These children are called "the second generation" in sociological literature, although those who were born in the United States have been labeled "the one-and-a-half-generation." This term refers to those children who try to live in the immigrant and the American world at once but do not fit in either. Those immigrant children or children of immigrants who are 6 to 13 years of age differ in many ways from those who came after reaching their 13th to 15th birthday. [232]

The immigration to the United States during the 25 years ending in 2005 came mainly from non-European countries. One fifth of these legal immigrants came from Mexico. One half of all illegal immigrants also came from Mexico and other South American countries. In addition, immigration to the United States came chiefly from Asia and included considerable numbers who came from China, Korea, the Philippines, Taiwan and Vietnam. Therefore, the foreign born population in the United States under age 18 is made up of 52% Latinos and 27% Asians.[233]

The new immigration differs from older immigrations to the United States in that a good number do not have to start on the bottom of the socio-economic scale but start in the middle class or even above. These are immigrants who earned a college education in their native land and have applied their education to good jobs in the US Since the children of immigrants and immigrant children are normally subject to the advantages and/or disadvantages of their parents, these adolescents do not necessarily have to work their way up the social ladder. This also demonstrates that the opportunities to work physically are almost exhausted in this country.

Unlike earlier immigrations, the new immigration is not concentrated on New York, Boston and Philadelphia. Instead, California accounted for one third of all immigrants during the years since 1980. Other Western states also received large numbers of immigrants while New York received only 14% of all foreigners.[234]

---

232. Ruben Rumbaut, "Ties that bind: immigraton and immigrant familiesin the United States," In: Alan Booth, Ann C. Crouter and Nancy Landale, eds., *Immigration and the Family*, (Mahwah, N.J. Lawrence Earlbaum, Assoc. 1997).

233. Roger Waldionger, *Strangers at the gate: new immigrants in urban America*, (Berkeley: University of California Press, 2001).

234. Alejandro Portes and Min Zhou, "Divergent destinies: immigration, poverty and entrepreneurship in the United States," In: Katherine McFate, ed.,*Poverty, Inequality and the Future of Social Policy*, (New York: Russell Sage Foundation, 1995)p.35.

Because the American economy has largely lost the need for physical laborers and unskilled workers, those immigrants who have little education and are not technologically competent are trapped in unemployment and poverty. This is also true of native-born Americans. These problems are aggravated by the failure of many immigrant children and children of immigrants to learn English. It has been estimated that in Los Angeles, San Francisco, New York and Miami at least one third of all children enter the school system speaking a language other than English. The overall poverty rate among such children is further increased by the growth in one-parent families during the years since 1980. This serious disadvantage for immigrant children and the children of immigrants is particularly pronounced among Mexican, Dominican, Cuban and Filipino children, whose single-parent families constitute upward of 40% of all families.[235]

Because the opportunities to work in low paying jobs have shrunk in recent years, there are many immigrant adolescents who now compete with adults for jobs once considered the province of high school students.

Andrew Sum, director of the center for Labor Market Studies at Northeastern University in Boston, claims that the job market for teens is the worst since 1948. His study of the job market in 2004 concludes that the average number of employed teens dropped 18%, although the number of teens increased five percent. In 2003 the ratio of employed teens to population fell 36.8 percent, according to Sum.

Sum attributes this disastrous situation to the recent increase in immigrants looking for unskilled positions and college graduates seeking jobs normally done by teens. Across all of the United States, 2.5 million immigrants found jobs between 2000 and 2003 even as the US economy lost 2.3 million jobs during that same time.[236]

In view of this dire situation, President George W. Bush has proposed that Congress fund a temporary work program for illegal immigrants. This proposal drew immediate criticism from those who do not want foreign workers encouraged to take the jobs Americans want themselves. Since nearly 2 million immigrants came to the US between 2001 and 2004 reliance on foreign workers has increased even as the economy slowed. This paradox may be understood to mean that the cheap jobs immigrants will take are not of interest to Americans.[237]

---

235. Landale and Oropesa, *Immigrant Children.*
236. Dana Bartholomew and Brent Hopkins, ""Teens job prospects bleakest in decades," *The Daily News of Los Angeles,* (March 26, 2004):N1.

Anyone who has been closely associated with American education is aware that there is a strong "anti-intellectual" trend in the American culture. This can be seen by the emphasis schools give to sports at the expense of academic success. However, among the children of immigrants this anti-intellectualism is even more pronounced and it works to their detriment. This has been called the "oppositional culture," which negatively affects educational outcomes. In schools dominated by children of Hispanic or Afro-American ethnic groups, academic effort is often derided as "acting white" and construed as disloyal to one's ethnic group. This makes entry into middle class or upper income professions almost impossible for many immigrant children and for many children of immigrants, although these attitudes support one's self-esteem among the minorities affected.[238]

Included in the immigrant population of the United States are numerous illegal immigrants, those who have no legal right to be in the country because they did not meet the immigration requirements normally enforced by the Immigration and Naturalization Service of the US

Because there are so many illegal immigrants in the country, about 65,000 illegal immigrants graduated from American high schools in the spring of 2004. These high school graduates cannot attend any American college because US immigration laws prohibit public financing of higher education for those who are in the country illegally. According to federal law, states may not use state financial aid to help undocumented illegal immigrants to attain a higher education in the United States.[239]

For example, the University of Connecticut denies admission to illegal aliens no matter how long they have lived in the United States or how good their high school grades may be. Students who are not legal residents of the state must usually pay three times the tuition paid by legal in-state residents.

In view of these restrictions, the National People's Action, based in Chicago, is demanding that Congress pass the Development, Relief and Edu-

---

237. Jennifer Held Powell and Jon Chesto, "Immigrant proposal draws fire," *The Boston Herald*, (January 9, 2004):29.

238. Bianchi Matute, "Ethnic identity and patterns of school success," *American Journal of Education*, (95, 1986):233-255.

239. Claudio Sanchez, "Illegal immigrant students find it difficult to go to college," *National Public Radio*, (April 21, 2004).

cation for Alien Minors Act, which would allow undocumented immigrants to gain legal US residency and therefore qualify for in-state tuition at institutions of higher learning.[240]

Those who are mainly concerned with the effort to allow illegal immigrants to benefit from these proposals are mainly Hispanics of Mexican origin. These immigrants differ from previous immigrants in that they come across the border and not from overseas. Therefore, these millions of immigrants can keep ties across the common border of the US and Mexico and are therefore less likely than the Europeans and Asians who came before them to assimilate American culture. It is evident that Mexican immigrants are therefore more likely than other ethnic groups to maintain the Spanish language over several generations. Nevertheless, like other ethnic groups, a third of the Latino population in the United States have married Anglos. Furthermore, many young Latinos have joined the US armed forces so that 10% of the American military is of Latino descent.

Nevertheless, compared to the majority of Americans, Latinos have a serious education problem which has nothing to do with the restrictions placed on their access to higher education. The difficulty here lies in the fact that only 55% of Latinos graduate from high school compared to 90% of non-immigrant adolescents. Likewise, only 8% of Hispanics get college degrees compared to 26% of the American population.[241]

There are 17 million Latin American immigrants living in the United States (2005). In addition there are as many native born Latinos in the country. This leads some observers to underscore that the Hispanic immigration of the late 20th and early 21st centuries differs from the earlier European immigration in several ways. First is the probability that, unlike all other immigrants, the Latino immigrants will never accept the Protestant/Anglo values which have heretofore governed America for over two hundred years. The reasons for this pessimism are that the US labor market is more difficult to enter now than was true in earlier years. In addition, Latinos are more visible than the Europeans who came earlier. Furthermore, cheaper transportation makes it easier for Latinos to retain ties to the countries of their origin. Additionally, there are now so many illegal immigrants that they face numerous barriers to full assimilation into American

---

240. Michelle R. Davis, "High Level Meetings," *Education Week*, 23, no.30, (April 7, 2004):22.
241. Editorial, "Hispanic Nation: Myth and Reality," *Business Week*, no.3874, (March 15, 2004):128.

culture for that reason alone. All of this impacts on adolescents more than any other age group because the adolescent is school age, the adolescent or young adult needs to enter the economic ladder or the freshman year at a college and the adolescent or young adult must decide whether or not to found a family and with whom to do so.[242]

SUMMARY

Homeless adolescents and children include those with families and those without families. These children are called "runaways" or "throwaways." These children live in the streets and face horrendous problems every day, aggravated by their inability to obtain any schooling. Many come from homes already involved in alcohol and drug abuse in which they too engage.

The Great Migration within the United States has created an excess of unemployment, violent crime and welfare dependency among the children and grandchildren of southern blacks who migrated north.

All of these problems and challenges are also associated with immigration. Immigration also provokes inter-generational culture conflicts and is responsible for educational deficiencies among the children of immigrants.

---

242. David Glenn, "Scholars cook up a new melting pot," *Chronicle of Higher Education*, 50, no.23 (February 13, 2004).

CHAPTER 6. SEX AND MORE SEX

SEX AND THE MEDIA

The use of sex appeal to sell any and all products is so common that it is hardly noticed by most American consumers. On occasion, the direct appeal to sexual appetites by aggressive advertisers raises a minor fuss, only to be soon forgotten.

One such example was the Abercrombie and Fitch catalogue which, in the winter of 2003, sought to appeal to young people. This catalogue included pictures of near-nude girls and boys together, with the suggestion that masturbation is a safe alternative to fornication.[243] This offended some customers and merchants so much that it was removed from stores after some "citizens" considered a boycott action.

In 2003, Seventeen magazine featured a shirtless young man and a girl in her underwear in bed. The advertisement sold "FCUK" scent and "Scent to Bed" fragrance. In addition, such magazines as CosmoGirl, TeenVogue and ElleGirl sell perfume by exhibiting near-nude popular actresses. There are even shirts for sale to teen age boys and girls with such inscriptions as "FCUK You 2."[244]

These excesses serve to highlight the conflicting views of sex in the US, one driven by the media together with the pornographic aspects of the culture, the other based in a sometimes hypocritical puritanism. The best example of the

---

243. No author, *The Economist*, 3780, no.8365, (March 6, 2004):10.
244. Allie Shah, "Sexy ads: what exactly are they selling to kids?" *Star Tribune*, Minneapolis, Minn. (December 23, 2003):1A.

puritan attitude concerning sex which lives side by side with the culture of pornography was the uproar over the exposure of one breast belonging to an entertainer at the 2004 Super Bowl. Whether by design or accident, Janet Jackson bared one of her lactic glands for a fraction of a second during the halftime "show," a negligible event that was made into such a scandal by the media that a vast audience sought out the website where this banality was posted.

In view of the uproar over the sighting of the Jacksonian globe, Paul Tagliabue, NFL Commissioner, proclaimed that the incident was "offensive and embarrassing to the NFL and its fans." This seems most hypocritical coming from the representative of an organization which is almost daily "embarrassed" by allegations of drug abuse, wife beating, violence including murder and other felony convictions associated with their players.[245]

The essence of the sex and violence associated with sports does indeed trickle down to the minds of children, as shown by an eight-year-old boy who declared, during a therapy session, that he wants to be a football player when he grows up. When the therapist asked for the reason for this ambition, he volunteered: "My cousin says if ya play good football you can bang them pretty cheerin' girls."

Another outcome of the Jackson scandal was the fine imposed on Clear Channel radio stations for broadcasting sex-tinged conversation by Howard Stern, including some gross descriptions of the human anatomy together with numerous "suggestive" themes. Consequently, six of the Clear Channel stations dropped the Stern broadcasts. This is of course a negligible loss for Stern. Furthermore, the FCC has evidently overlooked a number of Spanish language broadcasts which are so bizarre that their description would be sufficient to induce illness in the reader. The perpetrators of this filth are Enrique Santos and Joe Ferrero of WXDJ in Miami. Because they broadcast in Spanish, their audience is limited and evidently receives no attention from the FCC. Also, it is difficult to define what constitutes a "dirty" word in Spanish, particularly since Puerto Rican Spanish and Mexican Spanish are not the same.[246]

There was a time when the media shared an almost puritanical attitude towards sex. At the beginning of the new century, however, the opposite is the case. Indeed, even now the preoccupation with sex by the media is usually

---

245. Richard M. Berthold, "America hypocritical about sex," *Daily Lobo*, (February 2, 2004) Column section.
246. Joseph Contreras, "Under the Radar Radio," *Newsweek*, 143, no.18 (May 3, 2004):53.

accompanied by a minimal effort to distance oneself from the topic about to be discussed.

During the Clinton Administration, the sexual proclivities of President Bill Clinton, usually summarized as "the Monica Lewinsky scandal," occupied so much media space that it could not possibly have escaped the attention of adolescents any more than all the other sexual messages associated with the commercialism which drives our communications industry. More recently, the subject of "gay" or homosexual marriages has occupied a great deal of time and space in the media, thus ensuring that there is always some "scandal" feeding the sexual interests of the public, including adolescents.[247]

Radio and television broadcasts are by no means the only money driven enterprises feeding on sex. Clothing and cosmetics sales are equally anxious to use sex as a selling vehicle.

Twenty years ago, in the early 80s, the clothing manufacturer Calvin Klein introduced the model Brooke Shields, then only 15 years old, to the world of commercial sex. Over 400,000 pair of Calvin Klein jeans were sold in one week after Ms. Shields, dressed in extra tight jeans, proclaimed, "nothing comes between me and my Calvins," and added, "I've got seven Calvins in my closet and if they could talk I'd be ruined." By the end of the year following that ad, Calvin Klein had earned $12.5 million selling jeans.

Male models are also used to sell clothes and even perfumes by means of exhibitionism. A perfume manufacturer, Lacoste, shows a nude "hunk" sitting in an armchair drinking coffee. No doubt this appeals to women and gay men as do the male underwear advertisements appearing in super large format in New York's Times Square.

The influence of easily available pornography on adolescent sexuality cannot be overlooked. A report from an Internet filtering company shows that the viewing of pornography rose 1,800 percent, from 14 million web pages in 1998 to 260 million in 2003. Pornography is a $12 billion industry in the United States, of which child pornography yields $3 billion annually. Because much of this material is visible on the Internet, it has entered every home and is easily accessible to children and adolescents.[248]

---

247. Joel Mc Nally, "Media Love Sex-plitation." *Capital Times*, (February 21, 2004):8A.
248. Sonya Jason, "Scourbe of the valley: Pornography undermines decent society," *The Daily News of Los Angeles*, (May 23, 2004):V1.

This availability may be illustrated by the experience of a teacher at the Riverdale Public School in New Jersey, who found that 42 students in a class of 42 all reported that they had seen pornography on the Internet. The children were 13 years old.

The Henry J. Kaiser Family Foundation has released a study showing that 70% of 15- to 17-year-old children view pornography, including one million erotic web sites. Therefore it is a matter of fact that sex education for most American children comes from the porn industry as exhibited on the world wide web.[249]

A definition of pornography is difficult because there are so many opinions as to what constitutes pornography or at least what should or should not be seen by children. The United States has a long history of attempted censorship which seeks to shield children, and often also adults, from sex related information. These efforts at censorship have waxed and waned over the years. Before the arrival of the Internet, video rentals and DVDs, these efforts at censorship targeted movies and magazines. The most sensational diatribe against magazines and particularly movies was the 1954 book by Frederick Wertham, Seduction of the Innocent, which sought to convince its readers that there is a direct connection between literature and behavior. He argued that crime comics, then very popular, had a direct effect on youngsters and led to violent delinquency.[250]

In the 1960s there was an uproar among censorship minded Americans concerning such movies as Rebel Without a Cause and The Wild Ones, Blackboard Jungle and High School Confidential, etc.[251]

Meanwhile popular music kept the puritans busy. In 1954, Bill Haley launched the "rock and roll" revolution, leading to the hip swinging Elvis Presley, whose sexual innuendos caused the Jesuit magazine America to publish an article entitled "Beware Elvis Presley," which condemned this music roundly and predicted evil consequences.[252]

All of these efforts at censorship concerning sexually explicit or implicit messages were doomed to fail. However, the would be censors could not have known that the coming of the computer and the Internet would drastically alter

249. Richard Jerome et.al.,"The Cyberporn Generation," *People*, 61, no.16 (April 26, 2004):72.

250. Fredric Wertheim, *Seduction of the Innocent*, (New York, Rinehart,1954).

251. David M. Considine, *The Cinema of Adolescence*, (Jefferson, N.C. McFarland, 1985)pp.181-182.

252. Karal Ann Marling, *As Seen on TV: The visual Culture of Every Day Life in the 1950s*, (Cambridge, MA., Harvard University Press, 1994)p.196.

the sexual behavior of the American people and give the young and the very young a view of sex which no one could have foreseen and which would truly have convinced our puritan ancestors that the devil had finally won all arguments.

THE SOCIALIZATION-SEXUALIZATION PROCESS

It would seem ridiculous to argue that sexual behavior is learned when all the world "knows" that sex is an inherited drive which needs no study to be effective. Nevertheless, sociologists have long discussed socialization as the process by which we develop our human potential and learn culture. Therefore, it is evident that we superimpose cultural requirements upon the sex drive and that the means adopted by members of any society to gain access to the opposite sex are derived from the culture in which such expression is experienced. We shall therefore call the enculturated process by which adolescents experience sex for the first time the sexualization process.[253]

One aspect of this process is related to the impact of the media on the adolescent's sexual interests. The media impact may be classified as "informal" sex education, to which "formal" sex education is added in almost all schools.

Informal sex education is of course not limited to the media. Parents, peers and religious groups all participate in the sex education of American youngsters outside the classroom. This begins with learning one's gender identity. Gender identity is a social issue because the roles played by women and men are determined by the cultural requirements of each society and are not everywhere the same. American boys and American girls learn by observation and parental influence what is masculine and what is feminine in American culture. Such learning includes forming sexual values.

Whatever one's values may be in any area of life, sexuality included, behavior is largely colored by such values, although not altogether determined by them. Whether sex or food or drink, the satisfaction derived from meeting the demands of the hormones differs with each individual. Therefore, someone who derives a great deal of satisfaction from a first sexual experience is more likely to continue such conduct than someone who derives little or no satisfaction from

---

253. John J. Macionis, *Sociology*, 3rd *Edition,*(Upper Saddle River, NJ. Prentice Hall, 2005)p.115.

the first or subsequent experiences. Since sex is contingent on the behavior of one's partner, no one is entirely in control of his sexual satisfaction, so that adolescents may continue or cease sexual activity because they had a satisfactory or unsatisfactory experience on first intercourse.[254]

Sexual development is therefore only partially influenced by parents. Parents are likely to assume that the values they taught their children will govern them. This is partially true. Yet, in the area of sexual behavior this is difficult to determine because few parents are willing to talk to adolescents directly and bluntly about sexual matters. Furthermore, adolescent conduct regarding sex cannot well profit from childhood experiences as other areas of value orientation do, because children cannot interpret sexual knowledge as would an adult. Therefore, the key factor influencing sexual behavior is "dating" the opposite sex.[255]

"Dating" has led to a steady decrease in the age at which the majority of American young people experience sex. In fact, most American adolescents report at least one sexual experience before they graduate from high school.

There are now many adolescents who avoid "dating" because they do not want to get involved in a long term relationship and who look upon those who "date" each other as "losers." Among these adolescents, "hooking up" is more common than dating. Hooking up is a no-strings sexual encounter. It is often achieved through the Internet. Teenagers flirt with each other first "on line" and then meet for a sexual event without romantic overtones. Some participate with the same partner more than once. Such friends are called "friends with benefits." They "hook up" and then play video games or otherwise entertain themselves and each other. According to one report, girls are as aggressive as boys in accosting the opposite sex. The sites used by teenagers are called rating sites because the participants exhibit their pictures on them. These pictures are then rated by the strangers who view them, with the intent of finding a sex partner.

A 2001 survey conducted by Bowling Green State University found that of the 55% of 11th graders who engaged in intercourse, 60% said they had sex with a partner who was no more than a friend. That study did not ask about oral sex, which is far more common than intercourse among teens.

---

254. Graham B. Spanier, "Sexualization and Premarital Sexual Behavior," *The Family Coordinator*, 24, no. 1(January 1975):35.
255. Ibid. 39.

Because the "hook up" is sexual only, it is the rule that teenagers who participate in these encounters do not see each other for any other reason. There are no dates, no phone calls to just say "hi," no romance of any kind. Some teens become emotionally involved just the same and are hurt by the cold sex-only relationship. Others use these Internet relationships until they feel they are no longer sexually attractive and therefore have no choice but to date or even get married.[256]

There are those who attribute this decline in adolescent "morals" to a lack of religious attachment. Such concerns are often ridiculed by the humanist academic establishment. Nevertheless, a number of studies have found that religious individuals have first sex at a later age than those who are less religious.[257]

No value judgment need attach to the finding that strength of religious convictions and participation in religious activities predict whether or not an adolescent has sex. Such convictions are more important than the denomination to which one belongs, except that the use of contraceptives is more likely to be determined by denomination than sexual behavior per se.[258]

Because adolescence is an age at which the process of individuation is very important as the young seek to establish their own identity apart from their family, adolescents own attitudes concerning sex are more influential than the attitudes of their parents. Therefore, the influence of religion on sexual activity needs also to be examined reciprocally. Sexual activity and beliefs about sex no doubt influence religious behavior. There is evidence that sexual behavior also causes individuals to change their religious values, promoting a more permissive view than is customarily expected within almost all American denominations. Involvement of adolescents in activities outside the family therefore influence the age at which sexual behavior is first experienced. School attendance and religious involvement influence sexual conduct, so that young men who attend religious services regularly are less likely to engage in premarital intercourse than those who do not attend.[259]

---

256. Ibid. p.32.
257. Shusheela Singh and Jacqueline E. Darroch, "Trends in Sexual Activity Among Adolescent American Women; 1982-1995" *Family Planning Perspectives*, 31, (1999):212-219.
258. Leighton Ku, Freya L. Sonnenstein and Joseph H. Pleck, "Factors Influencing First Intercourse for Teen Age Men," *Public Health Reports*, 108, (1993):680-694.
259. Arland Thornton and Donald Camburn, "Religious Participation and Adolescent Sexual Behavior," *Journal of Marriage and the Family*, (51) 1989):641-643.

All research in this area concludes that the higher the religiosity, the less the probability of adolescents having sex. In short, religious adherence has an effect on first sex. This effect is far stronger for females but also concerns males. Those adolescents who have decided to have sex develop more permissive attitudes thereafter since it now becomes necessary to adopt a post hoc justification for having become involved in sexual behavior. It is also important to consider that the opportunity to have sex is not the same for all adolescents, so that those with greater opportunity will be involved sooner than those who have little chance of "dating" or otherwise gaining access to the opposite sex.[260]

There is, then, a significant association between dating and sexual activity. Therefore, since dating is initiated at an earlier age in 2005 than in the past, the overwhelming majority of adolescent Americans engage in sexual intercourse before age eighteen. Furthermore, one quarter, or 24% of females and 27% of males, have had sex by age 15, and the proportion of even younger teenagers engaging in sex has been increasing.[261]

Sexualization is not the same for males and females. Males, at least in American culture, view their first intercourse in a far more casual fashion than females, who romanticize such relationships. There are also racial differences in teenage sexual activity. A far larger proportion of black adolescents engage in sexual intercourse by age 15 than is true of non-blacks. This despite the fact that dating generally begins later for black females than white females.[262]

Research reveals that only 3% of children 11 to 12 years old engage in sex. This increases to 10% between the ages of 13–14, with 12% of males and only 8% of females engaging in intercourse at that age. By age 15–16, 34% of adolescents have engaged in sex.[263]

In view of the young age at which Americans generally begin sexual activity, it is obvious that the risk of disease and pregnancy has increased as the

---

260. Ibib.b 642.

261. John S. Santelli, Laura Duberstein Lindberg, Joyce Abma Clea Sucoff McNealy and Michael Resnick, "Adolescent sexual behavior estimates and trends from four nationally representative surveys, *Family Planning Perspectives*, 32, no.4 (July-August 2000):156-165.

262. George L. Donus, T.B. Heaton and Paul Steffen, "Adolescent life events and their association with the onset of sexual intercourse," *Youth and Society*, 25, no.1, (1993):3-23.

263. Elizabeth C. Cooksey, Frank L. Mott and Stefanie A. Neubauer, "Friendship and Early Relationships: Links to Sexual Initiation Among American Adolescents Born to Young Mother," *Perspectives on Sexual Reproductive Health*, 34, no.3, (2002): 121.

age of first intercourse has declined. These risks are taken by many adolescents, not only because dating begins earlier at the outset of the 21st century than was true before, but also because a number of social pressures create circumstances that lead to early dating and early intercourse. One of these is the large number of adolescents who live with only one parent. The evidence is that youth living with only one parent have higher rates of first sex at a young age than those living with both biological parents.[264]

The US Statistical Abstract confirms that in just 26 years the number of couples with children decreased 71% and the percent of adults who were married decreased from 75% to 56%. Meanwhile, the number of unmarried households with no children increased 230% and the number of children in single mother households increased 417% as the number of children living with neither parent increased 1,440%. Only 51% or 36.4 million of American children lived with two parents in 1998 and 18%, or 12 million, lived with a single parent at that time. Therefore, 31% or 22 million children in the US lived with neither parent. The Statistical Abstract uses the phrase "two parent family groups" rather than "parents" because 13 million of the 25.7 million children living with two parents in 2003 were actually living with stepparents, mostly stepfathers, thereby increasing the risk of sexual abuse seven fold.[265]

> *Katheryn Fox was living with her mother and stepfather. She did not know who her biological father was and from infancy she only knew Karl, the man known as "Dad," to herself and her two very young brothers. Kathy's mother was an alcoholic and the girl was frequently left alone with Karl, who was also a heavy drinker. Even as a very young child she had experienced sex in many forms. He would come into her room at night, sometimes sober, sometimes inebriated. When she was a little girl he would frequently hold and pet her before starting. Kathy seemed to enjoy this man's "affections" and participated willingly. As she grew, he continued making advances toward her, cuddling her most of the time to have her feel "loved." As she got older he told her not to share their "fun secrets" with her mother. Since Kathy had known nothing else, she did not reject this man's attentions and on the contrary enjoyed the "fun" she was having with him. By the time she was a preadolescent, they were having sex with Kathy. She came to her social worker's attention when she was living in a children's institution at age thirteen. She had*

---

264. Dawn M. Upchurch, Levy-Storms Lene, Clea A.Sucoff and Carol S. Aneshensel, "Gender and Ethnic Differences in the Timing of First Sexual Intercourse," *Family Planning Perspectives*, 30, no. 3 (1998):121-127.

265. US Bureau of the Census, *Current Population Reports*, (http://www.childstats. Gov/ ac2000poplhtm)

been placed there because she had been neglected by her alcoholic mother and had come to school in an unclean, disheveled state, complaining of hunger. Shortly after her arrival at the institution she told the therapist that she missed her "Dad" and his affectionate ways. Before that time she was not aware that there was something strange or different about her relationship with Karl. She lacked concentration, often appearing to be in "deep thought." This adolescent's moods changed rapidly and only after some time in her new environment did Kathy realize that her experiences were different from other children who lived in "normal" families.

Such abuse is not limited to stepfathers or, indeed, stepparents. A recent study of heterosexual relationships among American teenagers[266] found that nearly one third reported having experienced some form of abuse by their own partners. Researchers conducted that study by using data from the National Longitudinal Study of Adolescent Health. This showed that physical abuse occurred in 29% of cases studied, augmented by another 12% who reported verbal abuse.

Young people living in low income households have a higher rate of sexual activity than those living in wealthier homes.[267] In addition, maternal education and employment are predictors of age at sexual initiation. The lower a mother's educational level, the more hours she works, the younger the teenager will be when she or he initiates sexual intercourse. Early sexual intercourse is also more likely among teenagers with low self-esteem. [268]

Substance abuse also contributes to early sexual involvement because it impedes a youth's decision making ability. Barbara C. Leigh documented the fact that males aged 18–30 who smoked marijuana or cigarettes or drank a good deal of alcohol were more likely to engage in sexual escapades than those males who did not engage in substance abuse. Sexual activity can also predict delinquent behavior in that sexually active students aged 15–17 are more likely to be suspended from school than those who are not sexually active.[269]

266. Carolyn T. Halpern, "Partner violence among adolescents in opposite sex romantic relationships," *American Journal of Public Health*, 91, no.10, (2001):1679-1685.

267. Susan Newcomer and William Baldwin, "Demographics of adolescent sexual behavior: contraception, pregnancies and STD's," *Journal of School Health*, 62, no.7 (1992):265-270.

268. Lori Kowaleski-Jones and Frank L. Mott, "Sex, contraception and child bearing among high-risk youth: do different factors influence males and females?" *Family Planning Perspectives*, 30, 4 (July-August 1998):163-169.

269. Barbara C. Leigh, "The relationship of substance use to sexual activity among young adults in the United States," *Family Planning Perspectives*, 27, no.1 (1995):18-22.

Suspensions from school together with various delinquencies are more common in minority communities in inner cities than in the suburbs. In minority inner city communities, sex has become a bartering device. Sex is transactional. This means that poor girls will have sex with any man willing to buy them a pair of tennis shoes, an outfit or a trip to the beauty parlor. Consequently, men will "cruise" high school parking lots for young girls who will join them in their cars. The girls know that the men will pay them in return for sex and the men find this a lot cheaper than paying for a mature woman.[270]

Girls who have an older partner are more likely to have an early sexual experience than those who have male friends of their own age. Such girls are at a greater risk of pregnancy and diseases. Females have a higher risk than males of contracting a disease from an infected partner. Furthermore, an unwanted pregnancy is of course borne by the female. When Darroch and other researchers examined data from the National Survey of Family Growth, they found that the pregnancy rate for females whose sexual partners were older by six or more years was 3.7 times the rate for females whose partners were within two years of their age.[271]

Because of this increased risk, some now postpone sex or abstain altogether until marriage. While sexual abstinence may be highly commended among some Americans, it must be understood that all Americans do not live in the same culture. A daughter of an upper-middle-class professional family, for example, inculcated with traditional values, may reject premarital sex and finish her college and graduate education before considering a permanent husband-wife relationship. In many communities, among many whites as well as minorities, sexual abstinence is ridiculed. Furthermore, the poor do not easily respond to the argument that abstinence will "pay off" later because many minority adolescents do not believe they have a future.[272]

Abstinence may well be related to sex education in schools, provided it does not come too late. Some children begin their sex life early. The federal government budgeted $273 million in fiscal 2005 for abstinence education in US schools. This program began during the Clinton administration, when Congress authorized the spending of $250 million for sex education in 1996. This money was to be used for "abstinence only" as the exclusive purpose. It was also ruled

270. Susan Reimer, "Some teens in inner city barter with sex," *The Baltimore Sun,* (January 25, 2004) 1N.

271. Jacqueline E. Darroch, David L. Landry and Selene Oslak, "Age differences between sexual partners in the United States, *Family Planning Perspectives,* 31,no.4 (1999):160-167.

272. Reimer, "Some teens etc" p. 1N.

that the money had to be totally separate from any state program involving contraceptive information or services.[273]

Recently a Christian group based in Ohio was granted $400,000 in federal money to take its teen sexual abstinence program on the road. Earlier, the same group was given $700,000 in federal money to finance their program. This group distributes silver rings and Bibles to any teen willing to take a vow of chastity until marriage. Using high-tech lighting and video displays, the group seeks to enroll at least 2 million teens in their abstinence only program.[274]

SEX EDUCATION

In his State of the Union speech, January 20, 2004, President Bush proclaimed that "abstinence for young people is the only way to avoid sexually transmitted diseases." This message was most welcome among those who believe that there should be no sex outside of marriage but was very much criticized by the Sexuality Information and Education Council of the United States. That group believes that sex education curricula should include information about contraception in addition to fostering abstinence. SIECUS believe that an abstinence only education is not realistic, although some post-sex education surveys show that abstinence messages may reduce the number of students involved in early sex.[275]

Such educational efforts are widely supported by the American public. Not only is abstinence widely supported, but six out of ten Americans believe that sexually active young people should be given access to birth control devices. Therefore, public opinion is in agreement with sex education which holds that the "abstinence only" approach ignores the evidence that other programs are also effective in delaying the onset of sexual intercourse among adolescents. In fact, there is little evidence that "abstinence only" programs have either delayed or reduced sexual activity. The evidence is that the "comprehensive" approach to sex education is far more successful than the "abstinence only" approach,

273. Sexuality Information and Education Council of the United States, "Between the Lines: States Implementation of the Federal Government's Section (510b0 Abstinence Education Program, (New York, SIECUS, 1999).

274. Alisha Hipwell, "Federal grant to fund message of abstinence," *Pittsburgh Post Gazette*, (December 19, 2003):N1.

275. Darcia Harris Bowman, "Abstinence only debate heating up," *Education Week*, 23, no.22 (February 11, 2004):1.

because the "comprehensive" approach includes contraception for pregnancy and information concerning sexually transmitted diseases.[276]

. When Congress passed the Adolescent Family Life Act in 1981, it included money for the establishment of a counseling and service network designed to provide contraceptive services only to adolescents who already had a child and who were seeking to prevent another pregnancy. Such a network never materialized. However, the AFLA subsidized curricula that promoted abstinence-only education in schools.

As a result more than two thirds of all American school districts have a sex education program. The remaining third leave sex education to individual schools or teachers. School districts in the north are more likely to have a district wide policy to teach sex education than is true of the south or the west.[277]

Although a large number of teachers believe that sex education should begin in grades 7 or 8, and although some children clearly have sexual encounters before then, it appears that in most American schools sex education does not begin until the ninth or tenth grade. There is also a gap between what teachers think should be taught and what is really taught. There is a particularly wide gap between the belief of teachers that students should be told where they can obtain birth control. Yet, such information is only available in 48% of American schools. There is much more uniformity concerning the teaching about AIDS, which is "covered" by 90-96 percent of teachers, with abstinence a close second. Sex education teachers regard parental interference and pressure from school administrators as the major obstacles in teaching about sex.[278]

In California over $200 million was spent between 1994 and 2004 for sex education, leading to a 40% decline in teen pregnancy. This led to considerable savings for the California taxpayer in that fewer teen mothers and their babies needed public help. State officials and parents believe this success is the product of a comprehensive approach to sex education and are therefore unwilling to take federal money for an "abstinence only" approach.[279]

---

276. Anne Grunseit, "Sexuality education and young peoples sexual behaviors: a review of studies," *Journal of Adolescent Research*, 12, no.4 (October 1997):421-453.

277. Rebekah Saul, "What ever happened to the Adolescent Family Life Act?" *The Guttmacher Report on Public Policy*, 1, no2 (1998):5.

278. Jacqueline Darroch Forrest and Jane Silverman, "What public School Teachers teach about Preventing Pregnancy, AIDS and sexually transmitted diseases," *Family Planning Perspectives*, 21, no.2 (March/April 1989):65.

279. David Whitney, "Teen pregnancy rate improvement at risk," *Fresno Bee*, (May 7, 2004):B8.

Sex education is controversial. Critics of sex education claim that it leads to more sexual activity among teenagers and therefore to more teen pregnancy. Advocates of sex education claim that sex education prevents pregnancy and prevents sexually transmitted diseases. The sociologist Oettinger has made a detailed study of the effects of sex education on 'teen sexual activity and concluded that enrollment in sex education was associated with a significant increase in sexual activity for females and a smaller and insignificant increase in the pregnancy rate. Sex education is also more important to young women than to boys and men.[280]

The content of sex education courses across the United States varies somewhat depending on political considerations. It is however fairly certain that children will be told about abstinence as the best means of protection against the hazard of pregnancy and/or disease. In addition, birth control and sexually transmitted diseases are included in every sex education curriculum. Furthermore it is necessary to teach children the biology of reproduction beginning with the sex organs because few young people and few adults understand the process of human reproduction. Ignorance of human biology leads many young people to believe that they are somehow immune to sexually transmitted diseases and the possibility of pregnancy.

The Alan Guttmacher Institute collected statistics showing that teenage pregnancies declined in 2004 as compared to 1990 because both abstinence and contraceptives have become effective. In 1990, 116.9 of every 1,000 girls 15-19 years old became pregnant. From 2000 to 2004 the decline in teen pregnancies led to a rate of 83.6 per 1,000 girls. The Alan Guttmacher Institute was founded in 1968 as an offshoot of Planned Parenthood. It was named after Alan Guttmacher, M.D., an eminent obstetrician-gynecologist, teacher and writer, who was Planned Parenthood president for a decade until his death in 1974.

No doubt there are now some young people who reject the "sexual revolution" of the 1960s which led to many families being left without a father; however, it is of course unlikely that the United States will ever return to the conservative 1950s. However, Welfare reform which no longer finances incentives for pregnant teens, aggressive pursuit of child support from young fathers, the campaign for birth control and, above all, fear of sexually transmitted diseases have contributed to this new abstinence.[281]

---

280. Gerald S. Oettinger, "The Effects of Sex Education on 'teen sexual activity and Teen Pregnancy. *The Journal of Political Economy* 1`07,no. 3 (June 1999):606.

SEXUALLY TRANSMITTED DISEASES

The World Health Organization estimates that 30 million curable sexually transmitted diseases occur each year in North America and Western Europe. These diseases included syphilis, gonorrhea, chlamydia and trichomoniasis. This does not include genital herpes and other infections. Because of the extensive effort to find a cure for HIV and AIDS very little attention has been given these more traditional sexually transmitted diseases in recent years.[282]

Recent studies show that American adolescent females have a syphilis rate of about nine per hundred thousand, which is a good deal higher than in other "developed" countries. The female adolescent rate of syphilis is 8.6 per hundred thousand or double that of male adolescents, which is 4.3 per hundred thousand.

The rate of gonorrhea infection in the United States is phenomenal for adolescents 15-19 years old. The female rate is 758.2 per hundred thousand and the male rate 394.8 per hundred thousand. Compared to England at 95.7 and 59.1 respectively or Germany at 1.1 and 1.2, American gonorrhea rates are indeed extreme.

Adolescents in the United States account for at least one third of all who suffer these infections. The incidence of these diseases is higher among the young than the older and married population and is highest among the black population as compared to Hispanics and whites.[283]

The sexologists Panchaud et al. discovered in a study of sexually transmitted diseases among adolescents that overall syphilis, gonorrhea and chlamydia disproportionately affect adolescents and young adults. This means that in a number of countries visited by these researchers the adolescent age groups account for one fifth and sometimes one third of all reported cases for these diseases. It is noteworthy that the incidence of gonorrhea is higher in all countries studied by Panchard et al. than the incidence of the other two diseases. The United States displays a higher rate of all three of these diseases than

---

281. Suzanne Fields, "When teens say 'no' to sex; responsibility/restraint make comeback," *The Washington Times*, (March 15, 2004): A23.

282. D.T. Fleming and Judith N. Wasserheit, "From epidemiological synergy to public health policy and practice: the contribution of other sexually transmitted diseases to sexual transmission of HIV infection." *Sexually Transmitted Infections*, 75, no.1 (February 1999):3-17.

283. US Department of Health and Human Services, *Sexually Transmitted Diseases Surveillance*, (Washington, D.C. 2003).

Western Europe because the incidence of reported gonorrhea among Afro-American adolescents is 2,828 per 100,000, or 24 times the rate found among Euro-Americans.

Chlamydia is a disease most prevalent among young women. In most developed countries included in the Panchard study the reported rate of chlamydia is about 100 in 100,000. It is important to remember that girls and women are more often screened and tested by physicians than is true of males. Therefore the higher reported rate is not necessarily a reflection of an actual higher rate of infection.[284]

Disease is of course not the only risk taken by sexually active people. For females pregnancy and the possibility of abortion are additional considerations.

ABORTION

About one half of unintended pregnancies in the US end in abortion. About 45 out of every 1,000 women aged 15 to 44 find themselves with an unintended pregnancy, but the statistics are heavily skewed toward adolescents. In fact, of those surveyed 50% of those who do not use contraceptives are adolescents, and most of them had never practiced contraception. Furthermore, women whose income is far below the federal poverty level are far more likely than women with higher income levels to ignore contraceptives. This is also true of women with less than a college degree and women of Hispanic, Black or other minority cultures in the United States.

About 1.3 million American women have an abortion each year. Of these women, approximately 608,000 did not use any contraceptive, 610,000 used contraceptives on occasion but were unexpectedly involved in intercourse, while 95,000 used contraceptives but became pregnant nonetheless.[285]

Included in those who seek abortions because of an unwanted pregnancy are numerous adolescents. Although abortions are legal in the United States, for adolescents there are usually some restrictions as to availability of an abortion. The most common of these restrictions concerns parental consent. Thirty-two

284. Christine Panchaud, Sushela Singh, Dina Feivelson and Jacqueline E. Darroch, "Sexually Transmitted Diseases among Adolescents in developed Countries," *Family Planning Perspectives*, 32, no.1 (January 2000):24-32.
285. Rachel K. Jones, Jacqueline Darroch and Stanley K. Henshaw, "Contraceptive Use among US Women Having Abortions in 2000-20001," *Perspectives on Sexual and Reproductive Health*, 34, no.6, (November-December 2002):294-303.

states now restrict adolescent access to abortion because parental consent laws require that one or both parents be notified prior to the performance of an abortion on a minor. Included are 17 states which require that the parent, so notified, consent to the abortion and a few states allow a grandparent instead of a parent to give permission. Furthermore, there are 28 states which allow a judge to bypass parental involvement.[286]

The reason for allowing such a judicial bypass decision is the need to protect adolescents from making decisions which are harmful to themselves and their families. These decisions involve the health of the mother-to-be who is also a legal minor. Normally, parents are responsible for their children's well being, including the authorization for medial treatment. Nevertheless, all 50 states allow minors to consent to treatment of sexually transmitted diseases without the consent of parents. The reason is that many minors would not get any treatment if they had to inform their parents first. In thirty four states an underage mother can place a child for adoption if she so sees fit.

There are, however, many restrictive laws concerning adoption. Three rationales support these laws. The first is that abortion poses a significant risk; that adolescents are incapable of making an adequately informed decision; and that adolescents benefit from parental involvement that results from notification or consent.[287]

These three reasons for restricting abortion among adolescents have been examined in detail by professional psychologists who found that the data do not show that minors are at a heightened risk of serious adverse psychological responses compared with adult abortion patients.[288]

A study by Ambuel and Rapaport compared adolescents seeking abortion with those who carried to term. The study found that competence at decision making was more pronounced among those who decided in favor of abortion. The girls who underwent an abortion had higher educational achievements, had more educated mothers and were from families in better economic circumstances than those who carried to term.[289]

---

286. Heather Boonstra and Elizabeth Nash, ""Minors and the right to consent to health care," *Guttmacher Report on Public Policy*, 3,no.4, (2000)4-8.
287. Centers for Disease Control and Prevention, "Abortion surveillance-United States 1993 and1994," *Morbidity and Mortality Weekly Report*, 46(SS4):37-89.
288. Nancy Adler, Emily J. Ozer and Jeanne Tschann, "Abortion among adolescents," *American Psychologist*, 58, no.3, (March 2003):211-217.

The American Psychological Association has filed several amicus (friends of the court) briefs arguing against restrictions on adolescents' access to abortion because the scientific evidence does not provide justification for the assumptions made by restrictive legislation. That legislation is best exhibited by the Adolescent Family Life Act passed by Congress in 1981 and supporting the kind of state legislation which restricts abortion among adolescents.[290]

Pregnancy, abortion and disease become real possibilities for those adolescents who engage in sexual behavior at an age when these consequences are far less manageable than they are for adults. Because almost all high school students engage in sexual intercourse while those of younger years are also involved, it is of great interest to discover the factors associated with that kind of risk-taking behavior.

One of these factors is that adolescents are reported to more often have multiple sexual partners than is true of adults. No doubt those who have numerous sexual partners and have been called "sexual adventurers" are at greater risk than those who are serial monogamists or those who abstain altogether. These adolescent "sexual adventurers" are heavily over represented among those who develop sexually transmitted diseases. It has been estimated that of the 12 million new cases of sexually transmitted disease infections discovered each year in the United States, 3 million occur among people younger than twenty and another 4 million occur among those aged 20-25.[291]

Research reveals that sexual adventurers had lower grades, were less religious and had less positive relationships with their parents. Such risk takers are also more likely to question authority and social expectations and are engaged in other risk-taking behavior such as using drugs and drinking alcohol.[292]

Suicide is another risk taken by sexually abused children and adolescents. This is particularly true of those who were physically abused, i.e. beaten as well as sexually abused.

289. Bruce Ambuel and Julian Rapaport, "Developmental trends in adolescents' psychological and legal competence to consent to abortion," *Law and Human Behavior*, 16, no. 2 (1992):129-154.

290. Adolescent Family Life Act, Public Law 97-35, State 578, 42USC 302 1981.

291. William.J. Kassler and W. Cates, Jr. "The epidemiology and prevention of sexually transmitted diseases," *Urologic Clinic of North America*, 19, no.1, (1992):9-12.

292. Tom Luster and Stephen A. Small, "Factors Associated with Sexual Risk-taking Behaviors Among Adolescents," *Journal of Marriage and the Family*, 56, no.3, (August 1994):622-632.

Research has shown that as the use of alcohol increases, the probability of having multiple sex partners increases as well. One study shows that only 8% of currently sexually active females reported no alcohol use during a three month period. These non-drinking 8% had two or more sex partners in a month. Those 48% who reported many more sexual partners in the past three months also used a considerable amount of alcohol. The use of alcohol and other drugs is therefore significant in initiating boys and girls into sex.[293]

Failure to use condoms is another indication of risk-taking behavior. This focuses on the risk of pregnancy associated with failure to use contraceptives. The evidence is that low grades, poor academic ability, lack of knowledge about sex and contraception and extreme youth all contribute to this form of risk-taking. Furthermore, those teens who risk pregnancy the most are more likely to come from a family with low parental education, lack of communication between mothers and daughters, overall strained relationship between teens and their parents and parental use of corporal punishment.[294]

Parental support, then, plays a major role in adolescent risk-taking. Open mother-daughter relationships have been found to predict the delay of coitus and the delay of pregnancy. These facts conform to the control theory proposed by Hirschi. Hirschi's principal argument is that the bond of the individual to society has four components. These components are: attachment to conventional persons; commitment to conventional behavior; involvement with conventional people and belief in conventional norms. If these components are weak, then delinquent behavior is much more likely than if these components are strong. Applied to early sexual conduct, the Hirschi theory holds that adolescents internalize the attitudes of parents concerning sexual behavior. This internalization can then become a protective device leading to a reduction in sexual risk taking behavior.[295]

It is further understood that children whose parents encourage autonomous thinking are more likely to develop social competence than those whose parents are highly controlling. In any case, it is most important that parents

---

293. John S. Santelli, Nancy D. Bremer, Richard Lowry, Amita Bhatt and Laurie S. Sabin, "Multiple Sexual Partners among US adolescents and young adults," *Family Planning Perspectives*, 30, no.6 (November 1998):271-275.

294. Ibid. p. 623.

295. Travis Hirschi, *Causes of Delinquency*, (Berkeley, CA. The University of California Press, 1969)pp.16-34.

communicate information about sex to teenaged children if risk taking behavior is to be reduced or avoided altogether.

It is easily understood that runaway and homeless youth are more at risk concerning unsafe sex and substance abuse than children living at home.

SEX ABUSE

"A youthful sex offender is usually a pre-adult male or female who instigates sexual or assaultive sexual interaction with either a non-consenting partner or a child too young to understand the sexual behavior consented to." This definition focuses on the victims of sexual offenses perpetrated by adolescents.[296]

Adolescent sexual offenders received little attention from professionals until recent decades. Studies since the 1970s have revealed that the families of adolescent sex offenders are significantly associated with the origin of that behavior. When compared to the families of delinquents whose offenses are not of a sexual nature, several differences between the two groups emerged.[297]

A study by the psychologists Bischof, Stith and Wilson has shown that one difference between the two groups is age. The mean age for adolescent sex offenders is 15 while the mean age for violent and non-violent delinquents is 16. Mean family income for adolescent sex offenders was $38,400; for violent juvenile delinquents it was $41,000; and for nonviolent juvenile delinquents it was $52,000. In other words, sex offending youths came from families whose income was about 26% less than that of families of nonviolent offenders. The study found no differences among the mothers' and fathers' occupations, nor were there any significant racial differences among the three groups.

Although emotional engagement between family members was about the same for sexual offending delinquents and other delinquents, Bischof et al. found that emotional disengagement was far more common among sexual delinquents as compared to non-problem families.[298]

---

296. D. Kim Openshaw et.al., "Youthful sexual offenders," *Family Relations*, 42, (April 1993):222-226.
297. Gary P. Bischof, Sandra M. Stith and Stephan M. Wilson, "A Comparison of the Family Systems of Adolescent Sexual Offenders and Non-sexual Offending Delinquents," 41, no.3 (July 1992):318-323.

There is, however, an aspect of family relations which is very much linked to youthful sexual deviance. That is sexual abuse. A number of studies have shown that pregnant teenagers are more likely to have experienced abuse than the general population. The incidence of sexual abuse reports for women in the general population ranges from 7% to 50%, while reports of sexual abuse for pregnant teenagers range from 51% to 75%.[299]

The psychologists Roosa, Tein, Reinholtz and Angelini studied the sexual histories of 2,003 young women and discovered that sexual precocity coupled with sexual abuse is related to much higher incidence of pregnancy than is expected in the general population. These researchers also found that pregnant teenagers engage in far more high risk behavior than those who had never been pregnant. Smoking, the use of alcohol, the exchange of sex for alcohol, drugs or money are all associated with early pregnancy, as is sex on a first date, sex with strangers and failure to use birth control. Girls who are pregnant at an early age are also likely to have several sex partners in any one year. According to Roosa et al., 36% of teenagers who were sexually abused as children experienced a teenage pregnancy. This is true of only 21% of those not abused.[300] Sexual abuse is therefore seen as a major contributor to teenage pregnancy.

Professors Luster and Small of Michigan Sate University explored the relationship between sexual abuse history and problem outcomes in adolescence. Their study "shows a clear relationship between sexual abuse history and alcohol abuse and suicidal ideation among adolescents." Their study focused on current abuse. Teens who experienced both physical and sexual abuse exhibited more problems than those who had to deal with only one kind of abuse. These female adolescents were frequently involved in binge drinking while abuse increased suicidal thoughts among male victims of such abuse. Of course, sexual abuse also contributes to poor performance in school. This is true even after the abuse has stopped, because the anxiety and intrusive thoughts pertaining to abuse continue long after these events.[301]

298. Gary P. Bischof, Sandra M. Stith and Stephan M. Wilson, "A Comparison of the Family Systems of Adolescent Sexual Offenders and Nonsexual Offending Delinquents'" *Family Relations*, 41, no.3 (July 1992):318-323.

299. J. Anderson et.al., "Prevalence of childhood sexual abuse experiences in a community sample of women," *Journal of the American Academy of Child and Adolescent Psychiatry*, 32, no.5 (September 1993):911-919.

300. Mark W.Roosa, Jenn-Yun Tein, Cindy Reinholtz and Patricia Jo Angelini, "The Relationship of Childhood Sexual Abuse to Teenage Pregnancy," *Journal of Marriage and the Family*, 59, no.1 (February 1997): 119-130.

We turn now to the issue of sexual contact between adults and children. Research has demonstrated that the long range effects of adult-child sex lead to such symptoms as low self-esteem, depression, anxiety and sexual dysfunction. Furthermore, adult-child sex promotes risky sexual behavior in adolescence and in adulthood. This includes sexual activity at an early age, failure to block the sexual advances of others, teenage pregnancy, multiple sexual partnerships and sexually transmitted diseases. In sum, adult mental health is impacted by adult-child sexual contact, leading to a variety of psychological consequences.

Women who experience adult-child sexual contacts are clearly more sexually active in adolescence and adulthood than those who had no such contacts. Such women are also more likely to experience forced sex. [302]

Adult-child sex has a dimension which may best be called "the breach of trust" view. This means that adults who initiate children into sex disregard the interests of the child for the sake of their own satisfaction. This is a more plausible reason for rejecting adult-child sex than the argument that children cannot consent, since children do not consent to vaccinations or other health related forced activities which are good for them. Consent is not the issue. The issue is abuse. Children trust that adults have good reasons for their actions. Adult-child sex is therefore similar to an assault or a beating. Adults know that children cannot benefit from sex, so that the consent argument becomes spurious.

Children are powerless to reject adult sexual advances not only because adults are physically larger, but also because children fear that they may lose the love of the adult and/or do not want to hurt the adult's feelings. Even adults are "playing with fire" if they engage in sex with someone they don't know well. An adult who becomes a sexual aggressor may be known to the child from a different, nonsexual role. Furthermore, since a child must work toward learning to lead a life of his or her own, not dependent on parents, it is particularly injurious for a parent to have sex with his own child because that prevents the child from forming a mature heterosexual relationship outside the family as an adult. [303]

---

301. Tom Luster and Stephen A. Small, "Sexual Abuse History and Problems in Adolescence: Exploring the Effects of Moderating Variables," *Journal of Marriage and the Family,* 59,(February 1997):131-142.

302. Christopher R. Browning and Edward O. Laumann, "Sexual Contact between Children and Adults," *American Sociological Review,* 62, (August 1997):540-560.

303. Laurence Thomas, "Sexual Desire, Moral Choice and Human Ends," *Journal of Social Philosophy,* 33, no.2 (2003):177-192.

Summary

The media promote attention to sex as a means of advertising all kinds of products. In addition, pornography is readily available to young people on the Internet. Censorship of sexual material has been advocated in the US for years, but without much success. Therefore children are exposed to a sexualization process which competes with formal sex education delivered by schools and any guidance offered by parents.

Because the world wide web makes strangers easily accessible for sexual encounters, many adolescents no longer "date" but "hook up" sexually on a one-time basis. These, and other social forces such as the use of alcohol and other drugs, contribute to early sexual activity and consequently pregnancy and disease among young girls and boys. Although some effort has been made to teach children sexual abstinence, this has met with very limited success. Added to all these problematic outcomes of adolescent sexual conduct is adult-child sex, defined as sexual abuse.

CHAPTER 7. RELIGION AND ADOLESCENCE

The National Study of Youth and Religion was directed by sociology professor Christian Smith of the University of North Carolina and his student Phillip Kim between August 2001 and August 2003, "to research the shape and influence of religion and spirituality in the lives of US adolescents."[304] This study has reached several oft-corroborated conclusions concerning the influence of religion on American youths. Among these are that 11% of American youths in 2003 had families involved in daily religious activities such as church attendance or the reading of scriptures. These youngsters exhibit a number of characteristics which are seldom visible among the 36% whose families do not engage in religious activities throughout the week.

The characteristics reported by Smith et al are: that daily religious activities result in stronger relationships with the mother; that religious adolescents participate in family activities such as eating dinner together more often than non-religious youths; that few if any such youths run away from home. Furthermore, the Smith et al. study showed that children from religious homes have mothers who are strict with them but also praise them; have mothers who know their friends and know with whom they associate when they are not home; have fathers whom they respect highly and who are their role models; have fathers who are supportive of children and do not suddenly cancel plans with them;

---

304. Christian Smith and Phillip Kim, "Family Religious Involvement and the Quality of Family Relationships for Early adolescents," *Research Report of the National Study of Youth and Religion #4*, (Chapel Hill, N.C. 2003)p. 1.

have fathers who know at least something about their friends, their friends' parents and their lives in school.

Three dimensions of family and parental involvement in religion are significantly associated with positive relationship characteristics. These are family religious activities, religious service attendance and parental prayer.[305]

The Detroit Area Study of 1958 includes data collected during the first quarter of 1958. Published by Gerhard Lenski in 1963, The Religious Factor: A Sociological Study of Religion's Impact on Politics, Economics and Family Life is an exhaustive study that questioned 656 residents of the Detroit area concerning attitudes towards unions, class and ethnic distinctions, family and child rearing patterns, spending and saving, civil liberties, minority rights, moral issues, doctrinal issues, orthodoxy and the role of religious leaders in politics as well as daily life. No doubt some of the questions and answers would be altered if the study were conducted in the present decade. Yet, almost all of the questions asked then are relevant now and point to the conclusion that religion is more than ceremony. Religion determines outlook on life or what the Germans call Weltanschauung.

Studies on such questions usually look at six theoretical types of social structure in child rearing. These are:

1. autocratic (in which youth are not allowed to express any views or assert any leadership);

2. authoritarian (which allows children to express views, although all decisions are made by parents);

3. democratic (which allows children to make some decisions concerning their behavior, although final decisions must meet parental expectations);

4. equalitarian (which gives children as much right to decide their behavior as parents);

5. permissive (which allows the adolescent more freedom than his parents in deciding his behavior); and

6. laissez-faire (which allows the youth to subscribe to parental wishes or ignore them — which is a total absence of parental involvement in the adolescent's conduct.

Humans generally assume an ethnic-religious identity. We define that identity with Phinney as "that part of an individual's self concept that derives

---

305. Ibid. p. 6.

from his or her knowledge of membership in a social group...together with the value and emotional significance attached to that membership." Religious identity contributes to the identity development of all adolescents whose family is involved in any religious practices. Research shows that ethnic and religious identity are correlated with self-esteem, optimism or depression.

Adolescents reflect in their personality, "looking glass self" and view of the world those experiences which their religious background has determined for them. This means that religion is a socializing agent and that Jewish, Muslim, Catholic, Protestant or other religious groups leave their mark on their adherents in different ways.

DELINQUENCY

The Sumerian civilization flourished about 3,700 years ago, in an area now covered by Iraq. Archeologists know something about that civilization from the writing on clay tablets which have been found and translated into English. Such records reveal that even then parents worried about the bad conduct of adolescents, as exemplified by a young man who is told by his father to stop loitering in the streets and do his homework. The father even says that "I am tortured because of you" and recites the son's failings such as truancy, failure to do his homework and wasting money on pleasure. The father also complains that the son is not religious and ignores their god, Nana.[306]

The relationship between religion and delinquency was the focus of an extensive study by the sociologist Mark K. Regnerus, whose work sought to relate inter-generational religious influence to adolescent delinquency. He concluded in 2003 that parents who profess a conservative Protestant affiliation "are ... apt to directly prevent and reduce delinquency among their adolescent children."

The issue of religion and delinquency has been studied many times by sociologists, but research on this issue has led to conflicting results. In fact, Rodney Stark, one of the foremost students of religion, concluded in 1969 in a study called "Hellfire and Delinquency" that it made no difference how often children attended church, how often their parents did the same, or how profoundly they

---

306. Samuel Noah Kramer, *History Begins at Sumer*, (New York: Doubleday Anchor Books) pp.13-15

believed that hellfire awaited sinners. Religious youngsters, concluded Stark in 1969, were no less likely to be delinquent than their irreligious peers.[307]

Yet, the same Rodney Stark said in 1984 that "religion has truly potent effects on delinquency."[308]

Not only are there those who cannot find a relationship between the alleviation of delinquency and religion, there are even students of the sociology of religion who suggest that religion can cause crime and delinquency. Edwin M. Schur told his readers in 1969 that organized religion may "be held partly responsible for the magnitude of the American crime problem." Schur based his claim on the idea that American criminal law reflects private moral standards, and when those standards are translated into criminal law they make the crime statistics in the US look worse in comparison to crime statistics in countries that do not confuse vice with crime.[309] Intellectual games aside, the American focus on the individual does overpower the sense of responsibility to others in society.

A 1986 study by the sociologists Sloan and Potvin concluded that "religion had a strong effect on whether adolescents commit each of the offenses considered." Sloan and Potvin also found that religion had a strong relationship to status offenses and drug violations but had little impact on fighting and other interpersonal violence. They also concluded that only declining truancy is strongly associated with church attendance.[310]

In view of these confusing results concerning the relationship between religion and delinquency, it appears that the type of instrument used to measure that relationship makes a great deal of difference in the outcome. Furthermore, there is little agreement concerning the nature of delinquency. This is best illustrated by twelve questions used by Sloane and Potvin in their effort to define delinquency. These questions are: Did you: skip a day of school, without a real excuse? run away from home? engage in sexual intercourse? drink beer, wine and/or liquor without parents' permission? use marijuana? use a drug or chemical to get high? go onto someone's property knowing you were not to be

---

307. Travis Hirschi and Rodney Stark, "Hellfire and Delinquency," *Social Problems*, 17, (Fall1969):202-213.

308. Rodney Stark, "Religion and Conformity," Reaffirming a Sociology of Religion," *Sociological Analysis*, 45, (1984):273-284.

309. Edwin M. Schur, *Our Criminal Society*, (Englewood Cliffs, N.J. Prentice-Hall, 1969)pp.85-86.

310. Douglas M. Sloane and Raymond H. Potvin, "Religion and Delinquency: Cutting through the Maze," *Social Forces*, 65, no.1 (September 1986):87-105.

there? damage school property on purpose? take something not belonging to you worth under $50? Take something not belonging to you worth over $50? get into a serious fight in school or at work? take part in a gang fight?[311]

Not everyone will agree that skipping school one day is a delinquency or that a fistfight is an offense. It is axiomatic that differences in outcomes of studies concerning delinquency begin with differences in interpretation ipso facto.

The idea that religious beliefs can inhibit delinquency or, stated otherwise, that lack of religious commitment is more likely to lead to delinquent behavior, has been long debated. A number of sociologists have argued that there is little support for the view that religion inhibits delinquent behavior. Others have gone so far as to contend that religion actually promotes delinquency and crime. Among these were two of the "fathers" of criminology, Cesare Lombroso and Willem Bonger.[312]

If we are to understand the relationship between delinquency and religion we need to first look at the influence of a family's religion on the adolescent, who is of course at greater risk of being labeled a juvenile delinquent than anyone else.

THE ADOLESCENT, HIS FAMILY AND RELIGION

Religion is a socializing agent. That is by no means the only function of religion nor is religion the only socializing agent. In fact, the family is the most pervasive and powerful socializing institution, so that intergenerational trans-mission of religious beliefs and practices influence adolescents immensely.

Much of what a child learns is based on day-to-day observation of signif-icant others who serve as role models. These role models are usually parents or parental substitutes such as stepmothers and stepfathers. Because religion is learned in the home from parents, religious continuity can be expected between parents and children. Religious continuity is of course much more likely between parents and children who are emotionally close to each other than those who are not.[313]

---

311. Ibid.p. 104.

312. T.D. Evans, F.T. Cullen, V.S. Burton, R.G. Dunaway, G.L.Payne, and S.R. Kethineni, "Religion, social bonds and delinquency," *Deviant Behavior: An Interdisciplinary Journal*, 17, (January-March 1996):43-70.

313. Joan E. Grusec and Leon Kuczynski, *Parenting and Children's Internalization of Values*, (New York, Wiley, 1997).

Bao et al. conducted a study in 1999 concerning the family and religion among a rather homogeneous Protestant population in rural Iowa, where church attendance and general religiosity is somewhat greater than would be expected in an American city. The researchers found that both male and female children acquire their religious beliefs and practices from their fathers and mothers by imitating them. The study also found that mothers appeared to be more influential than fathers on both boys' and girls' religious beliefs. This is consistent with a number of other studies.[314]

Numerous studies of religion and the family indicate that the religious institutions in America provide support for both the formal and the informal social networks associated with family life. Religion also acts as a socializing agent which propels the young into the direction devised by the earlier generation. Religion also has a major impact on the interpersonal relationships needed to insure a family's well being. Most important among these relationships is the connection between mothers and their children, which has a direct impact on the lives of adolescents.[315]

Over the years, sociologists have documented a link between religious participation and a strong bond between husbands and wives and parents and children. As early as 1897, one of the fathers of sociology, Emile Durkheim, wrote that religion encourages shared values, interaction and strong social bonds, protecting individuals from anomie. By anomie Durkheim meant a condition in which society provides little moral guidance to individuals. That is, of course, precisely the problem for adolescents in American society at the beginning of the 21st century. This is a value neutral statement and does not imply that formal religion is the only source of moral guidance. In fact, John Dewey, the author of the Humanist Manifesto, provided moral guidance in his many writings and his enormous impact on American education.[316]

---

314. Wan-Ning Bao, Les B. Whitbeck, Danny R. Hoyt and Rand D. Conger, "Perceived Parental Acceptance as a Moderator of Religious Transmission among Adolescent Boys and Girls," *Journal of Marriage and the Family*, 61, no.2 (May 1999):362-374.

315. Dennis P. Hogan, David J. Eggebeen and Clifford C. Clogg, "The Structure of Intergenerational Changes in American Families," *American Journal of Sociology*, 98, (1993):1428-1458.

316. Emile Durkheim, *Suicide*, New York, *The Free Press*, (1966) originally 1897.

More recent sociological studies also provide evidence that religion is associated with family cohesion. Examples are the work of Bahr and Chadwick, Greeley and Stinnett and DeFrain and many others.[317]

These studies all show that religious institutions disseminate the idea that positive relationships among family members are desirable.

Religious organizations also provide formal support for families, leading to interaction and positive relationships between family members. One example is mutual attendance at religious events. In addition, most religious organizations provide counseling and study of holy scriptures, as well as travel to religious sites, all of which involve the bonding of family members.

In addition, religious organizations provide their members with social ties which link friends and family members in the same social group, so that married couples meet other married couples with similar interests and parents with children can meet other parents of similar religious backgrounds. Therefore, strong child-parent relationships are encouraged and become nearly inevitable, as involvement in religious institutions creates an emotional theme underlying the importance of family. Children who attend religious gatherings with their parents are exposed to the message of the importance of the parent-child relationship, which is also affirmed by their peers.[318]

Finally, we recognize that mothers who regularly attend religious services report more positive affective relationships with their children.

If lack of religious involvement is indeed positively associated with an increase in delinquency, early sexual behavior, alcohol abuse and drug use, then it may be possible that a precipitous decline in weekly church attendance could be related to deviant conduct among adolescents. That decline in church attendance is at least in part associated with a rise in Sunday sports activities among American youths. Clergy of all faiths have noticed this trend. For example, the Rev. Charles Rush, pastor in a wealthy New York suburban church, noticed a decline in weekly attendance because many of his parishioners were involved in

---

317. Howard M. Bahr and Bruce A. Chadwick, "Religion and Family in Middletown, USA." in D.L. Thomas, Editor, *The Religion and Family Connection: Social Science Perspectives,* (Provo, Utah, Brigham Young University Press, 1988)pp.51-65. See also: Nick Stinnett and John DeFrain, *Secrets of Strong Families,* (Boston, Little Brown & Co. 1985 and Andrew Greeley, *Faithful Attractions: Discovering Intimacy, Love and Fidelity in American Marriage,* (New York, Tom Doherty, 1991).

318. Alice S. Rossi and Peter H. Rossi, *Of Human Bonding,* (New York, Walter de Gruyter, 1990).

soccer and other sports on Sunday morning. He therefore asked coaches to delay sports until Sunday afternoon. Likewise, the sports director for the Catholic Archdiocese of Boston, Peter Williams, has asked coaches to schedule all sports activities after noon on Sundays. Similar problems face the Jewish community, and others whose holy day is not Sunday.

RELIGION AND THE SCHOOL

In addition to the influence of the family, education positively impacts the lives of adolescents. Teachers and schools, like parents, cannot avoid teaching values. Religious groups have a considerable stake in transmitting their messages to the young, particularly because the values of religious groups usually conflict with the goals of secular society, as diffused in public schools and in the media.

School is of course the venue where adolescents learn to define themselves and where they are taught how to fit into the majority culture. Some conservatives, whether Protestants, Catholics, Jews or Muslims, oppose secular education altogether. In order to support their children in learning and adhering to their religion and its strictures, they stay together in small, tight-knit communities, thus limiting the children's secular exposure. In addition, some Protestant fundamentalists fear that secular education promotes humanism and that as a result their children will burn in hell.[319]

In addition, legal issues surrounding religion and education are fought out in the American school. The First Amendment to the Constitution of the United States makes a final resolution impossible. Consequently, every generation of schoolchildren is confronted with the confusion which two paragraphs in the Constitution have provoked for many years.

"Congress shall make no law respecting an establishment of religion, or prohibiting the free exercise thereof...." This part of the First Amendment to the Constitution has caused endless debate and disputes as to its meaning. Those who dislike religion or fear its intrusion into the public schools emphasize the first, so called "establishment," clause of this sentence. Others interpret the second clause as conferring the right to pray or otherwise exhibit religious

319. Christopher G. Ellison and Darren E. Sherkat, "Obedience and Autonomy: Religion and Parental Values Reconsidered," *Journal for the Scientific Study of Religion*, 32 (1993):313-329.

conduct on school property. Apparently endless disputes have arisen concerning the First Amendment and its meaning. Almost all of these disputes have been concerned with religion in schools because children have no choice but to be in school as required by law.

Prior to the end of the Second World War, in 1945, it was taken for granted in this country that anything public was also Protestant. The Protestant point of view had dominated American traditions since the founding of the Republic. This may be seen by considering that in 1890, when the US had 63 million inhabitants, church membership was only 33% of the population. Of these, 14 million were Protestants and 6 million Catholics. It was then assumed that almost all of the 40 million unaffiliated Americans held Protestant sentiments and would attend a Protestant church if they were to attend at all. By 1906, this distribution had changed. Then, the US had a population of over 84 million and church membership had risen to 39% of the population. Then, 20 million were affiliated Protestant and 38% or 12 million were Catholics. With the great migration of eastern and southern Europeans to the United States between 1880 and 1923, the Catholic (and to some extent, the Jewish) segment of the population increased considerably. Nevertheless, in 1947 Protestants still outnumbered Catholics by a margin of 3.5 to 1. Forty years later, in 1987, this margin had declined to 2:1 and has remained there since. Among the age group 25-29, Protestants are now only a plurality, leading to the possibility that Catholics may be the dominant religious group in America by the middle of the 21st century.[320]

Since 1947, there has been an increase in religious diversity in this country. At that time only 6% of Americans viewed themselves as belonging to a religion other than Protestantism, Catholicism or Judaism. In 1987, that figure had risen 13% including Muslims, Hindus, Buddhists and others. This diversity has increased yet more during the past few decades, so that the potential for religious disputes in our schools involving children and adolescents has increased proportionately.

Since the Supreme Court decided the Everson case, more cases concerning religion in the schools have been heard than in all the years since the establishment of the court. The Everson case dealt with the practice of Ewing Township in New Jersey of reimbursing parents for money spent on bus trans-

---

320. Kevin J. Christiano, *Religious Diversity and Social Change*, (New York, Cambridge University Press, 1987) p.20.

portation to attend both public and parochial schools. By a majority of 5 to 4, the justices upheld this practice but nevertheless specified in their decision that aid to all religions is prohibited by the First Amendment and that no tax money may be used to support any religious activity whatever. Justice Hugo Black, speaking for the majority, declared that: "in the words of Jefferson, the clause against establishment of religion by law was intended to erect 'a wall of separation' between church and state."[321]

One year after Everson, the supreme court of the United States decided in McCullom v. Board of Education that release time programs operating in the public schools of Champaign, Illinois were unconstitutional. The program permitted parents who wished to do so to send their children to religious instruction held inside the school by clergy of diverse faiths. Although children who did not attend such classes were not excused from school, no one was forced to participate in religion classes of any kind. Nevertheless, the court held that the state compulsory education law operated to enforce religious instruction. Justice Hugo Black, speaking for the court, wrote: "Here not only are the state's tax supported public school buildings used for the dissemination of religious doctrine, the State also affords sectarian groups an invaluable aid in that it helps provide pupils for the religious classes through use of the State's compulsory public school machinery."[322]

Arkansas made it a criminal offense to teach Darwin's theory of evolution or use a book in any classroom which did so. This law was passed in 1968 in an effort to teach fundamentalist Christianity to Arkansas schoolchildren. In Epperson v. Arkansas, the court struck down this prohibition because it violated the establishment clause and "resulted from fundamentalist sectarian conviction."[323]

Seeking to circumvent these decisions, Arkansas and Louisiana declared the story of creation as told in the first chapter of the five books of Moses, i.e. Genesis, "creation science." This "science" became mandatory in the science classes of these states. By law, "creation science" had to be given equal time with evolution in science classes in these states. A lower court held this law unconstitutional as did a court of appeals. A similar ruling greeted the exhibition of the Ten Commandments in the classrooms of Kentucky.[324]

---

321. *Everson v. Board of Education*, 330 US1, 15, (1947)
322. McCullom v. Board of Education,333 US 203, (1948).
323. *Epperson v. Arkansas*, 393 US 97 (1968).
324. *Edwards v. Aguilard*, 482 US 578 (1987).

More recent is the Supreme Court decision of June, 1994 which dissolved the Kiryas Joel School District in New York State. Kiryas Joel is a village inhabited exclusively by a Jewish sect known as the Satmar Hasidim. The Court ruled that a school district which follows village lines and excludes all but Satmar Hasidim is unconstitutional because it violates the Establishment clause of the First Amendment.

In 2004, the Supreme Court sidestepped the issue of whether or not the phrase "under God" may be recited as part of the Pledge of Allegiance demanded of every American school child every day.[325]

All the decisions by the Supreme Court concerning these disputes maintained the separation of church and state (with the possible exception of the school bus decision) and seek to follow the tradition of keeping government out of religious practices and separating religion from government.

SECULARISM

The religious controversies which have affected American schools over the past 50 years may be traced to the religious diversity in the United States. There is, of course, a large proportion of Americans who do not participate in any organized religion.

Only about 160 million of 293 million Americans are in any fashion associated with a religious group; more than 130 million apparently have no interest in a religious establishment. Furthermore, it is reasonable to assume that many people of Christians or Jewish heritage have little if any connection to religion. Secularism is quite common and it influences the outlook and conduct of adolescents who come from such homes.

Sociologists Jonathan Kelley and Nan deGraf have conducted an international study of parental socialization and religious belief. This extensive study reveals that "the religious environment of a nation has a major impact on the beliefs of its citizens." Kelley and deGraf show that the pool of possible friends, teachers, work colleagues and marriage partners will be mostly devout or mostly secular and that this influences adolescents and young adults more than any other religious impact available to them. This means that in the relatively secular United States, secular beliefs are reinforced. That being said, in comparison to

---

325. *Board of Education of Kiryas Joel Village School District v. Grumet*, 93-517.

Western Europeans, Americans attend religious services with extraordinary frequency and show a surprising willingness to assume the existence of God.

To some extent, this "exceptional" status may be exaggerated by the way various polling organizations have conducted their surveys. Contacted by telephone and asked how often they attend a religious service, Americans have reported attendance of 40% — a figure that is longstanding and oft repeated. This polling method, however, is misleading, because self reports reflect over-representation based on the perception that it is socially desirable (in the US) to adhere to religion. Sociologists Hadaway, Marler and Chaves used far more sophisticated and objective methods of studying church attendance and discovered that only 20% of Americans participate in religious activities once a week. This resembles the Western European attendance numbers a good deal more than is claimed by self report studies.[326]

THE CIVIL RELIGION

There is a unique American solution to the great popularity of religion and the decline in church attendance. That is American "civil religion," which is taught to all schoolchildren.

The civil religion in the United States consists of myths, rituals, national holidays, celebration of the lives of national "saints," and the sacred treatment of sacred national symbols. This resembles every religion everywhere, except that the national civic religion is entirely non-denominational and available to all who live in the United States. The national civil religion teaches the kind of Americanism that is included in Martin Luther King's famous "I have a dream" speech, which includes the words: "when all of God's children, black men and white men, Jews and Gentiles, Protestants and Catholics, will be able to join hands...."[327]

Examples of the national civil religion may be found in American history and in the present. Thomas Jefferson compared the founding of the United States with the founding of ancient Israel, while comparing Europe with the

---

326. C. Hadaway, Penny Marler Kirk and Mark Chaves, "Over-reporting church attendance in America: evidence that demands the same verdict" *American Sociological Review*, 63, (1998) :122-130.
327. C. Eric Lincoln, *Is Anybody Listening to Black America?*)(New York, Seabury Publishing, 1968)p.65-66.

Egypt of the Exodus. Likewise, Katharine Lee Bates' great anthem, "America, America, God shed his grace on thee and crown thy good with brotherhood from sea to shining sea" is incomparable with the usual patriotic songs exulting military feats and aggression. This kind of mythology promotes unity in a diverse population, as do such civil holidays (or holy days) as Memorial Day, Independence Day and Presidential Inauguration Day. These holidays inspire a feeling of common purpose.[328]

The civil religion, like all religions, also includes national shrines such as the Washington Monument, the Lincoln Memorial, the Tomb of the Unknown Soldier and the Vietnam Wall. The most sacred object in the civil religion is, of course, the American flag. There is a prescribed handling of the flag and outrage at "desecrating" it — all of which seems rather silly and over-done to the rest of the developed world.

The civil religion also includes "sacred scriptures" such as the Declaration of Independence, the US Constitution, Washington's Farewell Address and Lincoln's Gettysburg Address. The saints of the civil religion are those who wrote or spoke the sacred words, as are all of the "Founding Fathers."

Even the money is engraved with the words, "In God We Trust," and the Pledge of Allegiance as recited each day by all American schoolchildren includes the words "under God"[329]

All of this inevitably causes American young people to adhere to that civil religion taught to them from early youth and reinforced every school day. It is the civil religion which makes it possible for orthodox Jews, Roman Catholics, agnostics and all the Protestant denominations to live together in stability.

SUMMARY

The National Study of Youth and Religion is a comprehensive survey of the influence of religion on the nation's youths. It reveals a good deal about the connection between religion, family and adolescence, including the role of delinquency in the lives of the young. The Jewish adolescent is portrayed showing some special issues which are unique to the American Jewish community. Likewise, Catholic, Fundamentalist Protestant, Mormon and Muslim adoles-

328. Keith A. Roberts, *Religion in Sociological Perspective*, (Belmont, Cal. Wadsworth/ Thompson Learning,2004)p. 356.
329. Ibid. p.357.

cents exhibit problems related to their cultures. Finally, all school age children are affected by the endless legal disputes concerning the practice of religion in American education.

The "civil religion" is a unifying force which serves to overcome the differences and disputes concerning religion in America. For many Americans, and particularly for adolescents, there is yet another source of unity and segregation from adult supervision and adult interference. That is youth recreation and amusement, which is the focus of our next chapter.

CHAPTER 8. RECREATION AND AMUSEMENTS

POST INDUSTRIAL SOCIETY AND ADOLESCENT "AT RISK" BEHAVIOR

After 1980, industrial society came to an end in America. This is visible in many ways but can best be seen by the collapse of the steel industry in the 1980s and its gradual recovery at the beginning of the 21st century. During the 1980s, the US steel industry appeared to be in an irreversible decline, as some 250,000 steel workers lost their jobs and production of unfinished steel in the United States declined by 12% while plant closures and downsizing reduced steel production by 25%. The reason for this collapse was that the US steel industry was no longer technologically progressive, a condition which at that time was also true of a good number of other manufacturing industries in the US.[330]

Since then, America has entered the post-industrial age. Electronic devices controlled by cybernation (*cyber* is Greek for *pilot*) and automation now dominate production in America. For young people this has made as big a difference as the invention of adolescence, at the beginning of the 20th century, which came about because industry allowed millions of teenagers to remain outside the labor force.

These teenagers went, instead, to school. This led to the separation of schooling and learning from practice, and also segregated the young from the middle aged and old. Now, at the beginning of another century, an almost

---

330. Richard J. Fruehahn, Dany A. Cheij and David M. Vilosky, "Steel" In: US *Industry in 2000: Studies in Competitive Performance*, New York: The National Academies Press, (1999)p. 75.

endless adolescence falling approximately between the ages of 14 to 22 (and up) has replaced the earlier concept of adolescence, which usually ended at age 18. This new, prolonged adolescence is made possible by technology. The "new adolescents" postpone adulthood and prolong dependence on parents and/or government. Many enjoy an ever-increasing amount of leisure time. This in turn leads to greater opportunity for self-expression and "self fulfillment," leading to a considerable amount of self-indulgence, the belief in omnipotence, great mobility from place to place and from job to job, and an intolerance (in fact, an abhorrence) for stasis or stability, and the banding together in youthful or not so young counter-cultures, all linked to freedom from obligations.[331]

Most 18- to 30-year-olds are not engaged in higher education. For many of them, full time work and a good deal of leisure time are all associated with an increase in drug use. Those who do attend college often have part-time work. The length of part-time work is also linked positively to drug use, so that more drugs such as tobacco, alcohol and illicit drugs are used by those working 20 hours or more than those who work less.[332]

This means that work intensity is associated with drug use. One clear reason for this relationship is that as adolescents earn more money, they can participate in behavior which some sociologists have called "pseudo-adulthood." This means that they can spend their money on drugs, luxury and consumer items. Unlike adults, adolescents do not have to pay for family living expenses. Instead they can gain status among other adolescents by exhibiting appropriate hairstyles, dress and music.

This is the essence of the youth culture, which values hedonism, irresponsibility and excitement and disparages delayed gratification and responsibility. This kind of conduct is by no means universal nor is it the province of the majority of adolescents, who, as we have seen, share adult values as held by their parents. Furthermore, the majority of adolescents who do indeed participate in the youth culture do so only on a limited basis.[333]

---

331. Kenneth Kenniston, "Heads and Seekers: Drugs on Campus, Counter Cultures and American Society," *American Scholar*, 38, (1968):97-112.
332. Laurence Steinberg, Suzanne Fegley and Sanford M. Dornbush, "Negative Impact of Part-time Work on Adolescent Adjustment: Evidence from a Longitudinal Study." *Developmental Psychology*, 29 (1993):171-180.
333. Margaret Stone and Bradford M. Brown, "In the Eye of the Beholder: Adolescents' Perception of Peer Group Stereotypes," In: R.Muuss editor: *Adolescent Behavior and Society: A Book of Readings*, (San Francisco, Jossey-Bass, 1998)pp. 158-169.

The current discussion is concerned with those who are involved in the youth culture full time. Many of these adolescents are using alcohol regularly and therefore are at greater risk of getting involved in other drugs than those who use alcohol sparingly or not at all. It has also been found that early drug use and long working hours frequently lead to early and unsuccessful entry into pseudo-adult roles involving sexual activity, marriage and parenthood. Entering such adult roles too early usually has negative implications for adult success. Working long hours is, of course, a form of adult conduct. It also yields money. Therefore, those adolescents who work a great deal like to spend their free time in activities which are not supervised by adults, but are adolescent-centered. Such activities may include riding around in cars for fun, going to parties and "hanging out" with friends. Their desire for independence is the main motive of such young people, who want to escape adult domination at all cost.[334]

Numerous adolescents work in low level service jobs which involve "shift" work. Therefore, these workers cannot subscribe to activities which meet at regular hours every day or every week. "Shift" work changes all the time and workers never know when they will have to be "on the job." Therefore, these adolescents cannot commit to sports teams and drama clubs but are dependent on structured activities and on friends who are available at the last minute. These unstructured groups present greater opportunities to use illicit drugs and/or alcohol. Lack of adult supervision also allows adolescents to gain an audience which appreciates deviant behavior and who do this themselves. Since nothing so soothes the conscience as the approval of others, it is easy to understand that those who spend more time among unsupervised friends will more easily become engaged in sex, drugs and other anomic conduct.[335]

YOUTH BEHAVIOR AND "AT RISK" AMUSEMENTS

The National Center for Chronic Disease Prevention and Health Promotion issues an annual report called Youth Risk Behavior Surveillance. This

---

334. Bradford B. Brown, Margaret M. Dolcini and Amy Leventhal, "Transformation in Peer Relationships at Adolescence: Implications for Health Related Behavior" J. Schulenberg, J.L.Maggs and K. Hurrelmann, Editors, *Health Risks and Developmental Transitions During Adolescence*, (Cambridge, UK, Cambridge University Press, 1997)pp. 161-189.

335. Judith S. Brook, Martin Whiteman, Lisa J. Czeisler and Joseph Shapiro, "Cigarette Smoking in Young Adults: Child and Adolescent Personality, Familial and Peer Antecedents," *Journal of Genetic Psychology*, 158, (1997): 172-188.

report showed that, in 2003, 70.8% of all deaths among persons aged 10-24 years resulted from only four causes. These were motor vehicle crashes, other unintentional injuries, homicide, and suicide. During the period of that study, 30.2% of high school students who died from one of these four causes had ridden with a driver who had consumed alcohol; 17.1% had carried a weapon; 44.9% had drunk alcohol and 22.4% had used marijuana. In addition, 33.0% of high school students had been in a physical fight and 8.5% had attempted suicide. Furthermore, in 2003, 46.7% of high school students had sexual intercourse, and 37% of those did not use a condom.[336]

Tobacco use is undoubtedly one of the amusements of adolescents. However, only 27.5% of all students nationwide reported current cigarette use or current cigar use to the Center for Disease Control in 2003. The Center also asked about alcohol use and discovered that nationwide 44.9% of students in all grades have used alcohol and that 28.3% of all students had five drinks of alcohol in a row within two hours on one of thirty days preceding the Center's survey. Somewhat more than one fifth of all students surveyed said that they had used marijuana one or more times during the 30 days preceding the Center's survey and over 40% had used marijuana in their lifetime.

The use of hard drugs is also not unknown to students in American schools. The survey of the National Center for Chronic Disease Prevention found that 8.7% of students had used a form of cocaine and that 3.2% of students had used a needle to inject an illegal drug into their body.[337]

One of the consequences of the use of drugs, and in particular the use of alcohol, is violence. Numerous studies of homicide have shown that about half of all homicide offenders have used alcohol at the time of the murder. Sociological research reveals that the social environment is a much more powerful contributor to youth violence than the pharmacological factors associated with alcohol use. [338]

The widespread use of alcohol and other drugs by adolescents has led to a sharp increase in spending on behavioral drugs for children and adolescents. Seventeen percent of expenditures for children's and adolescents' drugs were

---

336. Jo Anne Grunbaum et.al. "Youth Risk Behavior Surveillance-United States, 2003.(Rockville, MD, National Center for Chronic Disease Prevention and Health Promotion, CDC, 53(2003) p.1.

337. Ibid. p.5.

338. Robert Nash Parker and Kathleen Auerhahn, "Alcohol, Drugs and Violence," *Annual Review of Sociology*, 24, (1998) pp. 291-311.

spent on behavioral drugs in 2003 while antibiotics accounted for only 16% of spending on drugs for those under age 19.[339]

Sports are a form of recreation and amusement but, as discussed in other contexts in this book, they are far more than that. In this country, sports also function as a means of enhancing the power of adolescents who are normally under the constant supervision of parents, teachers and other adults. Adolescents are usually controlled by adults and suffer from a lack of power over their own lives. Sports, however, block out all the physical, mental, emotional and social difficulties bothering adolescents all the time. Sports are an escape from the realities of homework, sexual problems, peer pressure, parental control and failure to understand one's identity. Sports contribute a great deal to the construction of a sense of self for those who participate. Furthermore, sports, unlike academic performance, bring immediate gratification for those who are successful at such popular games as football and basketball. Recognition and status are important elements of American culture for all Americans but have tremendous meaning for high school students who cannot spend money like adults and do not have the power that adolescents perceive them to have.[340]

The sports field is the territory of the adolescent himself. There he rules and parents, teachers and others sit on the sidelines. It is on the sports field that boys and girls can earn the adulation of others, particularly that of the opposite sex.

Sports achievements are particularly important to male students. That importance attaches more to football and basketball than any other sport, although all sports achievements are given a good deal more credence in American schools than academic success. Sports are seen as signs of masculinity among adolescents and American adults although that term may be confined only to those who are winners. Losers can be badly maligned and may well see

---

339. Gregory K. Fritz, "Keep your eye on spending rising for children's behavioral meds," *Child and Adolescent Behavioral Letter*, (Providence, RI, 2004):2.

340. Lawrence B. Angus, "Women in a male domain: gender and organizational culture in a Christian Brothers college: In: Lawrence b. Angus, *Inequality and Social Identity*, (Washington D.C. Palmer Press, 1993).

themselves as failures if their parents and "significant others" define the situation in that way.

Youth sports has become the fastest growing entertainment in America. More than 20 million children compete in this industry in which millions of dollars are spent on equipment, uniforms, and recreation fields. The benefits of this entertainment may be visible but many of its drawbacks are not well known. Included in the vicissitudes of children's sports are the 5 million injuries suffered by schoolchildren who need emergency medical care. These range from broken arms to concussions and spinal injuries and even death. In addition, parents can become a real problem for their child athletes, although parental support is of course desirable as long as it remains within the bounds of civility. That is sometimes disregarded, as adults get far too involved and anxious to have their child win. [341]

There are numerous examples of parental and coaching abuses imposed on children only because the adults want their child or their team to win at any cost. These abuses involve violent parental behavior, which is so common at children's sports events that 89.4% of 3,300 parents surveyed by *SportingKid* magazine said they had seen such abuse towards children, coaches and officials. Similar surveys in South Florida and Minnesota discovered that name calling, insults and even physical violence are not uncommon. For example, in Port Orange, Florida, a "Pop Warner" football game for small boys ended in a brawl involving more than 100 parents, coaches and players. Police filed charges against a 31-year-old mother for resisting arrest and a 15-year-old for battery on a law enforcement officer. In Villanova, Pennsylvania, about 100 parents from two youth football teams fought in a "free-for-all" at the end of a championship football game and in Jacksonville, Florida, a coach threw a ten-year-old player to the ground. The child broke both of his arms and the coach was arrested for aggravated assault. In Coppell, Texas, a 56-year-old father was arrested for felony injury to a child after he knocked his son's teammate to the ground. In view of all this violence, the drop out rate for children from organized sports is said to be 70%. [342]

Many parents are of the opinion that they can create a child star by starting their child early. By early, they may mean age nine or less. Many children

341. Kimberly Davis, "Sports and Your Child: What Every Parent Should Know." *Ebony*, (June 2000):88.
342. Dana P. O'Neill, "Open Season on Discord," *The Philadelphia Daily News*, (August 12, 2001):1.

are so disgusted by sports that they drop out before they reach high school age.[343]

That leaves those who succeed at sports. Sports are so important in American high schools that anyone who reads the popular press, watches television, reads magazines or listens to the radio must come to the conclusion that the only purpose of education in America is to conduct sports events. All newspapers have sports pages which recite the achievements of football and basketball players and occasionally mention other sports as well. There is, however, no regular news feature dealing with the academic achievements of our adolescents.[344]

One outcome of this tremendous emphasis on sports is bullying. That term is best defined as the legitimization of aggression against anyone seen as a defenseless target. Bullies are often those who have the ability to play popular sports in high school and who have become convinced by the adulation they collect that they can do no wrong. Two examples of extreme bullying were presented above: the Glen Ridge, NJ scandal in 1989 and the Columbine, CO killings in 1999. The Glen Ridge crime was publicized only after a black football player who was excluded from the violent "in" crowd exposed this atrocity. The "in" crowd at that high school, as at so many American schools, allowed no one to "act differently" and made life miserable for any student who did not belong.[345] At Columbine High School, the two students who caused the massacre were seeking to "get even" with the athlete-bullies in their school. Both students were not athletically inclined and were therefore not in the good graces of the school "in-crowd." These are only the most sensational examples of a widespread trend in nearly every school in America.[346]

Another consequence of the sports culture and anti-intellectual atmosphere in high schools is the construction of academic inadequacy. This inadequacy is learned, in that high schools and, later, colleges indicate to their athlete-students that athletics are important and that academic learning is less

---

343. Peter Cary et.al. "Fixing Kid's Sports," *US News and World Report*, 136, no. 20, (June 7, 2004);:44.
344. Murray Sperber, *Onward to Victor: The Crisis that shaped college sports*, (New York: Henry Holt and Co. 1998)p.505.
345. Bernard Lefkowitz, *Our Guys: The Glenn Ridge Rape and the Secret Life of the Perfect Suburb*, (Berkeley, Cal. The University of California Press, 1997)p.113.
346. Lorraine Adams and Dale Russakoff, "Columbine jock culture probed," *The Washington Post*, (June 12, 1999).

important. Athletes, and in particular football and basketball players, frequently skip classes, without any repercussions. Some athlete students even walk out in the middle of a class without the teacher saying anything. Other teachers give athletes "extra" chances to "make up" for poor performance on examinations. Because athletes have so much prestige in high school and in college, many teachers have given up on their academic performance and "pass" them despite their inability to meet the minimum requirements. The failure of many athletes to perform well in school is not only the fault of the students themselves, but is produced by the anti-intellectual culture of the American high school *ipso facto.*[347]

ELECTRONIC ENTERTAINMENT

The belief that violence in the media can be responsible for violent behavior among young people is at least as old as the invention of the first newspapers, and has been convincingly documented. Today, in the electronic age, this connection has received a considerable amount of attention and continues to be a focus for research and opinion.

Over many years, nearly 300 studies have been conducted to deal with the issue of media violence and violence among youths. The overall consensus among 284 such studies strongly supports the proposition that media violence does influence aggression.[348]

Almost all the studies relating media violence to aggression are based on television and movie content. However, the sociologists Anderson and Dill made a study of nonviolent and violent video games and aggression and found that violent video games are also positively correlated with aggression. They used a rigorous experimental test that found evidence for short-term increases in aggressiveness as a result of using violent video games. These video games actually allow the players to engage in violence in a fantasy context and, together with similar Internet sites, provide social support for violent conduct. While

---

347. Kristen F. Benson, "Constructing Academic Inadequacy: African-American Athletes' Stories of Schooling," *The Journal of Higher Education,* 71, no.2, (March-April 2000):223-246.

348. Brad J. Bushman and Craig A. Anderson, "Media violence and the American Public: Scientific facts versus media misinformation," *American Psychologist,* 56, (2001):477-489.

television has been the most common provider of violent entertainment in the past, the newest versions of such activities used by teens are the interactive media.[349]

There are some youths who are disposed to violence even without stimulation from any electronic media. Those so disposed are more likely to entertain themselves with violent media productions than those not so disposed. It is evident that risk-takers and sensation seekers are more likely than others to prefer aggressive entertainment, so that there is some possibility that those already predisposed to violence are more likely to participate in media generated violence.[350] Research suggests that people select media content that meets their psychological needs. In other words, more aggressive teens would be more likely to seek out violent media content and vice versa, so that aggressiveness and the viewing of violence in the media may be said to be mutually reinforcing and cumulative.

Media violence has been blamed for desensitizing people to real human suffering. Furthermore, the sociologists Eron and Huesmann have shown that exposure to television can be particularly deleterious before age eight. They demonstrate that the effects of children's watching of violence last into adulthood and increase aggressive behavior both for males and females. Children identify with same-sex characters on TV and believe that TV is realistic, i.e. "tells it just like it is." The work of Eron and Huesmann also indicates that violent children are most likely to view TV violence as supportive of their own behavior because it makes their violent conduct appear normal. There are of course factors other than watching TV violence which affect children. However, the work of Eron and Huesmann leads to the view that TV violence has the greatest effect.[351]

During the thirty years ending in 2001, a number of researchers concluded that televised violence leads to aggression, desensitization and fear. In sum, these researchers found that viewing televised violence can lead to increases in aggressive behavior and/or changes in attitudes and values favoring the use of aggression to solve conflicts. In addition, extensive violence viewing may lead to

---

349. Craig A. Anderson and Karen E. Dill, "Video games and aggressive thoughts, feelings, and behavior in the laboratory and ion life," *Journal of Personality and Social Psychology*, 78, no.4 (2000):772-790.

350. Marina Krcmar and Kathryn K. Greene, "Connections between violent television exposure and adolescent risk taking," *Media Psychology*, 2, (2000):195-218.

351. Ibid. p.220.

decreased sensitivity to violence and greater willingness to tolerate increasing levels of violence in society. Thirdly, extensive exposure to violence may produce a "mean world syndrome" in which viewers overestimate the risk of victimization.[352]

Over the years, television programming has devoted about one third of its time to crime. Innumerable reruns such as the Rockford Files, Dragnet, Columbo, Hill Street Blues, Walker: Texas Ranger, etc. are constantly visible by day and by night. As a result, adolescents, and adults as well, have a mythological knowledge of the American criminal justice system generated entirely from TV entertainment — and largely unrealistic.

Television also over represents crimes of violence, particularly murder. Murder is the least common American crime, but young viewers must come to the conclusion that it is far more prevalent than official statistics indicate. Researchers have found that 22% of prime time television shows depict murder while 8% depict robbery. Rape is another favorite television crime.[353]

Children and adolescents view television more than adults, since they have more free time. Young people are therefore most likely to have a distorted idea of crime in America. In fact, the social psychologist Carlson found that adolescents who are heavy viewers of crime shows have more erroneous beliefs about the criminal justice system than those who view little television. This is of course true of all forms of "information" gathered from the media, whose interest is entertainment and not factual educational material.[354]

Video games are the fastest growing form of entertainment in America in 2005, as demonstrated by the fact that there are 100 million gaming consoles in American households and 60 million handheld games. In addition, there are a growing number of game-enabled cell phones. Video games are a $9.4 billion business in the US, larger than the movie box office income.

---

352. George Gerbner, Michael Morgan and Nancy Signorelli, "Growing up with television'" In: Bryant G.Zillman, ed., *Media Effects: Advances in Theory and Research* (Hillsdale, N.J. Laurence Earlbaum Assoc. Inc. 1994)

353. Paul G. Kooistra, John S. Mahoney and Saundra V. Westervelt, "The World According to COPS." In: G.Fishman and G. Cavender, Eds., *Entertaining Crime,* (New York: Aldine de Gruyter, 1998)pp. 141-158.

354. James M. Carlson, *Prime-time Law Enforcement,* (New York: Praeger Publishers, 1985)p.33.

Adolescents now rank these games, together with the Internet, as more important sources of entertainment than movies or television. A cable channel called G4 has developed programming around video games which is now sent to 15 million homes. Corporations such as Coca-Cola, Procter and Gamble, and Best Buy are sponsors of these games, increasing the advertising income of the producers by 200% in two years. Video games are now the principal entertainment of adolescent boys, who spend as much as four hours at a time with one game.[355]

Those video games which target young men and boys and are teen-rated usually contain significant amounts of violence. A study conducted by The Entertainment Software Rating Board found violence in 98% of games seeking a youth audience. Forty-two% of the games included blood; deaths from violence occurred in 77% of games, at an average of 122 deaths per hour of game play, with half the deaths involving human characters. Most of the dead were police officers, security guards and postal workers.[356]

Kimberly Thompson, Kevin Haninger and Seamus Ryan, researchers at the Harvard Center for Risk Analysis, found that 90% of a random sample of video games rewarded or required the player to injure characters, 69% rewarded or required the player to kill and 69% rewarded or required the player to destroy objects. The researchers observed 11,499 character deaths in 95 hours of game play. Of these deaths, 5,689 were human.

Thompson et al. also found that 88% of games depicted weapons, 73% depicted use of the body as a weapon and 59% allowed players to select weapons. The authors of the study believe that these games lead adolescents to simulate acts of violence which can and do result in actual violence, including deaths and permanent injuries.[357]

The entire media industry is of course driven by the desire for profit. Therefore, the interests of children are given no consideration by those seeking to make money from television and video game entertainment. It is therefore no exaggeration to say that some children are "lured into aggression, under-achievement and apathy" by these electronic devices.[358]

---

355. T.L. Stanley, "Joystick Nation," *Advertising Age,* (March 22, 2004):1.
356. Mary Ellen Shay, "Teen rated Video games loaded with violence," *AScribe newswire,* (March 10, 2004):1.
357. Ibid. p.2.
358. Jane M. Healy, *Endangered Minds: why your children don't think,* (New York: Simon and Schuster, 1990).

In 1988, the then president of the Los Angeles Writer's Guild, David W. Rintels, said: "the network not only approves of violence on TV, they have been known to request and inspire it." Evidently, the media executives' decision to offer televised violence is based on the assumption that violent programs will attract viewers and subsequently sponsors.[359]

Advertisers are of course heavily involved in creating desires in children and particularly adolescents with money for items they cannot afford. These tactics include using famous athletes such as Michael Jordan to push expensive basketball shoes. This sometimes even leads to violence in order to acquire such equipment. Since programs including violence improve their ratings during "sweeps week," a period which determines how much advertisers will have to pay, violence is almost certain to be included in TV entertainment during that time.[360]

Because television and video games are an escape from reality, poor children and many teenagers watch more TV and play more at video games than do affluent children. In fact, there is an inverse relationship between socio-economic status and favorable attitudes towards the media. This is in part true because watching TV is inexpensive. TV also serves as a babysitter for latchkey children and for those whose parents are busy or worn out. As a result, many children play video games or watch TV for hours and hours and become "hooked" on these devices. It is entirely possible for youngsters to become so obsessed with the unreal world of TV and/or video games that they live in a pleasurable, almost catatonic state.

Programs especially designed for children include violence more often than programs designed for adults. For every four acts of violence of prime time television, 32 violent acts occur on children's TV programs every hour. Violent characters are found in 56% of children's programs but in only 34% of prime time programs.

A 1995 study revealed that 75% of Houston's black public school children watch television for three or more hours every weekday with minimal or no supervision. The demographer Waldrop considers this excessive viewing of television to be responsible for more social isolation, diminished family time, less time for social activities, and less-than-desirable social skills. Furthermore, it has

359. Daniel Schorr, "Go get some milk and cookies and watch the murders on television," In: Erwin N/ Hiebert and Christian Reuss, *Impact of Mass Media*, (New York, Longman, 1988)p.137.
360. John Waldrop, "Shades of black," *American Demographics*, 12, (1990):30-34.

been determined by a great deal of research that those who are excessively involved with video games and television lose the ability to read a book or concentrate on anything that does not change by the second as do electronic devices. This failure to read must contribute to academic failure, *ipso facto*, and therefore has far reaching effects on the life chances of those engrossed by the electronic drug.[361]

Because these dangers have been recognized for some years, Congress passed the Children's Television Act in 1990. This Act was amended in 1992 and again in 1997. The law demands that stations broadcast three hours of "educational and informational" shows for children 16 and younger each week. Stations must also not exceed 12 minutes per hour of advertising during children's programs. Although this law appeared to support children's programming, it actually had the opposite effect. The "Three Hour Rule" induced the networks to provide all affiliated stations with the entire three hours required for educational programming. Therefore the incentive for stations to dc shows of their own was eliminated. As a result, 29% fewer stations submitted applications for the Annual Service to Children Award of the National Association of Broadcasters, reflecting the decrease in the number of children's programs the Children's Television Act produced. Likewise, network shows proclaimed as "educational" are seldom instructive at all. According to the Annenberg Public Policy Center, the number of children's shows labeled "highly educational" has fallen from 80.6% to just 28.3% since the passage of the Children's Television Act. Meanwhile, violence continues unabated on TV and in video games, which are enhanced by "music" whose lyrics are as bloody as an Italian opera.[362]

Teen Movies

The number of teen movies produced in the past fifty years, beginning with such stars as Frankie Avalon and Elvis Presley, is staggering These movies included *American Graffiti*, *American Pie*, *The Wild One*, *I Was a Teenage Werewolf* and other bizarre titles.

American Graffiti shows Richard Dreyfus, Paul Le Mat and Harrison Ford as young men getting into all kinds of trouble. *Animal House* became one of the best-known youth movies, as it depicted a gang of drunk fraternity "men" who lose

---

361. Ibid. p.33.
362. Andy Levinsky, No kidding: Locally produced children's shows have all but vanished," *The Boston Phoenix*, (December 17-24, 1998):1-3.

their 1960s fraternity house. *Fast Times at Ridgemont High* is undoubtedly the "father of all teen movies," following the daily lives of students at a California high school as they flip burgers, surf, party and party on and on. The star of the movie is Sean Penn, who is depicted as using drugs, drinking to excess and having sex.

Sixteen Candles, popular in the 1980s, introduced "the teen queen of the 80s," Molly Ringwald, who portrayed a girl whose family forgot her 16th birthday. There ensues a series of boy-chases-girl, girl-chases-boy events as well a drunken party, insensitive grandparents and at least some humor. In 1986, Molly Ringwald also starred in *Pretty in Pink*. This movie deals with the adventures of high school lovers, peer pressure, the annual "prom" and social class differences.

Sometimes, the title says it all: Don't tell Mom the Babysitter is Dead; Dude, Where's My Car?; Road Trip; Whatever it Takes; Coyote Ugly; Ten Things I Hate About You... Almost all teen movies attempt to be humorous. Not Another Teen Movie satirizes all the others. It includes nudity, a great deal of drug use and considerable gambling.[363]

An extensive study of movie portrayals of juvenile delinquency was conducted by the psychiatrist Dr. Scott Snyder in 1995. Snyder reports that these movies are seen by a large number of adolescents, who comprise 40% of all admissions to American movie theaters. In addition videocassette recorders and DVD players have increased the audience for such movies and therefore their influence, including their influence in encouraging aggressive behavior.

The use of aggression to solve problems begins early in life, and the more aggressive child is likely to become the more aggressive adult.[364] One means by which a child may become most aggressive is known as "observational learning." This term refers to the tendency of young children and older adolescents to model their conduct on the behavior of violence as depicted in movies. This modeling becomes most important when the viewers of movies have had experiences similar to those shown on a screen. The picture may become congruent with the experiences of the onlooker and therefore invites violence on his part. This perspective also sees the depiction of violent pornography as a danger when boys are already supportive of violent behavior. Because the media portray a good deal

---

363. Gareth Olds, "Favorite Flicks," *Anchorage Daily News*, (July 16, 2004):F6.
364. Scott Snyder, "Movie Portrayals of Juvenile Delinquency," *Adolescence*, 30, no.117 (March 1995):53-65.

of violence as justified, some viewers can become desensitized to the pain and suffering violence can produce.[365]

Movies concerning juvenile misconduct were already produced in 1938 when *Girls on Probation* addressed that issue. During that decade a number of such movies blamed parents for the misdeeds of adolescents, an attitude which continued into the Fifties with *Reform School Girls*. As late as 1985, *Bad Girls' Dorm* continued this message and blamed sexual abuse for the delinquency of the "bad girls."

In 1973 the film *Badlands* told the story of Charles Starkweather and his girl friend Carol Fugate. These two adolescent mass murderers were responsible for the deaths of ten innocent people. The sexual abuse of teens was depicted in the 1985 film *Streetwalking*, followed that same year by *Streetwise*, a documentary which deals with the subject of runaway, abducted and abandoned children.

In 1979, *Hardcore* examined the world of teenage pornography and *Taxi Driver*, a 1976 movie, dealt with the life of a 14-year-old prostitute.[366]

The Music of the American Youth Culture

When the waltz was first introduced to Vienna in 1800, Viennese society was "shocked" at the immorality such dancing represented. Prior to the waltz (German for *rotate*), men and women did not touch each other while dancing. Therefore, the "new" dance, which allowed the dance partners to be physically close, was viewed as the "cause" of all the social ills of that time.

More than two hundred years later, many "decent" people still suspect that the music of the young has dreadful consequences, particularly because some of that music contains lyrics that shock polite society. Most egregious of all the music now popular among teens is "rap" music. This music is broadcast on cable MTV. "Rap" is a segment of "hip-hop" music which first became popular among youngsters in the 1970s.

"Hip-hop" is not only music. It includes a subculture which is characterized by droopy pants, hats to the back, laceless sneakers, hood and loud radios. A subculture is defined by sociologists as any group which sets itself apart by use of some culture pattern. Language is the most distinctive device used to exhibit such differences, so that those who live in foreign-speaking enclaves, or those who follow a minority religion such as snake worshippers, are a subculture. This is also true of opera lovers and "hip-hop" musicians.[367]

---

365. Ibid. p.54.
366. Scott Snyder, "Movie Portrayals etc." p. 2.

Rap music is a form of self-expression for those who live in urban slums where drugs, violence, poverty, poor schools, family breakdown and racial animosities are part of daily life. In addition to "rap," hip-hop includes rhythm and blues, new jack swing, reggae and others. "Rap" consists of story telling which seeks to gain power through symbolic verbal action. It demeans women, promotes drug use and praises violence. This music is sold to blacks and whites. For blacks it may have the advantage of pseudo-empowerment. The upper- and middle-class whites who buy this music allow themselves the feeling and belief that they have done something about poverty, racism, etc. without having to enter the ghetto or "soiling their hands" by dealing directly with blacks.[368]

"Rappers" speak in street language and therefore attract those who, like the rapper, have been rejected by the mainstream. The language of rappers is generally aggressive and insulting to women. An example is music written by a rapper who calls himself "Dr. Dre." His lyrics call women "bitches" or "whores" and relate sexual encounters in explicit terms. Black rappers also use racist language which whites avoid religiously. Street language has a different meaning than standard English, because it is the expression of a subculture.[369]

Rap singers also promote the use of drugs and sing songs demanding the legalization of marijuana. One rapper was indicted for murder, but the charges against him were dismissed. He then delivered numerous additional records with aggressive lyrics which made him a "star," leading to movie roles and heavy sales of his recordings. Other rap artists also convey the image of a "gun totin'" weed fiend.

Rap artist Tupac Shakur was noted for frequent arrests. Specializing in "gangsta rap," his lyrics endorse holdups, drinking beer and smoking pot together with the girlfriend, who is of course called a 'ho.[370]

In September of 1996, 25-year-old "rapper" Tupac (or 2Pack) Shakur died in a Las Vegas hospital after having suffered multiple wounds during a drive-by shooting a week earlier. Shakur had been the target of a previous shooting and had himself been arrested a number of times in addition to having spent eight

---

367. Franklin B. Krohn and Frances L. Suazo, "Contemporary Urban Music: Controversial Messages in Hip-hop and Rap lyrics," *Review of General Semantics*, 52, no.2, (Summer 1995):139.

368. David Samuels, "The Rap on Rap," *The New Republic*, (November 11, 1991):24-29.

369. Krohn and Suazo, p.3.

370. David H. Yoffie, "An Open Letter to the Music Industry," *Reform Judaism*, 23,. No.1, (Fall 1994):88.

months in a New York prison for sex abuse. His "gangsta rap" records sold by the millions, promoting such lines as "the power of a gun can kill" or "Life through my bloodshot eyes; would scare a square 2 death; poverty, murder, violence and never a moment 2 rest." Poems of this nature made Shakur a hero among many young people whose musical knowledge is usually limited to the cadences of these angry expressions.[371]

Although popular music is most admired among the youth of America, there are some who have an interest in music generally called "classical." There are hundreds of youth symphony orchestras in this country that participate in learning and presenting the music of Haydn, Mozart, Beethoven, Mendelssohn and Mahler. There are young opera singers who maintain the music of Verdi, Rossini and Donizetti. They may be in the minority in choosing their musical entertainment, and they affirm thereby the ancient Latin proverb, *de gustibus non est diputandum.*

The Teen Market

In the course of one year, the 32 million American teenagers spend $172 billion, or $104 per teenager per week. Obviously, anyone who has anything to sell will want to reach the teen market. That includes the sale of teen books, which focuses on those aged 14 to 17. In 1997, 35 million books were sold to that age group. By 2000 that volume had declined 15.4% to 29.6 million books. In 2001 the number of books sold to teens increased again to 35.6 million only to decline by 8% to 32.8 million in 2002. The $309 million spent by teens on books represent 2% of the entire American book market per year. Over 60% of teen books that are bought are intended as gifts. These books are usually bought in the large chain bookstores, who sold 41% of all teen books bought in 2002.[372]

Teen books are advertised on the Internet and include books about "sex and desire," such as *Empress of the World*, by Sara Ryan. This book tells the story of a girl, seeking to become an archeologist, who meets a "beautiful dancer from North Carolina." A book about teenage love, *Annie On My Mind*, has a lesbian protagonist. Horror stories such as *Demon in My View* are also common.

---

371. Walter Edwards, "From Poetry to Rap: The Lyrics of Tupac Shakur," *The Western Journal of Black Studies*, 20, no.2, (2002)61-70.
372. No author, "Teen Book Market in Flux," *Bookselling This Week*, American Booksellers Association, (October 1, 2003):1.

The greatest success ever enjoyed by an author of adolescent literature is that of Joanne K. Rowling, whose Harry Potter books (seven volumes, by 2005) have sold 80 million copies and have made Rowling the wealthiest woman in England (except, of course, the Queen). A number of the "Potter" books have been made into movies. The stories deal with "wizardry" and the frightful adventures of a boy who overcomes all fears and all obstacles because of the loyalty of his friends and his immense courage.[373]

Despite all the books and magazines targeting them, many American adolescents (and many adults) cannot read. Literacy rates aside, many "literate" people will not read when they can stare at TV and/or the Internet instead. As a result, the failure of high school and college students to read and write good English has reached phenomenal proportions. It is possible that the US President makes frequent reference to "nucular arms" and newscasters talk about events in "Febuary" specifically to create a closer bond with their semi-literate audiences, even if they know better; but this does nothing to encourage higher standards among the public.

Teen Vogue has an annual distribution of 1.5 million, while even a minor circulation magazine such as *Elle Girl* sells 300,000 copies annually. Because the US census estimates that the teen population of the US has reached 31.5 million in 2005, magazine sales are expected to reach an all time high. According to the market researcher "Teenage Research Unlimited," 80% of teenagers age 12-19 read a teen magazine once a week. American teens spend about $155 billion each year, a sum from which advertisers benefit greatly.[374]

Magazines for adolescents cover every aspect from *American Cheerleader* to *Boys' Life* and *Soccer*; but the magazines are almost entirely aimed at girls. Despite the few words telling girls to "be yourself," that is hardly noticeable amidst pages that are almost entirely devoted to the efforts of advertisers to induce young girls to try to be what they see in the magazine, and *not* themselves. Many of the stories are illustrated with passionate kissing scenes, updates on "what's cool," and lots of advertising. Perhaps the most prominent of all teen magazines is *Seventeen*, which claims 14.45 million readers a month. The contents of *Seventeen* include "back to school fashion," "the best way to get rid of acne," "the best summer date ideas" and a story about actress Hillary Duff. A few stories depicting juvenile romance constitute the scant reading matter in this adver-

---

373. Wikipedia: The Free Encyclopedia. http://en.wikipedia.org/wiki/J.-K.-Rowling
374. Jennifer F. Steil, "Youth Market Bustling," *Folio*, (February1, 2001):1.

tisement extravaganza. It is surprising that the circulation of this magazine is so large.

The shared readership of all teen magazines is over 10 million. The average price of these magazines is $4.00, so that the profits, including advertisements, is indeed immense.

There is also a subculture of adolescents who call themselves "punks" or "hippies" and "rockers" and who try to move as far as possible from the middle-class lifestyle practiced in schools and among that silent majority which make up most American families.

SUMMARY

Post-industrial society has created the electronic age, which in turn permits American youngsters to have more leisure time. This leisure is used, by some, for drugs. There are also those who work part time or full time, and some of those spend their money on drugs, video games and other entertainment.

Sports are also an important aspect of the American youth culture, as are movies and music. Electronic entertainments show a great deal of violence, from which advertisers benefit.

Separate electronic games, separate music, and reading material just for adolescents all tend to segregate that age group from the middle aged and old. This segregation is by no means total nor universal. It becomes more severe, however, when adolescents join the punk subculture, a life style seeking to gain a distinct identity at any cost.

Chapter 9. Hippies, Punks and Rockers

Origin of the Hippie Movement

"He's an old hippie and he don't know what to do; should he hang onto the old, should he grab onto the new." So sang the Bellamy Brothers in 1990.

The word "hippie" may be derived from the older term, "hip," used at the beginning of the 20th century among San Francisco opium smokers who reclined "on the hip" while smoking. It may also stem from the West African word "hipicat," meaning "one who has his eyes wide open."[375]

Like all subcultures, the Hippie subculture has a language of its own. John Bassett McCleary has published a Hippie Dictionary, which defines such terms as "Doctor Feelgood" and "Doctor Dope," and contains the remarkable statement that if the country had only listened to the hippies then the attack of September 11, 2001 would not have happened.[376]

The "hippie" social movement originated on the West Coast in the 1960s in response to alienating events like the Vietnam War. Opposition to that war was chiefly fueled by the anger of college students (but others, as well) over the drafting of young men for duty in a war that had hardly any popular support.

The "hippies" led the anti-war movement in the 1960s and 1970s, and were willing to fight physically with law enforcement officials. There are those who believe that the "hippie" movement was only about sex and drugs. In fact,

---

375. Michael Quinion, "What is the origin of the word 'hippie?" *World Wide Words*, (New York: Michael Quinion, (August 12, 2000).
376. David Gates, "Me Talk Hippie," *Newsweek*, 144, no.2, (july 12, 2004):15.

"hippies" had a political agenda, although they may have had many superficial imitators, as well. There was no one monolithic "hippie" movement. Some only held up signs while others became physically aggressive, invaded schools and burned bureaucratic records. Others placed flowers into the gun barrels of the police or sang songs.

The "hippie" movement then and now opposes war and is active in supporting lifestyles and political views that are sometimes called extreme but are always concerned with issues of freedom and the right to self expression.[377]

The first major event concerning the "hippie" movement which caught the attention of the media was The Summer of Love in 1967. The event which triggered so much attention occurred in the winter on January 14, 1967 when 20,000 activists gathered for a "human be-in" at the San Francisco Polo Field. Although people of all ages attended that gathering, the great majority of those who participated in the "hippie" subculture were adolescents.

In San Francisco, these young people had settled in the Haight-Ashbury district of the city east of the Golden Gate Park. That area had swelled from 15,000 to 100,000 inhabitants between 1965 and 1967. A good number of these girls and boys had no means of support and they prostituted themselves or sold and used drugs. Some begged on the street. In the words of the musician George Harrison, "...what I saw were hideous, spotty little teenagers."[378]

In the summer of 1967 the "hippie" movement hit its peak. Although the most important engine driving the "hippie" movement of the 60s and 70s, the Vietnam war, is long over, there are even now "hippies" living in the Haight-Ashbury section of San Francisco. These folks resemble "dropouts" in other cities, some of whose drug addicted citizens are also living in the streets. In San Francisco, however, the aura of the "hippie" revolution continues into the 21st century.

Rock Ninja, writing in the *SFWeekly*, described an encounter with a current "hippie": "The characters ... wear patchwork clothing and beads, twisted tangled hair, ... gazing with glossy retinas. These are the "hippie" panhandlers of Haight street."[379]

No doubt, the most remembered event of the "hippie" movement was the "Woodstock Music and Art Fair" of 1969. From Friday, August 15 until Monday,

---

377. Marilee Movius, "Hippie Movement Misunderstood," *Daily Forty-niner*, (May 13, 2004):8.

378. Damien Cave, et.al. "The Hippie Takeover" *Rolling Stone*, 951, (June 24, 2004).

379. Rock Ninja, "The Good Deed," *SFWeekly*, (March 17, 2004):1.

August 18, more than 450,000 people, mostly adolescents, congregated in a muddy field at Bethel, NY, near Woodstock, a small town south of Albany and 100 miles from Manhattan. The word "Woodstock" has now become synonymous with youthful hedonism. Financed by the multi-millionaire John Roberts and three other wealthy young men, the event cost $2.4 million, as numerous professional singers and bands were signed to participate in "Three Days of Peace and Music." It was understood that "music" meant "Jefferson Airplane," "Creedence Clearwater Revival," "The Who," "Wavy Gravy" and others known in the psychedelic music community at that time.

Once the festival began, the crowd became so immense that route 17B was jammed for nine miles and part of the New York Thruway had to be closed. Because many adolescents came to the concert without tickets or money, the vast majority paid no entrance fee. These "hippies" left cars in the middle of the road, used drugs, and engaged in sex publicly, but had too little food. Therefore New York residents made sandwiches and airlifted the food to the thousands who had come without a plan and without any foresight. There were insufficient "necessary rooms." Much of the food consisted of cold "hot dogs" and hamburgers which many of the "hippies" working the concessions gave away free. The crowd slept outdoors on the farm, and the rain made it a quagmire.

Meanwhile such entertainers as Arlo Guthrie, Tim Hardin, Bert Sommer and Melanie, Sly and the Family Stone, Canned Heat and others sang and played guitars. While these musicians played, the mud increased to two inches deep. Cigarette butts and clothes were lying in the mud as sewage accumulated in the portable toilets. When a tractor came to remove the sewage, it ran over 17-year-old Raymond Mizak, who was hidden under his sleeping bag, and killed him.

The Woodstock festival had 5,162 medical cases, 797 documented cases of drug abuse and two deaths from drug abuse.

After the 36 years which have passed since Woodstock, true believers still call that event a source of human advancement; others say it was the end of an era of human stupidity and some merely view it as "one hell of a party." [380]

To sociologists Woodstock was one manifestation of a social movement that they define as "an organized activity that encourages or discourages social change."

In the 1960s, the "hippie" movement built on several earlier phenomena, including the rejection by younger Americans at the end of the 1950s of the dom-

---

380. Elliot Tiber, "How Woodstock happened," *The Times Herad- Record* (1994).

inance of the older generation and the sexual repression which marked the first half of the 20th century. Beginning in 1950, the New Left were those who participated in the voter registration drives which lasted until about 1965. The Free Speech Movement developed during the 1960s at the University of California and all across the United States to New York. The Free Speech Movement was mainly interested in university reform. Their complaints were intensified by the "hippies" who conducted a revolt against the "middle class" tyranny of the '50s and defied the bureaucrats in (and outside of) Washington, D.C. They developed a counter culture around drugs, sex, music and mysticism. This in turn was co-opted by the New Left, which dreamt of social revolution but finally exhausted itself and ended with the Woodstock formation. Thousands of communes developed from these sources. These communes practiced vegetarianism, talked about organic food and proclaimed that "everything is free" as they denounced the stock market and capitalism in general.[381]

The Beatles, a group whose "singing" consisted of repetitious monotones, insisted that "all you need is love." The message downplayed the material culture; and the word "love" became the catchword of the hippie culture in the 1960s and led to the development of communes, collectives, encounter groups and "group marriages." Associated with all that "love" were drugs of all kinds, as getting high was the symbol of final liberation.

Some in the youth culture of the 1960s claimed that drugs such as LSD provided them with a "higher state of consciousness"; the practice of yoga and meditation also increased. Sexual liberation was regarded as the best means of showing opposition to the established "middle class" social order. The hippie slogan, "make love, not war," emphasized this departure from the expectations of the earlier generation.[382]

The "hippie" movement also denounced all authority. Opposed to school rules, to parental authority and the formalities of the courts, "hippies" denounced pay toilets (which were certainly problematic; although perhaps better than the utter lack of public toilets that prevails today) and refused to stand up when a judge entered a courtroom. Because of these "radical" ideas and because of some radical conduct, the hippie movement was largely exhausted at the end of the 1970s.

---

381. David L. Foss and Ralph W. Larkin, "From the Gates of Eden to Day of the Locust: An Analysis of the Dissident Youth Movement of the 1960s and its heirs of the early 1970s-the post-movement groups." *Theory and Society*, 3, no.1 (Spring 1976) 45-64.
382. Ibid. p.49.

That exhaustion came about because hedonism and immediate gratification of the body did nothing to change society. As a result, all kinds of formal organizations developed, many with pseudo-religious aspects. These organizations promoted a hierarchy of leaders. Some followed eastern mysticism; others called themselves "Jesus freaks." There were also "The Holy Spirit," "Krishna," and a number of Marxist sects.

By the beginning of the 2000s, the "hippie" movement has largely disappeared. Nevertheless, it has had an impact on American society that is not often recognized thirty-five years after Woodstock. One such impact has been the sexual revolution. This "revolution" is of course not only the product of the '60s "hippie" movement. Instead, it may be much more the outcome of new methods of birth control, the publication of *The Feminine Mystique* and the founding of the National Organization of Women, the last two both achieved by Betty Friedan in 1973.[383]

Together with a number of government-sponsored initiatives, efforts by women themselves have resulted in an immense increase in women's rights and opportunities during recent decades. Furthermore, much of the repression concerning sex has been eradicated from the American psyche. Advertisements include women's and men's underwear at one time called "unmentionables," pills to defeat erectile dysfunction, and an immense flood of pornography both on television and on the world wide web. Whether this is desirable may be debated; but it is a fact.

The mysticism of the 1960s is also still alive, although in somewhat altered form. There are still a good number of followers of invented "oriental-inspired" cults. These are often people who have become dissatisfied with the structures and teachings of traditional religions. The latest freak adventure into mysticism involves the top star, "Madonna." Raised a Catholic, she produced a "rock" video in which she calls herself "the Kabbalah girl." As earlier stars, including the Beatles, sought wisdom among Indian gurus, Madonna (like a number of other Hollywood celebrities) has visited the Kabbalah center in New York City, claiming to be interested in the mystical Jewish tradition dating back centuries.

---

383. Mary P. Ryan, *Womanhood in America: From Colonial Times to the Present*, 3rd Edition (New York; Franklin Watts, 1983)pp.305-323.

THE PUNK CULTURE

In 1623, Shakespeare' *Measure for Measure* used the word "punk" to refer to a prostitute. Since then, punk has become part of American slang, altering its meaning to include "worthless," or a young person seeking to represent a rebellious subculture.[384] In the 1980s, the word still defined prostitutes — the first customers of the "punk" music played at CBGB's on the New York Bowery were allegedly male prostitutes.[385]

That subculture began in the early 1970s in New York City and has since then spread mainly to adolescents all over the United States. Its visible manifestations are hairstyles including a so-called "Mohawk." That hairstyle was reputedly worn by the Mohawk tribe of Native Americans. It consists of shaving all the hair except for a single narrow stripe of varying length running from the forehead straight back. Some "punks" dye their hair brilliant orange, pink, light green or red. Some also wear the center strip of hair pointing straight up.

More recently, "punk" hair styles have been altered. More fashionable and wealthy "punks" wear the Mohawk somewhat shorter. Grease is used to keep hair down on the side of the head, which is no longer shaved, while women wear a "pony tail" and sculpt the "punk" look on top.[386]

Hair is a powerful symbol of individual and group identity. It can be changed easily, and allows people to portray different identities at different times. The importance of hair in the United States is reflected in the $2 billion income of the hair industry in this country. Hair has gender significance, as male hairstyles generally differ from female hairstyles.[387]

Among hippies and punks, hairstyle became a means of protest against the "Puritan" sex ethic, the "Protestant" work ethic and all kinds of oppression. Beads and jeans replaced suits, peace signs replaced ties and marijuana replaced alcohol. Likewise, hair became a symbol of rebellion. Girls associated with the punk movement wear long, straight, natural hair without dyes or curls or "permanents." Young men wear their hair long, in rebellion against their fathers' styles. Boys in the punk movement may also wear beards and mustaches and by

384. *The American Heritage Dictionary of the English Language, Fourth Edition*, New York: Houghton Mifflin Co., 2000).
385. Wikipedia, the Free Encyclopedia, http.//en.wikipedia.org/wiki/Punk
386. Olivia Barker, "Mohawk isn't as hair-raising as it used to be," *USA Today*, (June 27, 2002):1.
387. Curtis Pesman, *How a Man ages*, (New York: Ballantine Books, 1984) pp.26-27.

these means demonstrate their opposition to the majority. The rock musical "Hair" celebrated the movement.[388]

Then came the "skinheads," whose purpose it is to protest the hippies and punks whose men they view as effeminate.

The "punk" subculture has other features now mainly embraced by teen-agers of all social classes. Some "punks" pierce their noses to accommodate a ring. Others pierce their "belly buttons" and adorn them with colored studs. Some even pierce their tongues or lower lips, and place a stud there, thus slurring their speech. This is a guaranteed way to shock one's parents.

Studded belts and bracelets are important parts of the costumes worn by those aspiring to the "punk" look. So are hooded black sweatshirts and bullet belts and dresses with chains. "Punks" also like to wear numerous buttons depicting revolutionaries like "Che Guevara." Combat boots and so-called bondage pants and "bondage straps" complete a "punk's" appearance. (A "bondage strap" joins the two legs together at the knees.[389])

Some punks also wear tattoos. The word "tattoo" is derived from the Tahitian language and refers to the coloring of the skin by hand. Tattooing has been used in Borneo and other South Asian societies for centuries. Tattooing was known in the United States but was not popular before the end of the 20th century. *Life* magazine estimated in 1936 that approximately 6% of the American population had a tattoo; these were mostly ex-Navy men. In 2003, the Harris Poll estimated that the "punk" subculture has increased the number of Americans with a tattoo so that 36% of young people now have a tattoo and 28% of those over 30 also are tattooed. While some say they became tattooed to be more "sexy," the largest number of those interviewed wanted to be more rebellious by showing their tattoo.[390]

Punk also refers to music. The lyrics to these songs are a mixture of aggression and sentimentality. One song is called, "I Wanna Sniff Some Glue." Similar lyrics accompany other songs by the Ramones, once more supporting the sociological view that the best indicator of a subculture is that it has its own lan-guage. The Ramones performed wearing black motorcycle jackets and punk

---

388. Barbara M. Lieberman, "Growth Patterns: Reshaping Facial Angles with Beards and Moustaches," *Gentlemen's Quarterly*, (July, 1987):

389. Helene Stapinski, "In punk rock's birthplace, a new breed of devotees," *The New York Times*, February 23, 2004):2.

390. Joy Marie Sever, "A Third of Americans with tattoos say they make them feel more sexy," Harris Poll # 58 (October 5,2003).

haircuts. They played loud music described by one listener as having "a raunchy, ripping quality, ...the bass had a driving piston feel."

The Pattie Smith Group, The Talking Heads, Teenage Lust, and others are sometimes considered part of a "united musical field" (although, of course, aficionados may disagree). Reviews of these bands were not initially friendly. A local newspaper, *SoHoWeekly*, described Television as "loud, out of tune and with absolutely no musical or socially redeeming characteristics."[391] One of the distinctive characteristics of most of these bands was loud noise and the constant use of crude language with sexual overtones.

The "punk" scene has its own magazines, abbreviated as "zines." Over eighty such magazines are published in the United States and England, such as *The Little Cracked Egg, Gene Simmons Tongue,* or *Pitchfork.*

SLAM DANCING AND THE "MOSH PIT"

The word "mash," mispronounced as "mosh" by a punk singer, Darryl Jennifer, has entered the language of the punk scene to refer to the dancing conducted by followers of this kind of noise. A "mosh pit," therefore, is an area of a dance floor nearest the orchestra where the crowding is most severe, leading to dancers slamming into each other. Those who practice slam dancing call it an art. (Of course, any human activity can be called an art!) Slam dancing is done without regard to the music, which in any event is sometimes no more than random noise. As dancers slam into one another, some fall down and may need help to get up.

The purpose of slam dancing is to promote aggression. This includes the use of some traditional "four letter words" while bouncing off other people, without necessarily hurting anyone. Some slam dancers are more aggressive than others. These faster dancers are called thrashers. There are videos by bands called "Minor Threat," "Suicidal Tendencies" and 'Red Hot Chili Peppers" which include this activity.[392] Teenagers report that they get a thrill from slam dancing and enjoy the closeness with other people.

---

391. Bernard Gendron, *Between Montmartre and the Mudd Club,* (Chicago: The University of Chicago Press, 2002)pp. 249-259.
392. James Cook, "Zen and the Art of the Mosh Pit: A Beginners Guide to slam Dancing," www.altx.com/gangsta/mosh.html.

Slam dancing sometimes results in fighting and violence; and some groping may occur. There is also the possibility dancers may meet someone they like. In fact, slam dancing, like all dancing, serves the function of providing sexual initiation to the young.

Slam dancing also functions to maintain group boundaries and impose an ideology and gain prestige. This was true when the waltz was king and continues to be true today when adolescents dance to reggae, indy, house, disco, rap and punk.

Dancing is a form of language. Slam dancing therefore seeks to comment on the society in which it occurs. The comment that slam dancers and punks are making is one that opposes the ordinary, middle class, striving, diploma chasing, repressive culture which they feel dominates American society. Slam dancing is a ritual or social drama which permits the participants to belong, in the same fashion as is true of a religious ceremony. Religious ceremonies are also rituals which provide communion or a sense of unity to diverse people who shed their differences once a week and attain a sense of belonging through that ritual.[393]

One of the most aggressive bands on the punk scene were the Sex Pistols. These performers included gross lyrics in their songs which were designed to explode every taboo and insult big business, government and just about everyone. The anger they portrayed related their young followers to all their frustrations in a faceless world in which jobs are hard to find and many felt they had no future. No doubt the Sex Pistols, an English group, sought to display their hostility toward the British class system which, in somewhat disguised form, also prevails in America.[394]

Despite its chaotic appearance, slam dancing, like all human activity, is organized around a set of expectations or norms. If that were not so, it could not exist. For example, if someone needs help in getting up, it is provided by other dancers. If someone leaps from the stage, other dancers catch him. Slam dancers do not hit people from behind but only from the side or the front. These rules are learned by participation and not by formal schooling.

It is significant that the average age of slam dancers is 22 and that a large percentage of slam dancers are students. A good number of them consider them-

393. Ed Christman, "Inside Mosh: Understanding America's No.1 Dance," *Billboard*, 1, (May 16, 1992):22.
394. Greil Marcus, "God Save the Sex Pistols," *Rolling Stone*, (March 9,1978):68.

selves musicians, although it is unlikely that very many are fans of Mozart, Verdi or Tchaikovsky.

The punk subculture raises the question: "Why do only some youths get involved in that subculture while most young people don't?" The answer is that although the majority of high school students do not belong to the punk sub-culture, punk nevertheless articulates what the "silent" majority feels as individuals.[395]

Recently, some punk musicians have entered the political arena and pro-moted a "Rock Against Bush" Tour with over 200 punk musicians and thousands of punk fans. The tour was sponsored by Music for America. The principal message was that "the dictatorship of Saddam Hussein was better for the world than the Bush administration."[396] Another group of punk musicians launched a web site called conservativepunk.com. This group supported President Bush and the war in Iraq. These musicians embrace freedom, individuality, and a limited role of government in the lives of Americans. Although the so-called Johnny Ramone, a.k.a. John Cummings, was a Republican, the liberals who oppose con-servative efforts send hate mail to Nick Rizzuto, the founder of conserva-tivepunk.com.[397]

THE SOCIOLOGY OF THE ROCK CULTURE

In 1983, the Scottish sociologist Simon Frith published *Sound Effects: Youth, Leisure and the Politics of Rock 'n' Roll*. In that book, Frith examined the relationship between the rock industry and its listeners. Simon Frith argued that popular music, most recently incarnated as rock music and the punk lifestyle, developed when the music industry sought to find a new market and the young sought a means of expressing themselves. The need for youthful expression came about during the years 1900 to 1930, as the separation between home and work accel-erated, as parental influence diminished over children's job opportunities and

---

395. Ralph Larkin, *Suburban Youth in Cultural Crisis*, (New York: Oxford Press, 1979):79.
396. Scott Goldstein, "Punkboter.com Rock against Bush Tour to Start Tonight in Seattle," *US Newswire*, (March 29,2004):1.
397. Shweta Govindarajan, "Conservative Punk Rockers Rallying Message through the Web," *Cox News Service*, (April 7, 2004):1.

marriages, as the importance of the high school grew as the center of adolescent activities and with the rise of the adolescent consumer.[398]

Frith believed that the youth culture is classless. This is not the case. It is, however, true that youths have many difficulties which they share with other youths rather than with adults. Frith's main thesis is that understanding a sub-culture's use of music is a key to understanding that subculture.

Of course, any assertion concerning youth must first define what is meant by youth. From a biological point of view, youth is a stage of life centered on the attainment of maturity or reproductive ability. From a sociological point of view, youth or adolescence is the age group that has reached biological maturity but is not yet economically independent. In pre-industrial societies, one is either a child or an adult. In post-industrial America, that is by no means the case. Because of constant innovations, an almost entirely knowledge-based economy, considerable geographic mobility, a surplus economy and considerable leisure time, marginalized youth are living "in limbo" between childhood and adult responsibilities. Now, adolescents are faced with lengthy schooling and a restricted labor market that leads to the need to acquire still more education and a great increase in the length of economic dependency.[399]

All this has led youth to become a distinctive subculture. Young Americans have developed distinctive values, ideals, sentiments and activities. Beginning with the "jazz age" of the 1920s, "youth" became a cultural construct that was practically institutionalized by the mid-1950s. As the electronic mass media increased in popularity, more and more young people were able to affiliate with the youth culture, which became a mass market in a mass society. In part, the youth subculture was created by the adolescents themselves; in part, it was the product of the consumer goods industry.[400]

Any subculture differs from the dominant culture, just as religions and lan-guage differ. The American and even worldwide youth culture not only differs from but is opposed to the general American culture. From its inception, the "rock" culture sought to resist mainstream values, leading in the 1960s to violent rebellion. Although that rebellion had a great deal to do with opposition to the

---

398. Craig Meyer, "Youth Culture and Alternative Rock Music," *Senior Thesis*, (College of Wooster, 1995):2.

399. Deena Weinstein, "Alternative youth: The ironies of recapturing youth culture," *Young*, 3, no.3 (1995):1.

400. Lawrence Grossberg, "I'd rather feel bad than not to feel anything at all:Rock and roll, pleasure and power," *Enclitic III*, 1-2, (1984):94-111.

war in Vietnam, it was also directed at all authority, such as the police, teachers and the clergy.[401] Mind-altering drugs became the vogue in the counter culture, which proclaimed the slogan, "Turn on, tune in, drop out."

Attempts to Protect the Young

All this alarmed many adults and particularly politicians. The US Senate finally held hearings concerning the popular record industry in 1985. Those hearings were introduced by the chairman of the Committee on Commerce, Science and Transportation, Sen. John Danforth of Missouri. It is noteworthy that Sen. Danforth is also an ordained Episcopal minister. In his opening statement Senator Danforth let it be known that the hearings were to be a forum for the airing of complaints about the records produced by the punk-rock music industry. The senator anticipated that the words to be used by witnesses concerning the lyrics in punk-rock songs would "shock the sensibilities of many of us."

These hearings were stimulated by the Parents Music Resource Center, a committee formed in 1985 by the wives of several members of Congress. They embarked on a mission to "educate parents concerning the alarming trends" in popular music. The committee believed that rock music, some of which glorifies drugs, violence, suicide and criminal activity, were harmful and that parents should be afforded some means of protecting their children from it, if they chose to do so.

Opposing the Parents Music Resource Center were several witnesses who told the Committee that the First Amendment to the Constitution protects all speech, including the obscene language found regularly on punk rock records. The principal witness for the porn-rock-punk music culture was Frank Zappa, who had formed a band called "The Mothers of Invention."

Sarcastic and as certain of his superiority and right to judge the world as any other bigot, Zappa expressed disgust with the United States and everything in it. Nevertheless, he earned his considerable income through the capitalist system which sold his recordings. This is not to say that the average musician earns much money. Only 60% of American musicians work full time at that occupation. The median income of American musicians in 2002 was $37,000.

---

401. Keith Roe, "The school and music in adolescent socialization," In: James Lull, Editor, *Popular music and communication,* (Newbury Park, Cal. Sage Publications, 1987)pp. 212-230.

Since a few, like John Denver (born Henry Deutschendorf), make millions, that means that most make very little. Denver also testified at the 1985 congressional hearings, although his music was far from the punk rock promoted by Zappa. Denver had earned millions from his recordings and was known for his extensive philanthropy. He died in an airplane accident in 1997 at the age of 54.

The hearings did not result in any legislation, but the record industry did agree to put labels on records containing "explicit content" so that some stores would not sell labeled records.

On September 19, 1997 the Senate Commerce Committee held additional hearings on the entertainment industry on the urging of the National Political Council of Black Women, who were alarmed at the evidence that rock music and other aspects of entertainment for youths led to "declining morality." Senators Sam Brownback and Joe Lieberman chaired the hearings, with particular reference to the effect of violent lyrics on children. The Senate committee heard a number of witnesses, including Raymond Kurtz, who testified that his son had committed suicide at the age of 15 after hearing the lyrics of an album entitled *Antichrist Superstar*, recorded by Marilyn Manson, a.k.a. Brian Warner. This male performer couples the name of Marilyn Monroe with the infamous murderer Charles Manson. The lyrics of his songs include references to child molestation, homosexuality, devil worship, sex crimes and an assortment of violence, including suicide.[402]

The hearing emphasized that the 1996 Telecommunications Act already mandated that any television set sold after July 1999 must be equipped with "V chips." A "V chip" allows a parent to block unwanted television programs. Thereafter, the television industry provided the Federal Communications Commission with a rating system designed to allow parents an opportunity to prevent children from viewing violent and sexually insinuating material.[403]

Suicide

Suicides by adolescents are by no means unusual in the US. These, however, tend to be anonymous statistics. When celebrities kill themselves, as a considerable number of rock musicians have done during the past forty years, they receive a good deal of attention. One of the most spectacular may have been the suicide of Kurt Cobain, leader of a group called "Nirvana." This may indicate

---

402. US Senate, *Committee on Governmental Affairs*, (Washington, D.C. 1997).
403. US Senate, *Committee on Commerce, Science and Transportation*, (Washington, D.C., 1985).

a change in his mindset, since his first band was called "Fecal Matter." Be that as it may, in 1994, Cobain blasted himself in the head with a shotgun in his room above a garage. His apartment had been decorated with blood-spattered dolls hanging by their necks. He also spray painted his neighborhood with the slogans "abort Christ," "God is gay," and "homo-sex rules." [404]

A long list of other rock related suicides includes Janis Joplin, Del Shannon, Ephraim Lewis, Janet Vogel, Bobby Bloom, Nick Drake, Joe Meek, Phil Ochs and at least fifty others, most of whom were in their mid-thirties when they died of self inflicted wounds or drugs.

Suicide is the third highest cause of death for Americans between the ages of 14 and 24. There are more than 30,000 suicides in the United States each year, of which about 3,900 are committed by adolescents. The overall suicide rate in the United States is about 11 per 100,000 residents. The suicide rate among rock musicians is far out of proportion to that of the general American population. [405]

One sign of an impending suicidal gesture among teenagers is cutting of the flesh, usually with a razor blade. People who engage in this activity are unhappy, and seek to suppress their depressive feelings by concentrating on their self-inflicted wounds. These do not hurt nearly as much as the psychic pain they are experiencing at the time.

There are many admirers of "rock" musicians who find it hard to understand why rich, successful women and men would kill themselves at a young age. Yet, one of the founders of sociology, Emile Durkheim, had the answer long before anyone ever heard of electronic music. In his 1897 book, *Suicide*, Durkheim showed that people with strong social ties rarely committed suicide while those whose success permitted them an almost unlimited freedom to do as they chose had high suicide rates. Extreme individualism without limits was then, and is now, a dangerous lifestyle. [406]

Gerontophobia

That segment of the young who promoted the punk viewpoint in the 1970s was obsessed with aging. This fear is called gerontophobia, and manifests as fear

---

404. Ernest A. Jasmin, "Kurt Cobain: what was might have been" *The News Tribune*, (April 4, 2004):DO1.

405. R. N. Anderson and B.L. Smith, "Deaths: Leading Causes for 2001," *National Vital Statistics Report*, 52, no.9, (2003):1-86.

406. Emile Durkheim, *Suicide* (New York: Free Press, 1966, org. 1897).

and hatred of those who are old. Using the slogan, "I hope I die before I get old," they labeled anyone or anything connected with the established social order as BOFs, or "boring old farts."

Those who were most involved in the safety pin, mohawk, and neon-hair color scene were no longer working-class adolescents by the end of the 1970s. By then, the upper middle class had adopted punk and had developed "heavy metal" music as a means of once more excluding the "old." The noise of heavy metal is considerable. Few adults are willing to expose themselves to this extreme volume. The producers of these sounds therefore pitch the slogan: "If it's too loud, then you're too old." In view of this ageist bigotry, those who were young in the 1970s must be most disappointed that in the early 21st century they are fifty years old or more.[407]

In the 1980s, the appropriation of punk and rock by the middle class and even "old" people led the college-age crowd to look for some other means of expressing their ideology, still emphasizing their contempt for established institutions. Capitalist greed was once more denounced by this "hip" college youth who were best represented by four bands, Husker Du, the Replacements, Sonic Youth and REM.[408] The anti-capitalist youth overlooked the fact that the money they paid for this music made it a highly successful capitalist endeavor. Some are so naïve that they enjoy a well-known rock group whose music seems to express the mood of, and stand up for, the poor and downtrodden while despising the "long-haired, money-making music which is for the rich and powerful." They will happily spend $40 each for a ticket to a rock concert.

Nevertheless, the "counterculture" of the 1980s never succeeded in convincing its followers that they were the revolutionaries of the 1960s. Instead, the late 1980s and the 1990s developed "alternative rock," which consists of immense diversity supported by college radio stations and independent record labels.

The Decline of "Rock"

"It is with heart gripped despair that I inform you of Lollapalooza's disbandment for the summer of 2004." So wrote Perry Bernstein, a.k.a. Perry Farrell or Peripheral, to "my fellow Artisans, Activists, and Feverish Supporters."

---

407. Ellis Cashmore, "Shades of black, shades of white," In: James Lull, Editor, *Popular music and communication,* (Newbury Park, CA. Sage Publications, 1987):245-265.
408. Parke Puterbaugh, "Crackers with attitude: when the alternative gets predictable crackers get weird," *Rolling Stone,* 679, (1994):67-69.

Farrell-Bernstein is the co-founder, with Marc Geiger, of a music festival named after a word borrowed from a Three Stooges movie. The first tour of the Lollapalooza festival was held in 1991, in an imitation of Woodstock. Although Lollapalooza claims the legacy of the poor, the underdogs, the minorities and the rejected of the 1960s, it was a big, profit-making enterprise. Highly organized, the music was provided by major label alternative groups and featured Farrell's band, called Jane's Addiction. During that tour Farrell was so "strung out" on drugs that he got into a fistfight with another performer.[409]

Included in that concert tour were bands with names like "Nine Inch Nails," "Throbbing Gristle," "Einsturzende Neubauten" (German for "end, collapse, new construction") and "Ministry." There was also "Ice T" and "Living Color," the "Red Hot Chili Peppers" and the "Beastie Boys" alongside "Soundgarden" and "Smashing Pumpkins," the "Vulgar Boatmen," "Mutabaruka" and "Possum Dixon"[410]

The music produced by these bands consists of loud guitars, accompanied by fist-pumping gestures. The audience were mostly 18- 24-year-old white suburban young adults, with very few blacks in the audience. The reason for this segregation may well have been the cost of tickets, which ranged from $29.50 for general admission to $49.50 for reserved seats.[411]

Only because the 2004 tour of Lollapalooza was cancelled, it was not possible for the organizers to use these concerts for political purposes as intended. Farrell hoped to include in the festival the "Revolution Solution." That segment of the festival would have featured political speeches concerning renewable energy, artistic expression, free speech, media deregulation, unemployment, world trade, voting rights, public education and other issues, all based on the opinions expressed by "MoveOn," a web site devoted to the defeat of George W. Bush in the 2004 election.[412]

Part of the apparent reason for the collapse of the Lollapalooza festival is the competition from such shows as Weenie Roast, a radio show; Cochella

---

409. Simon Reynolds, "Woodstock for the lost generation," *The New York Times*, (August 4, 1999): Section H, pp. 22 and 28.
410. Alan DiPerna, "Sold Out-A Brief History of Lollapalooza," *Guitarworld*, 13, no.11, (November 1992).
411. Renee Graham, "Slow ticket sales cancel Lollapalooza" *The Boston Globe*, (July 23, 2004):D1.
412. Susan Jones, "Left-leaning Summer Music Tour Canceled," *Cybercast News Service*, (June 23, 2004).

Valley Music and Arts Festival, "Warped" (which is a Lollapalooza inspired performance), and "Ozzfest," a traveling road show organized by Ozzy Osbourne. A severe alcoholic and cocaine addict, the English-born Osbourne has spent some time in jail for "breaking and entering" and "assaulting a police officer." Osbourne's shows include such gestures as throwing calves' livers and pigs' intestines into the crowd, followed by the crowd throwing meat and even live animals onto the stage.

The concerts continue for 14 hours of music. Ticket prices range from $100 to $313. Therefore, it is reasonable to conclude that rock and heavy metal and other music associated with this kind of entertainment has now been absorbed into the mainstream culture of 2005 America and that the aggressive messages of its lyrics are quite distorted imitations of the hippie music of the 1960s.

SOCIAL MOVEMENTS

The hippie, punk and rock culture is a social movement. Sociologists define a social movement as "organized activity that encourages or discourages social change." Social movements are a form of collective behavior, deliberately organized with a view of attaining a lasting effect on a society. Using shared symbols such as music or clothes, those who seek to promote their agenda usually believe that they are deprived and that they cannot achieve change individually. It has long been understood that those who are the most deprived are seldom in a position to bring about social change. Instead, those who have at least some means are more likely to demand change and succeed in getting it. This observation applies directly to the punk-rock subculture, whose most vocal advocates are middle-class youths who are able to pay for attendance at rock concerts and/or who earn a considerable income for performing in them.

Sociologists therefore hold that *relative* deprivation is a far more powerful incentive in bringing about social change than absolute deprivation. Relative deprivation is defined as a perceived disadvantage rising from some specific comparison.[413] A sixteen-year-old may even feel deprived if he does not have his own car — or a "good" car — if he lives in a middle-class neighborhood and many of the boys in his high school class have cars of their own.

---

413. John Macionis, *Sociology*, (Upper Saddle River, N.J. Prentice-Hall, 2001)p.610.

Social movements often attract otherwise isolated people who feel personally insignificant. This is most certainly true of many "rock" concert performers and followers. The shocking and aggressive language used in the lyrics of punk-rock songs indicates a strong need to exhibit power and strength among those who believe they have neither.

Many of the suggestions of social consciousness within this segment are cynical, false and exploitative. An example would be Eric Boucher, a native of Boulder, CO, who calls himself Jello Biafra. (Biafra is a segment of Nigeria whose population has been murdered and otherwise persecuted by the Nigerian government. Both the perpetrators and victims of this genocide are Black Africans.) The so-called Biafra, Eric Boucher, gives the impression that his "liberal" political agenda, which consists largely in making the most extreme accusations against the US government, would be somehow comparable to the suffering of the Biafran people. In fact, he and others like him earn large sums from their record sales and concerts. His band is called The Dead Kennedys, and the cover of their album *Frankenchrist* features a picture called Penis Landscape. The lyrics included in the songs in that album are the usual collection of obscenities, which are now so expected that they shock no one.[414]

True social movements are, in deed, fostered and supported by the youth culture, including some generous contributions by musicians who have put on many enormous benefit concerts. While social movements were at one time limited to a specific place, recent social movements have become international, particularly in the post-industrial countries of Western Europe and in the United States. Included in these international issues are the rights of women, gay people and animals. There are also international social movements that promote bigotry against religious minorities, such as Jews or Muslims.

In the 20th century, social movements such as labor unions generally dealt only with economic issues. These economic concerns drew support from the working class but were seldom of interest to the middle and upper classes. In recent decades the new social movements draw support from the middle and upper classes and one favorite topic of concern is the environment, including global warming. Affluent people control the agenda of most social movements. Typically, these people are conservative on economic issues but find that they can relieve some social pressure by supporting other aspects of the "liberal" agenda. This dichotomy between conservative and liberal attitudes has spread

---

414. Jodi Van der Molen, "Jello Biafra," *The Progressive*, (February 2002):2.

from a small elite toward the middle of the social spectrum as a result of the increase in education and the professionalization of the workforce in America.

The spread of social movements across the whole world has come about in response to worldwide communication. The computer, the television screen and numerous other electronic devices have developed international political connections. Information technology unites people around the globe to support worldwide social movements.

All this has happened to the social movement represented by rock 'n' roll music. That music is a symbol of the social movement called "the 60s rebellion." This is also true of the clothes, hairstyles and violent lyrics needed by the "rock" subculture. Yet, there are those who support Italian opera and German symphony generally and who have a different political agenda than the politicians on the "left" who seek radical changes in American life, but who are more than willing to make a profit on concerts devised to demean the very system that provides their profits.

There can be little doubt that social movements including protests will continue in the United States. Protest is part of the American culture and is the province of the young in every generation. Therefore the subculture of adolescence and youth will produce other forms and other means than have heretofore been used to express the protest of the young against the Establishment, or the "old." To do this requires language capable of expressing the distinctions the young must make between themselves and the perceived autocracy suppressing their wishes and desires. We turn next to that special language.

Summary

The "hippie" movement in the United States developed mainly as a protest against the Vietnam War. That protest culminated in the "Summer of Love" in San Francisco and the Woodstock Festival, followed by the development of the "Punk" subculture. "Punk" includes tattooing, the use of body piercing, "punk" magazines, obscene language and "slam dancing."

"Punk" leaders also have a political agenda which usually, but not always, denounces American institutions. An unusual number of these denunciators have committed suicide.

On two occasions the US Senate has taken action, albeit minimal, to limit the documented harmful effects of media violence and other deleterious facets of today's culture, especially rock and punk, on children.

In the last couple of years numerous rock concerts and tours have had to be canceled because of poor ticket sales. This seems to indicate that the punk-rock culture is fading in the United States, probably because it has been preempted by the middle and upper class of American young people, whose social protest may be more effective than the protests of those who founded "rock 'n' roll" a half a century ago.

CHAPTER 10. THE LANGUAGE OF YOUTH

THE SAPIR–WHORF HYPOTHESIS

In one sentence, the linguists Roger Brown and Eric Lenneberg summarized the extensive work of Edward Sapir and Benjamin Whorf concerning the impact of language on "world view": "The structure of anyone's native language strongly influences or fully determines the world-view he will acquire as he learns the language."

Sapir (1884-1939) was a student of Franz Boas (1858-1942), the founder of American anthropology and the originator of "cultural relativism." Sapir's student, Whorf (1897-1941), a chemical engineer, studied linguistics in his spare time and together with Sapir developed the hypothesis that culture influences language and language influences culture. Whorf wrote that language affects how people perceive their reality and that language coerces thought. Hence, the content of a language is directly related to the content of a culture. We shall now apply this insight to the youth subculture which, like all subcultures, has developed a partial language of its own.[415]

---

415. Paul Kay and Willett Kempton, "What if the Sapir-Whorf Hypothesis," *American Anthropologist*, 86, no.1, (March 1984):65-79.

Language and Identity

American speech has been greatly influenced by the use of terminology first employed by adolescents in an effort to maintain an identity separate from that of adults. Because those who employ such sub-cultural language become adults themselves, it is inevitable that many expressions at one time the province of teens have become the language of adults.

The linguist Mary Bucholtz calls language "a set of resources" and claims that the symbolic use of language to perform identity will endure as long as language itself. She shows that the media facilitated the dissemination of distinctive hairstyles, music, dance, clothing and language of the young in the 20th and 21st centuries and that this trend has been accelerated by the Internet. Inasmuch as the young are the most proficient and the most frequent users of the digital media, it is to be expected that new forms of language will continuously evolve from that source.[416]

Media used by adolescents have helped create the language of youth. First, there is web-based communication as used in the so-called "chat rooms." In addition, there are the expressions created by the lyrics in rock-punk songs. There are "zines," erstwhile magazines, and graffiti (derived from Greek, *graphein*, to write). In addition, foreign expressions enter the language of the youth culture, in part because the Internet is worldwide (despite the obvious fact that English is the dominant international language used in the electronic media).[417]

In addition, there is a new Asian influence as the direct outcome of the "new immigration" which has brought 13.1 million people of Asian origin to the United States. They constituted about 5% of the American population in 2000. Since then the Asian population has grown another 9%, the highest rate of growth of any group in America today. Asian cultures are now impacting American youth in an unprecedented way.

The youth culture influences language just as it influences choices in clothing, hairstyles, recreational activities and musical tastes. Of course, all youths are not interested in the punk culture or in rock music or slam dancing. In fact, there are many adolescents who seek good grades in school; who want to emulate parents; and who dress and speak conservatively. Such youngsters are

---

416. Mary Bucholtz, "Language and Youth Culture," *American Speech*, 75, no. 3 (2000):280-283.
417. Ibid. p. 281.

called "nerds," in the slang of the adolescent world. [418] Many, of course, are somewhere in the middle.

THE USES OF SLANG

"Slang" is related to the Norwegian phrase "slengja kjeften," meaning "to sling the jaw" or to use abusive language. English "slang" consists almost always of "four letter words," which may be considered obscene if they pertain to bodily functions. "Four letter words" are considered casual or disrespectful in comparison with the "educated" Latin- or French-derived words meaning roughly the same thing (for instance, longer words ending in "-tion"). This goes back to the time of the Norman-French victory at the Battle of Hastings, in 1066. Having invaded England, the Norman-French ruled there and constituted the upper class. The local Anglo-Saxons spoke a Germanic language, which primarily consisted of short words. That language was viewed as inferior. The two languages merged into modern English, but the short words continued to bear a negative overtone. [419]

Adolescents use "slang" in part to evade adults. This may be compared to the way lawyers use Latin terms (such as *amicus curiae*, "friend of the court," or *certiorari*, "to be informed" or *stare decisis*, "to stand by a decision"). Such phrases partially hide the legal profession from its clients, making it somewhat mysterious. Physicians and all other professions use the same device. This permits the subculture to set boundaries between itself and the "lay" world. In the case of adolescents, adults are the "lay" world.

Language also indicated status. It labels some people admirable and others reprehensible. The prestige of any youngster in school or other adolescent gathering may be gauged by the language used to describe his group affiliation. The language used refers, then, to the amount of respect an adolescent can expect in his social system. [420]

---

418. No author, "Asian Pacific American Heritage Month," *Facts and Features*, (Washington: D.C., US Census Bureau, April 19 2004):FF06.

419. No author, *Webster's Dictionary of English usage*, (Springfield, Mass. Merriam – Webster.1989).

420. Paul Kay, "Ethnographic Semantics: A Preliminary Survey," *Current Anthropology*, 7, (February 1966):20-21.

The outstanding anthropologist Clyde Kluckhohn wrote: "how people behave toward one another is, in part, a function of what they call each other and how they conceive objects, themselves, other people and types of events which enter into their relations."[421]

Adolescents enjoy a limited amount of autonomy; they are no longer children under the constant supervision of adults, nor are they adults responsible for their own sustenance and that of a family. Adolescents may sometimes conduct themselves in a raucous and ridiculous manner, demonstrating freedom from adult supervision and group autonomy. The youth culture contains a distinctive social reality. It includes norms or expected, admirable behavior for boys and for girls. Because the very structure of adult society generates at least some rebellion among adolescents against adult authority, it may appear that the expectations or norms of the youth culture are the result of intergenerational conflict. In fact, such rebellion against the older generation is rare.

Instead the existence of the youth culture may be attributed to an unspoken agreement between the generations that each will leave the other alone and not interfere in its activities. Teenagers then become self centered as they concentrate on issues of importance to them. These are friendships, the opposite sex and such activities as school, music, dancing and sports. The segregation of the young from working adults leads many adolescents to the conclusion that only their peers can understand them. That dependence on other adolescents can then result in either gratifying or mortifying experiences.[422]

These experiences are concentrated in high schools, where adolescents live most of the time. In America, academic interests rank lowest even among the best students. Instead, personal worth depends on sex role identification. For boys, physical strength and athletic ability are of most importance. In addition, masculinity requires willingness to fight and sexual and drinking prowess. Feminine virtues, according to adolescents, are physical attractiveness and, most of all, the ability to manipulate interpersonal relationships.

Adolescent language reflects these realities for adolescents, just as professional "slang" reflects any professional subculture from accountants to zoologists. For example, the word "trip" was coined in the 1960s to refer to a very good or very bad experience with LSD, a psychedelic drug which gained some fol-

421. Clyde Kluckhohn, "Culture and Behavior," In: Gardner Lindsay, Editor, *Handbook of Social Psychology* (Reading, Mass. Addison-Wesley Publishing, 1954)p. 938.
422. Frank Musgrove, *Youth and the Social Order*, (Bloomington, Ind. Indiana University Press, 1965).

lowing in the Sixties. Although outlawed in the US, LSD has become part of the American vocabulary. At the beginning of the new century, LSD is once more as popular as it was in the 1960s, despite a decline in popularity among high school students in the '70s and '80s. In the 1990s, one study reported 8.8% of all high school students claimed to have made an annual "trip" on LSD.[423]

While the word "trip" was at one time associated only with LSD, it has now come to mean anything unusual, including the designation of someone deemed to be peculiar. Such a person may be referred to as a "dude" as in "that dude is a real trip." (The word "dude" is derived from the word "dud," meaning a delicate weakling.[424] Think of a "dude ranch.")

Some slang used by adolescents appears rude and deliberately rebellious. The phrase "pissed off," meaning "angry" or "upset," is an example.

The word "geek" may have been used first in Shakespeare's *Twelfth Night*, Scene I, as Malvolio says to Olivia: "Why have you suffered me to be imprisoned, kept in a dark house, visited by the Priest; And made the most notorious gecke and gull That e'er invention played on?"[425]

Some slang has been used for many years and can be found in old dictionaries of historical slang, such as a 1785 book by Francis Rose called A Classical Dictionary of the Vulgar Tongue.[426]

The use of slang may evolve in four ways. First, the term may persist over a long time although it changes its meaning. This is true of "punk," which in Shakespeare's time meant a whore but now means an immature "wise guy." Second, the slang term could be elevated to relative respectability. Examples are "yankee," "eavesdrop" or "crony." Third, the slang can keep the same meaning but only among a few "insiders." An example is "ding," a word used by pickpockets. Fourth, words disappear from the language entirely. Examples are "grunters" and "mopuses," which both meant money.[427]

423. The Trustees of Indiana University, "LSD Makes a Comeback in the 1990s" *Current Issues in Drug Abuse Prevention*, (Bloomington, Ind., Indiana Prevention Resource Center, January 13, 2004):1.

424. Eric Partridge, *A concise dictionary of slang and unconventional English*, (London, Routledge, 1989).

425. Bruce Colville, *William Shakespear's Twelfth Night*, (New York: Dial Books, 2003).

426. Francis Grose, Eric Partridge, Editor, *A Classical Dictionary of the Vulgar Tongue*, 1785 (New York: Barnes Publishing Co., 1963).

427. David W. Maurer and Ellesa Clay High, "New Words-Where Do They Come From and Where Do They Go?" *American Speech*, 55, (1980):184-194.

As adolescents molt into adults, younger people have to renew adolescent slang by adding terms or changing the meaning of earlier neologisms.

Slang terms may label people. Slang may also be used to evaluate people or events positively or negatively and slang may be used to label how time has been spent. The latter use of slang refers to spending time at parties, having sex, using drugs, or doing nothing.

Slang is also related to the several youth subcultures found in all American communities. This means that there is no one youth subculture but that the youth subculture is as diverse as the adult culture. In every high school and college there are some students who have been called the "leading crowd" or the "in" crowd, who are envied or even respected by other students. Usually these are the "jocks" or sports heroes or are at least identified by engaging in some sport; then there are "motor heads," i.e. students who are constantly talking about cars; and thirdly there are "flea bags" or drug users, both male and female.[428]

In other high schools somewhat different terms may be used, such as "intellectuals," "politicos," "jocks" and "rah-rahs"; or "academics," "fun" and "delinquents." Whatever the labels, the use of slang is certain in each group as an identifier and as a means of speaking of matters not always known to outsiders and particularly dealing with the use of drugs.

Slang is differentiated by gender. Boys are more likely than girls to use slang concerning cars, motorbikes and money, while girls will use slang in connection with clothes, styles, appearance and boys. The number of terms used in a study by Nelsen and Rosenbaum of 2000 youths in Madison, Wisconsin increased from grades 7 to 12 for both males and females, the older adolescents producing more terms for alcohol, drinking and the opposite sex.[429]

Slang is used by individuals as a means of identifying with a group. Therefore, slang reflects the social structure of a school, at parties, at home, at sports events and at work. In all these situations adolescents talk incessantly and make use of adolescent slang.

---

428. Matteo H. Leona, "An Examination of Adolescent Clique Language ion a Suburban Secondary School," *Adolescence*, 13, (1978):495-502.

429. Edward A. Nelsen and Edward Rosenbaum, "Language Patterns within the Youth Subculture: Development of Slang Vocabularies," *Merrill-Palmer Quarterly*, 28, (1981):273-284.

THE LANGUAGE OF INCARCERATED YOUTH

The young commit a disproportionate number of crimes of violence in this country and are therefore far more often incarcerated than the middle aged or the old. This is best understood by comparing the percentage of adolescents and young adults to the percentage of those arrested. Consider first that only 4.3% of Americans are between the ages of 13-15. Yet, 8.0% of persons arrested in this country belong to that age group. This becomes even more disproportionate in the age group 16-18. That age group are only 4.3% of all Americans but they constitute 13.9% of all arrested. Likewise, 19- 21-year-olds amount to 4.1% of the population with an arrest rate of 21.4% of all arrests.[430]

Incarceration rates as reported by The Bureau of Justice Statistics reflect this trend. These statistics show that those age 16 to 24 are most frequently incarcerated for violent crimes and that a large number of children under the age 18 are in American prisons.[431]

The language of American prisoners is also the language of a segment of American youths. Prison language is as old as prisons themselves. It is also based on social class and race. Although only 13% of Americans are of African descent, Afro-Americans make up 29% of all incarcerated youths. The disproportion of minorities in American prisons leads directly to the far greater use of prison argot among black youths than white youths.[432]

Prison language is sometimes called argot ("slang" in French). This slang plays a role in establishing a prisoner's identity just as it identifies other young people not incarcerated. The use of such language, as always, is to exclude outsiders. If the meaning of words is known only to the initiated few, the group reinforces its shared identity.

Codes are also used by prisoners and by youths on the streets. A code is a means of keeping one's business away from others and thereby reducing the chance of being arrested (in the community) or being sent to the hole (isolation) in prisons and mental hospitals. Sometimes a small group of youths uses a code which they change if it becomes apparent that others are also using it. Codes are

430. Roy Lotz, *Youth Crime in America*, (Upper Saddle River, N.J., Pearson-Prentice Hall, 2005)p.37
431. Kevin J. Strom, "Profile of State Prisoners," *Bureau of Justice Statistics Special Report*, (Washington D.C., U.S Department of Justice, February 2000).
432. Jack E. Bynum and William E. Thompson, *juvenile Delinquency*, (Boston, Allyn and Bacon, 2002)p.63.

not only used to insure secrecy, but are also symbols of identity as "cons," "outlaws" and/or "inmates."

Secret languages have been called "cant." In prison, cant is particularly useful in segregation. Cant is used wherever there is a great deal of suspicion and mistrust between two different populations as between prisoners and guards, patients and doctors, teachers and students, men and women.

THE USE OF SUBSTITUTIONS

There are also aspects of adolescent speech that substitute whole phrases for normal American English. Most common among these phrases is "I'm like" or "she's like" or "he's like" for I said or she said or he said.

The words be+ like function much in the same way as the verb "say" to report speech. The phrase "be+like" can also infer thought rather than speech. "I saw the movie and I'm like, what a bore."

The use of "like" as a substitute for "say" or "think" is mostly promoted by teen girls and seldom used by boys. In fact, 83% of those who use "like" to indicate speech are female. Because adolescents in the US are mainly socialized in a single sex peer group, it is not surprising that an expression can be mainly limited to one sex or another. Since the word "like" tends to "communicate affect and emotional involvement, ...it is associated with the female communicative style."

Adolescents also use the word "go" to indicate speech. Suzanne Romaine and Deborah Lange exhibit a conversation between two teenage girls: "I go, 'why'? She goes: 'Her Mom's makin' her,' I go: 'ah, ah, ah.' She comes back and goes: 'Nancy's left.'"[433]

Romaine and Lange call the use of "like" in its new meaning as accepted by young women an instance of "grammaticalization." They define this word as "an unidirectional historical process whereby lexical items acquire a new status as grammatical...forms.[434]

---

433. Suzanne Romaine and Deborah Lange, "The use of like as a Marker of Reported Speech and Thought: A Case of Grammaticalization in Progress. *American Speech*, 66, no.3, (Autumn 1991):227-279.
434. Ibid.p. 257.

GOSSIP

Gossip has been defined as "evaluative talk about a person who is not present." Gossip is universal among adolescents and has been viewed as a means of strengthening "in-group" bonds by projecting a positive self-image at the expense of the "out-group"[435] or individual outsiders.

Some researchers have discovered that adolescent gossip functions to solve personal problems, although it also promotes group solidarity and defines group norms (expectations). Girls, more than boys, engage in gossip as a substitute for open hostilities, and bring about consensus in a group.

As an example of how gossip can enhance one person's image at the expense of another, while promoting solidarity (among all but the target of the gossip), consider the case of Caitlin and Jennie. They are rivals and vie for attention from the boys in their eighth grade class. Caitlin sees Jennie as more attractive than herself, although both are very nice looking thirteen-year-olds. Caitlin convinced herself that Jen had "stolen" the so-called boyfriend of Jane. She did not hesitate to inform her classmates as well as Jane of this "fact," since she had observed Jen speaking in close proximity to the boy in question and "putting her hands on him." All of Jane and Caitlin's friends ostracized Jennie and added to the gossip. Jennie was soon shunned by the other girls in the class. Caitlin's story and gossip made her very "important" and classmates avidly repeated her "juicy" details of the unforgivable behavior of the unsuspecting Jen.

Gossip is primarily negative, although this will not remain so if someone among the gossipers challenges the negative evaluation that gossip normally produces.[436]

The key elements that identify gossip are the identification of a target who is not present. Groups of adolescents engage in gossip particularly against those with low status. Such gossip strengthens group bonds.

The main topic of gossip among adolescent females is appearance of other students and "conceited" behavior of a particular girl. Among boys, the principal topic of gossip deals with athletic prowess.[437]

---

435. Niko Besnier, "Information Withholding as a Manipulative and Collusive Strategy in Nukulae Gossip," *Language in Society*, 18, (1989):315-341.

436. Donna Eder, " The Role of Teasing in Adolescent Peer Culture," In: S. Cahill, Editor, *Sociological Studies of Child Development*, 4, (Greenwich, CT, JAI Press) pp. 179-195.

MINORITIES AND LANGUAGE

In 1979 a Federal District Court handed down a decision in favor of eleven African American children in Ann Arbor, Michigan. According to that decision, the Ann Arbor School District Board was held responsible for failing to prepare teachers at the Martin Luther King, Jr. school to adequately teach children whose native tongue was "African-American English." Judge Charles Joiner objected to the teachers treating Afro-American students like all students because such equal treatment failed to take into account that Afro-American English constitutes a language barrier that impeded the students' educational progress.[438]

This meant that the court held the school board and the teachers responsible for the inadequate educational progress of the black children involved. The decision was further interpreted to mean that the court considers Black English to be a distinct language that should be respected like any foreign language. The court allowed that Black-English speakers are at a disadvantage in schools, in business and in the general community.

Teachers and others generally consider Afro-American English to be a product of low education, and tend to believe that those who speak that way ought to learn to "speak properly." Therefore, students who use that English are constantly corrected and admonished to improve. Children who use "black" English at home may have difficulty reading; they also find it awkward to interact with speakers of standard English. Thus, they shut themselves out of the opportunities standard English would afford them.

Black English has been called "Ebonics," a word derived from ebony and phonics. An example of the use of black English in school is the following: "Bobby, what does your mother do?" "She be at home." "You mean she *is* at home." "No, she ain't." "You aren't supposed to say: 'she *be* at home'; you say, 'she *is* at home'. "Why you tryin' to make me lie? She *ain't* at home."

In Afro-American English, "she be at home" means an ongoing status. "She is at home" means a present condition existing now. This distinction doesn't exist in standard English.[439] The existence of patterns like this sets this lan-

---

437. Lynne Smith-Lovin and Charles Brody, "Interpretations in Group Discussions: The Effect of Gender and Group Composition," *American Sociological Review*, 54, (1989):424-435.

438. Memorandum, Opinion and Order. Martin Luther King Elementary School Children v. Ann Arbor School District Board. Civil Action No. 7-71861. 473 F. Supp. 1371 (1979).

guage or dialect apart from mere "sloppy" language; however, it remains a topic of debate how significant the distinction is and, indeed, what to do about it. The millions of American children and adolescents who speak this way are rein-forcing the solidarity of their community but at the expense of being able to join or at least pass through the community of "success," including educational attainment and better jobs. For this reason, many Black leaders do not support the promotion of Ebonics, as it becomes just one more means of keeping people down.

No better example concerning the controversy surrounding Ebonics exists than the decision of the Oakland School Board of Education to teach Standard American English proficiency based on Ebonics or Pan-African Communication Behaviors or African Language systems. The idea was to use Ebonics as a tran-sition to Standard American English. This, however, was roundly denounced by the Rev. Jesse Jackson, by Kweise Mfume, a.k.a. Frizell Gray, President of the National Association of Colored People and a former congressman, and by the comedian Bill Cosby. Jackson called Ebonics "garbage language," Mfume called it "a cruel joke" and Cosby called it "Ignobonics."[440]

The American Speech-Language Hearing Association has labeled Ebonics a legitimate variety of English. Whatever their motivation for doing that may have been, the fact is that a large number of Afro-American children and adoles-cents cannot speak and/or write an English that is acceptable in the business world or in higher education.

A second group of youths who have considerable difficulty because they lack a good knowledge of the English language are those generally called His-panics.

It is important to recognize that all Latino children do not come from the same ethnic background, because Puerto Rican civilization is quite different from Mexican culture, and both differ from other Spanish-speaking countries such as Colombia and Cuba. Meanwhile, Brazilians do not speak Spanish but Portuguese and Haitians speak a French. Keeping these differences in mind, there are nonetheless some general language problems encountered by Latino school children.

---

439. Harry N. Seymour, Lamya Abdulkarim and Valerie Johnson, "The Ebonics Contro-versy: An Educational and Clinical Dilemma," *Top Long Discord*, 19, no.4 (1999):66-77.
440. Ibid.,p. 68.

The Mexican-American Opportunity Foundation reports that an achievement gap exists between academic performance of Hispanic children and non-Hispanic children. According to the MAOF, Hispanic students perform below their non-Hispanic peers in reading, math, and science by age nine and more than one third of Latino students of high school age are enrolled below grade level.

One aspect of this gap is the failure of Hispanic students to keep up with the reading skills of other students. Hispanics lag behind other students in reading achievement by an average of 30 points.

Hispanics are the largest minority group enrolled in US public schools; one of every six children attending public schools in the US is of Hispanic origin. Forty nine percent of Hispanic children are the children of immigrants who do not speak English at home. In 1970, one million Hispanic children were enrolled in US public schools; in 2000 that number was 8.6 million. They comprise three quarters of the population with limited English skills. Furthermore, many Hispanic children attend schools in which over a third of students have limited English skills.

Budget cuts add to the problem. In Buffalo, NY, a $28 million budget cut directly impacted the services to English language learners as five full-time classroom teachers and one administrator were eliminated from the English program. Similar budgetary difficulties faced numerous other cities with large Hispanic populations.[441]

NO CHILD LEFT BEHIND ACT OF 2001

In 2001, Congress passed the No Child Left Behind Act, which President George W. Bush signed on January 8, 2002. This act included support for English language learners and new accountability for Hispanic and Afro-American children.

The act addresses the particular problems of adolescents in the Hispanic community, whose students have the highest "dropout" rate of any group in the country, i.e., 27%. This may well be related to the failure of many Hispanic children to learn to read, as shown by the fact that only 16% of Hispanic students

---

441. No author, Hispanic Education Report, *Mexican-American Opportunity Foundation,* (July 2002):1-24.

scored at or above proficient in reading as reported by National Assessment of Educational Progress.

Only 12% of Afro-Americans children scored at or above proficient on reading tests while 40% of European-American children did so.[442]

There has been a good deal of controversy concerning the "No Child Left Behind" Act. That law mandates annual testing of all students receiving federal funds. As a result, some school districts have tied teachers' and administrators' pay to the results of these examinations. Therefore, teachers in several states have altered students' exam papers, helped students during exams, failed to count dropouts or special education students, and allowed students to share answers during exams.

Those who defend the law claim that the illegal practices of some teachers are not the fault of the law but of the faculties who engage in them, and that overall these tests will improve English usage and mathematics proficiency.[443]

Because of the criticism concerning the "No Child Left Behind" legislation, a significant relaxation of testing requirements for students with limited knowledge of English was allowed in February of 2004.

READING AND WRITING AT RISK

One aspect of youth language which is widespread in secondary schools and colleges appears truly irrational. This is the strange phenomenon sometimes called "mangled vocabulary." It is found in all American high schools and colleges and has been summarized by Professor Anders Henriksson in a book entitled *Non Campus Mentis*. His examples are taken from term papers and examinations involving history. However, the writings of students of other subjects are equally peculiar. Teachers in all parts of the country, teaching all subjects, report that they have seen the kind of writing which Henriksson has published. A few of his examples will serve to illustrate the nature of "mangled vocabulary" and the addled thought process that could produce it.

• Judyism ... had one big God named Yahoo;

---

442. US Department of Education, "Promoting Educational Excellence for All Americans," Washington, D.C. 1-5.
443. Brina Grow, "A Spate of Cheating: ---by Teachers," *Business Week*, 3890 (July 5, 2004):3

- the Book of Exodus describes [this] trip and the amazing things that happened on it, including ... the building of the Suez Canal;
  - Plato invented reality;
  - a German soldier put Rome in a sack;
  - the McDoughal Empire grew on the Indian submarine continent;
  - death rates exceeded 100% in some towns;
  - an angry Martin Luther nailed 95 theocrats to a church door;
  - deism was the belief that God made the world and then stepped on it;
  - the airplane was invented and first flown by the Marx brothers;
  - that Prussia's army was well brained;
  - that we should give peas a chance.[444]

This pattern includes far more than spelling and grammatical errors alone; irrational statements are not uncommon, such as the assertion that the Second World War "Big Three" consisted of Roosevelt, Truman, Churchill and Stalin. Such writing indicates not only a lack of interest in the subject matter but an inability to concentrate on the written word, whether a book or a sentence one is writing, oneself. This inability to focus on the written word comes from a lack of practice, mostly because so many teens have been raised on television and/or the Internet.

The full explanation for this astounding lack of writing skills on the part of American youth are not readily at hand. However, several possible contributing factors can be listed as having at least some influence.

It is safe to say that those who read a good deal of literature cannot help but acquire language competence, including good writing. But the National Endowment for the Arts reports that the steepest decline in reading has occurred among young adults, ages 18-24.

In a report published in June of 2004, The National Endowment for the Arts listed some key findings that relate to reading skills among young Americans. These findings are first, that over the 20 years ending in 2002, the percentage of adults reading literature has dropped from 56.9% to 46.7%. This means that less than half of the adult population of the US now reads literature and that the decline of 10% of literary reading represents a loss of 20 million, mostly young readers. The decline in literary reading parallels a decline of 7% in total book reading. Further, the NEA report shows that the rate of reading has declined, from –5% in 1992 to –14% in 2002. This decline is greater among men

---

444. Anders Henriksson, *Non Campus Mentis*, (New York, Workman Publishing, 2001).

than women and is most severe among Hispanic Americans, followed by Euro-Americans and least among Afro-Americans.

Although higher education levels are associated with higher reading rates, reading among every group has declined over the twenty years ending in 2002. This means that 66.7% of college graduates read, but only 37.7% of high school graduates read. Among grade school graduates the reading level is 14% as of 2002. The percentage of decline of readers at each level does not entirely follow educational levels. Thus, the rate of reading decline for college graduates and those with some high school is 15.4% while high school graduates exhibit a reading decline over twenty years of 16.5%. However, the reading decline of those with some college was 20% during the same twenty year period.

All age groups show a decline in literary reading. This is most severe among those 18-24 years of age whose reduction of literary readers amounted to −17% while those over 65 suffered a decline of only 1.9%.

Most remarkable is that the decline in literary reading foreshadows an erosion in cultural and civic participation. Literary readers are more likely than non-readers to visit art museums, attend performing art events and attend sporting events. The difference is considerable, as 49% of literary readers attend performing arts events but only 17% of non-readers do so.[445]

The decline in reading correlates with an increase in the use of a host of electronic media. These include the Internet, video games, portable digital devices and television. Of course, non-readers watch more television than readers. This is illustrated by the fact that in 1990 book buying constituted 5.7% of all recreational spending while spending on electronic devices was 6%. In 2002, electronic spending had quadrupled to 24%, while spending on books declined slightly to 5.6%.

The average American child lives in a household with three televisions, two video cassette recorders, three radios, two CD players, one to two video games and one computer; books can hardly meet that immense competition.

All of this has a direct influence on high school and college writing and "functional illiteracy." A functional illiterate is someone who may be able to read and write his name but who cannot read and comprehend a book. (The word "cannot," in this sense, does not apply to a physical disability but to a state of mind. The television state of mind.)

---

445. Tom Bradshaw, Bonnie Nichols and Kelly Hill, *Reading at Risk: A Survey of Literary Reading in America*, (Washington, D.C. National Endowment for the Arts, 2004).

American children ages 2-17 watch television about 25 hours per week. Twenty percent of 2- 7-year-olds have a TV in their bedroom. This increases to 46% of 8- 12-year-olds and 56% of 13- 17-year-olds. Children spend more time watching television than doing anything else except sleeping.[446]

Early cognitive development is influenced by the development of brain neural networks. Those networks are subject to heavy television viewing on the part of children ages 3-5. The time spent viewing television is not spent on verbal interaction and that in turn influences the development of speaking, reading and writing skills. Reading and writing fluency comes with practice. Reading becomes a pleasure for those who have spent a good deal of time doing so. This is not the case for those who are constantly engaged in electronic viewing. Television, the Internet and electronic games constantly change. They inhibit the development of an attention span sufficient to read a book (in which the letters are supposed to remain still on the page). That leads to a dislike of books and homework, so that nationally, across the United States, students spend four times as much time watching television than reading school assignments. Those who are the heaviest television watchers show the greatest decline in reading and writing ability. Furthermore, the impact of television on reading and writing ability depends not only on how much is being watched, but also the content of what is watched.[447]

The consequences of television watching snowball as children get older. Those who are already heavily into TV at a young age have an ever greater difficulty divorcing themselves from that entertainment long enough to attend to schoolwork. The exception are those who have seen a good number of educational programs. Such TV viewing is associated with higher grades, more reading, less aggression and more value placed on academics in high school.[448]

446. D.A. Gentile and D.A. Walsh, "A normative study of family media habits," *Applied Developmental Psychology*, 23, (January 2002):157-178.

447. David Reinking and J.H. Wu, "Re-examining the research on television and reading," *Reading Research and Instruction*, 29, (1990): 30-43.

448. David.R.Anderson, A.C. Houston, K. Schmitt, D.L. Linebarger and J.C. Wright, "Early childhood television viewing and adolescent behavior: the re-contact study," *Monographs for the Society for Research in Child Development*, 66, no. 264 (2001).

SOCIAL PROMOTION

The gradation of school experiences into classes based on age began with the development of universal public education around the time of the First World War. Prior to that era, many American children still attended a one room schoolhouse during those months when they were not needed on the family farm.

With the advent of age gradation, it became necessary to promote children from one grade to another with the presumption that the child had learned the lessons of the previous grade and was now ready to absorb more advanced material.

As more and more American children were unable to meet the requirements for promotion to the next grade, "social promotion" was substituted for academic promotion in areas and school districts where parents adamantly insisted that their child be promoted, competent or not. The notion is that it is socially detrimental to a child to keep him back to repeat a grade.

The Chicago school system is a good example of an American public school because it includes children of many different races, ethnic groups and religions. It serves 431,000 children of every economic level. Prior to 1997, Chicago schools, like many other schools across the US, routinely promoted children who had learned very little from one grade to another with their classmates. Fourteen states have used this "social promotion" in the past. As a result employers no longer trust the school system to furnish them with educated adults; many of the graduates of the Chicago schools could not even fill out a job application.

Since 1997, Chicago has adopted the Iowa Tests of Basic Skills, which are given to all 3rd, 6th and 7th graders each May. Those who do not achieve a reasonable score on these tests are sent to summer school for six weeks of intense work. Then, another test is administered; those who still do not pass are retained and not promoted to the next grade. The Iowa Tests of Basic Skills were devised by the faculty at the University of Iowa. The tests include a test that measures "listening vocabulary." There is also a word analysis test and a reading comprehension test. This is augmented by a listening test and a language test. The language test measures students' ability to understand linguistic relationships.

This method of weeding out poor learners has its critics. There are children who may know the subject matter but who are "not good at taking tests." Others have poor vision and need eyeglasses, which parents cannot necessarily afford. Because retained children receive extra help, about one third are

222

admitted to the next grade at midyear. Others do even worse on retention than before, because they are discouraged at having to repeat a grade.

Reading difficulties are by no means limited to Chicago. The *New York Times* reported in 2004 that nationwide 25% of ninth grade students are unable to read well enough to take high school courses. Many of those who cannot read well drop out of high school because they cannot compete in the higher grades. Often, a poor reader may slip through the system and go unnoticed until the higher grades, when guessing and faking it are no longer sufficient to get by.

While most schools emphasize reading in the third grade, adolescents are faced with a real educational and vocational crisis if they cannot read adequately when they reach 12th grade. To alleviate the reading problems of high school age children, the Phoenix, AZ school system has arranged for 3,600 high school 9th and 10th graders with low reading scores to spend 110 minutes a day in a reading program. Most of the students in that program never liked reading, had poor educational experiences and no academic success. The Phoenix program is one of the few in the country dealing with adolescent illiteracy.[449]

In sum, 80% of teachers favor the retention program as a better solution than social promotion, which passes failure from one grade to another until students who can neither read well nor write adequately may even enter college, without a minimum of language skills.[450]

THE CONTRIBUTION OF HIGHER EDUCATION TO POOR WRITING SKILLS

Those who come to college without the ability to write good English are seldom challenged to do better. One reason for this is the abandonment of the liberal arts. The "liberal" arts were so named because those free to study without needing to learn a vocation were "liberated" from economic worries and studied for the sake of knowledge alone. Such studies as philosophy and history, mathematics and sociology allowed students to read classic texts in these fields and absorb good language. At the beginning of the 21st century, however, specialization is in vogue, leading even those who have written a doctor's dissertation to write in professional jargon. Such language, if it makes sense at all, is known

449. Tamar Lewin, "In Cities, A Battle to Improve Teenage Literacy," *The New York Times*, (April 14, 2004)Sec. B:11.
450. Beth Nissen, "Ending Social Promotion," *US News*, (June 28, 2000):1-4.

only to a few specialists who use these esoteric phrases to exclude everyone else. This love of jargon makes academic journals almost unintelligible to students.

An additional obstacle to learning good writing skills is that almost all freshman composition courses are taught by part-time instructors, whose ability to impart good English to youngsters may not be their greatest skill.[451]

Even full-time English teachers are usually overwhelmed by the size of classes and the need to read a vast number of papers every week. Teachers of English and of other courses are constantly confronted with imprecise language, poor punctuation, dreadful grammar and confused thought bordering on the laughable.

Nevertheless, there is another side to all of this. In the past several years, many high schools and colleges have made a major effort to teach the English language to that vast number of "functional illiterates" who annually move from grade to grade, from year to year, without developing language skills that are essential to their vocational aims and to their standing as capable adults.

THE OTHER SIDE

At the end of the 1980s, some small liberal arts colleges instituted a program to improve writing skills among their students. The program was called "Writing Across the Curriculum." Today, in 2005, large public universities and Ivy League schools alike have introduced the program, thereby changing the entire educational process at the higher education level.

"Writing Across the Curriculum" follows the teachings of John Dewey (1859-1952), the philosopher of "progressive education," and also supports the more modern demand that education consolidate several fields of knowledge. Students often believe that job preparation is all that they want from their college education. Therefore, accounting students or engineering students or students in any area usually overlook the need to learn good writing.[452] "Writing Across the Curriculum" links writing to the special subject matter in which a student is enrolled, and makes students aware that writing is a frequently used skill, no matter what their occupational goals.

---

451. George H. Douglas, "Why College Students Can't Write," *Liberal Education*, 79, no.3 (Summer 1993):3.
452. Susan McLeod, "Defining Writing Across the Curriculum," *WPA: Writing Program Administration*, 11, no.1-2, (Fall 1987):19-24.(Fall 1987):

It is fairly certain that those now in high school or college will face more than one career change during their working years. That fact alone should induce everyone to learn to write a reasonable letter of application and to sustain employment thereafter. The use of good English is required in every field, and provides an edge in job competition. Police captains have complained that they cannot read the reports of some of the officers reporting to them because the narrative makes no sense and cannot be interpreted; citizens filing complaints have observed that some desk officers seem unable to work their way through a two-page letter.

The inability to write well enough to convey to others what is meant is illustrated by the Philadelphia experience. The public high schools of that city enroll about 1,200 new students in the 9th grade each year. On average only 200 of these students receive high school diplomas and hardly any enter a four-year college. A large contingent of these students are of Latino origin. These failures then contribute a great deal to the public welfare rolls and to juvenile crime, and may well be called a social catastrophe.[453]

"Writing Across the Curriculum" involves numerous disciplines. For example, at the State University of New York College at Buffalo, numerous departments maintain courses which require the student to write, instead of administering only multiple choice tests. Anthropology includes a course on Folklore and Life that demands written work. Likewise, Creative Problem Solving, Broadcast Copy Writing, Seminar in Criminal Justice, Micro-economics, School and Society, Medieval Europe, Experimental Psychology and Social Thought all require writing. This means that in all these courses and others, student involvement is paramount. These courses use writing as a means of learning outside of the standard English instruction. In WAC classes, each student engages in a specific project within the discipline under consideration. The projects also teach critical thinking, the lack of which is apparent in such writing as this: "The Civil Rights movement in the US turned around the corner with Martin Luther Junior's famous 'If I Had a Hammer' speech." Or, "One index of this situation is a poor infant morality rate.[454]

In sum, a Writing Across the Curriculum program will have the salutary effect of encouraging students to learn to think clearly and express thoughts precisely.

---

453. North Philadelphia Community Compact Data Report, 1995-1996.
454. Henriksson, *Non Campus Mentis*, pp. 134-135.

REMEDIAL ENGLISH

In addition to the Writing Across the Curriculum effort, almost all colleges and universities now include "remedial English" in their programs. To discover who needs remedial writing courses, the City University of New York Writing Assessment Test was introduced to all seventeen colleges in that system several years ago. Students who failed that test had been required to enroll in a basic writing course, even if they have been accepted by one of the senior colleges in the system. Such acceptance rests on SAT scores, junior college or high school achievements and/or class rank. Although one half of the CUNY students are of foreign birth, the same test is applied to them as to native speakers of English.

While remedial or basic English courses have many supporters, there has been a good deal of criticism of this effort on the part of those who view the need for remedial English as a consequence of the open admission policy of the City University of New York. This policy was altered when, in 1988, the Trustees of the City University of New York approved a resolution requiring that all students wishing to enter one of the senior colleges to first pass CUNY's reading, writing and math skills assessment tests.[455]

Then, on May 26, 1998, that same board of trustees passed a resolution phasing out all remedial course instruction. It also barred from the senior colleges anyone who had failed even one of the three skills tests required by the university. Writing is, of course, one of these. Consequently the enrollment at CUNY fell by 25% over six years.

Those who object to these policies and support open admissions point to former students who improved immensely upon entering a college, despite poor high school records and failure to pass the several admissions tests.

There can be little doubt that the experience concerning remedial English courses at the City University of New York involved racial and ethnic differences. Poor whites, blacks and Hispanics were and are more severely affected by the ending of the remedial English program than are more affluent students. In fact, social class, status and role make a good deal of difference among all Americans and among adolescents both in and out of school. The role of social class

---

455. Karen Arenson, "With New Admissions Policy, CUNY Steps into the Unknown." *The New York Times,* (May 28, 1998):A1.

and status among American adolescents will therefore be the topic of the next chapter.

SUMMARY

The Sapir-Whorf hypothesis holds that language is influenced by personality and vice versa and that culture predetermines language. Language promotes identity. This is also true of slang which is so widespread that several authors have published dictionaries of slang. Slang is gendered. Slang may include grammatical shifts and substitute words, such as the contemporary use of such as "go" and "like" for "said."

Since language distinctions are an important part of identity, it both confirms belonging to one group and heightens exclusion from other groups. This can be a liability for those who are not in the "in group" in society at large, namely the largely white, educated middle and upper classes. At the same time, it is true that students who are not accustomed to standard English when they enter school will have a handicap in learning the subject matter. Thus, there is controversy over whether accommodations should be made, and to what extent, for non-English speakers and those who use the form of English sometimes called Ebonics.

Schools can contribute to the failure to learn standard American English by allowing social promotion; but the principal reason for that failure is lack of reading. Colleges have had to make up for students' poor language skills by instituting the "Writing Across the Curriculum" method to improve the use of English among college students and graduates.

CHAPTER 11. STATUS, CLIQUES AND GANGS

STATUS DEFINED

Status may be defined as any position in any social arrangement. Examples are husband and wife, teacher and student or senior and junior. Every status involves a role. A role is here defined as the sum of the obligations incurred by assuming any status. A husband and a wife are expected to play a role, such as supporting each other financially, emotionally and physically. Likewise, "teacher" is a status. In his role, the teacher is expected to impart new skills and information to a student, whose status-role requires that he make an effort to attend class, complete assignments and pass examinations. The concept of "master status" is the status that identifies a person even to strangers. For example, being a Rockefeller or a Kennedy is a master status that outweighs any other role the individual might fulfill. People hold a status and perform a role.

A status may be either ascribed or achieved. An ascribed status is beyond the individual's control. It is given at birth, and includes such characteristics as female or male. An achieved status is gained by one's own action. An example is high school or college graduate.[456]

The most important means of measuring status in the United States is occupation. Occupational status is prestige. The National Opinion Research Center polls Americans almost every year to discover the prestige rankings of

---

456. John J. Macionis, *Sociology*, (Upper Saddle River, N.J. Prentice Hall, 2001)p.147

various occupations. According to their reports, as mentioned in Chapter 4, physician ranks first among 70 occupations. Bank teller and telephone operator rank approximately in the middle.[457]

Because the occupation of American adolescents is "student," it would seem that all student-adolescents have the same status in this country. That, however, is not the case. Student-adolescents reflect American culture and have developed a status-prestige system of their own which operates in every school and is based on a number of ascribed and achieved characteristics.

Some male students look like men at age 16. Some female students have the physical attributes of women at that age. Other students, also aged sixteen, look like children. Some students have great athletic prowess and therefore gain a great deal of status-prestige in the high school scheme of things. Others may shine academically or be the lead in a school play. For the vast majority of schoolchildren, none of these outstanding roles are available, so that they have to be content with the status-role assigned to them, like it or not. Children are more direct and far less subtle than adults. Therefore, the injuries of social class are more crudely expressed and more cruelly enforced in high schools and among adolescents than is general among adults.

THE HIGH SCHOOL SOCIAL SYSTEM

The high school status system reflects the values of American society, and so the lowest status in high school belongs to the so-called "nerds." "Nerds" are students who openly seek academic success. Equally low in prestige are those students who have few social skills and are called "geeks." Then there are "goths" or "freaks" or "punks," students who reject middle-class values and conventional conduct. The term "preps" or "preppies" may be used for those students who are generally more mature than others, are sexually active, use drugs and alcohol and hide all this from adults. Most of them are also concerned about the fashions they wear.[458]

Adolescents have no choice about being high school students. They must be in school for most of the day. They cannot change the teachers. They cannot change the administrators. They cannot influence the curriculum. The only

---

457. Ibid. p.274.
458. Carlos Santos, "High Schoolers Create Castes," *Richmond Times Dispatch*, (May 10, 2004):B-1.

power students have is to evaluate one another and thereby create their own status system. That system impinges on almost every child, since there is no escaping it. In high school, status becomes a "zero-sum" game. The only way anyone can be up is if someone else is down. There is a good deal of cruelty in the world of the high school student, as those who manage to hold onto high status must constantly keep others "in their place." That is done by constantly altering what style of music is "in," emphasizing one kind of hairstyle over another, or displaying fashionable clothes.

American youngsters are well aware of social class differences, although this awareness is usually obscured in the United States where it is customary to act as if social classes do not exist. It is considered offensive to acknowledge differences in rank, the way the British do. The pretense runs deep that making class distinctions is offensive and cannot be allowed in this democracy. Thus, there is a widespread belief in this country that nearly all Americans are middle class. Almost everyone, except for some unusually wealthy individuals and those living in the streets, will claim middle-class status. Yet, the same adolescents who deny social class and seek to evade class consciousness to the extent possible still answer written questions about social class in the US by asserting that they are well aware of the differences between the rich and the poor.[459] And that is an awareness that comes with adolescence.

By the time American children have reached high school they are certainly acquainted with occupational stratification and the positions of their families within that scheme. However, the egalitarian beliefs taught in American schools lead to status confusion in this country. American youths become convinced of everyone's potential for status improvement and for advancing one's career. This in turn excites the wish to improve one's condition by accumulating wealth. The United States, unlike most societies, has no aristocracy. Instead, status is largely acquired through material wealth. Competition for high status becomes more intense as one moves up in the stratification system, so that there are everywhere all kinds of signs of status achievements such as expensive cars, swimming pools, and club membership. All of this was already known to Alexis de Tocqueville in 1835, when he wrote in his classic book *Democracy in America*, "When inequality is the general rule in society, the greatest inequalities attract no

---

459. Roberta G. Simmons and Morris Rosenberg, "Functions of Children's Perceptions of the Stratification System," *American Sociological Review*, xxxvi (1971):244.

attention. When everything is more or less level, the slightest variation is noticed."[460]

European visitors have long commented on the American custom of behaving as if subordinates are fully equal to those above them. This may be seen in the use of first names even for bosses and others in positions of authority. This is a nod to the idea that "all men are created equal," in all aspects of human existence and not only as a matter of political rights. In keeping with this ideal, the "elevator" called education must be opened to all so that all can at least have a chance at becoming "rich and famous." The American population is indeed obsessed with upward mobility.[461]

That upward mobility is expressed in many ways, including residential segregation, in that those who can afford to do so live in the suburbs outside the cities and occupy far more land than is needed to accommodate their houses. The proliferation of gated communities is just the latest version of this. Families with little income squeeze into apartments or in houses crowded together in "poor neighborhoods."

Because adolescents are keenly aware of social class differences, they too practice class segregation based on such visible symbols as clothes worn to school. That in turn can lead to a good deal of resentment.

CONSPICUOUS CONSUMPTION

In 1899, the American sociologist Thorstein Veblen coined the phrase "conspicuous consumption" in his influential book, *The Theory of the Leisure Class*. Veblen meant the tendency of the wealthy and even the not-so-wealthy to buy expensive clothes and other products, not because they need them but because they exhibit the wealth of the user. Conspicuous consumption is well known in American schools.[462]

Some high school and even middle school children spend a great deal of money on expensive school clothes which others (and, sometimes, they) cannot afford. Such expenditure assures the consumers prestige and high social status

460. Alexis de Tocqueville, *Democracy in America*, George Lawrence, Translator, J.P. Mayer and Max Lerner, Editors, (New York, Harper and Row 1966)p.510.
461. John J. Macionis, *Sociology*, p.283.
462. Thorstein Veblen, *The Theory of the Leisure Class*, (New York: The New American Library, 1953, org. 1899).

in school. In order to prove how much was spent on clothes, some students insist on buying clothes with specific labels that all their peers will recognize.

Abercrombie & Fitch has already been mentioned. That chain of stores seeks the attention of adolescents by blaring rock music into the malls where they do business. They hire great-looking college age students to sell their goods. Each store is decorated with the pictures of well-built male and female entertainers of the "rock and roll" variety. The customers are junior high and high school girls and boys, who usually arrive in a group.

In these stores the youngsters find T-shirts and other clothes with sexual innuendos printed on them. The cost of these clothes is no doubt prohibitive to some, while easily affordable to others. For example, a poncho at A&F costs $49.50 and a velvet blazer with a ribbon costs $99.50. Jeans can cost as much as $133, although there are also some jeans for $98 and $70.

There is also Scoop, which sells cashmere sweaters for $195 and cashmere ponchos for $245, and a whole league of others. All are very expensive and sell not only clothes but also social prestige.[463] With prices like that, it is obvious that the average household cannot afford books. Comparable clothes do not cost that much in most department stores. For example, a poncho can be bought for $25-$30 at Sears and other such stores. Likewise, jeans can be had in the vicinity of $25.

It is not only the wealthy who buy clothes from these high-priced stores. Far from it. A good number of high school students buy the most expensive clothes with their earning from babysitting, car washing and slinging hamburgers. Parents also augment their income. The purpose of such expenditures is unquestionably "conspicuous consumption." Students who wear such items in school seek to attract the attention of the opposite sex and to enhance their status with both genders.

At the same time, there are some students who spend a great deal of money to wear dark, "gothic" clothes. These clothes may be ripped and/or exhibit safety pins or other features that are extreme contrasts to the sleek, finished fashions described above. Tough-looking boots and chains may be part of these "outfits." These clothes can also be extremely expensive, at such stores as Hot Topic.[464]

---

463. Julie Zeveloff and Lesley Messer, "WWDWALKTHROUGH: A Lesson in B-T-S.", *WWD*, (August 12, 2004):6.
464. Interview with Gabrielle Balderman, a sophomore at Kenmore West High School in Erie County, N.Y. August 29, 2004.

The function of this kind of "conspicuous consumption" is peer group seg-regation, leading to the selection of best friends and membership, both formal and informal, in socially homogeneous groups. The desire to consume is therefore the most important lesson taught in the American high school, even if that is not part of the curriculum.

THE MEANING OF FRIENDSHIPS

On reaching adolescence, young people spend more time with their friends than with their parents. This new association functions to allow youngsters to try on new identities and roles and to seek the approval of friends who serve as "looking glass selves." Thus, friends allow adolescents to assume more and more responsibility for themselves and distance themselves gradually from their parents. Still, parents continue to have a great deal of influence at the same time and usually survive as influential individuals adolescents need to use as their role models.[465]

Because social anxiety is at its height during mid-adolescence, friendship is most important during the ages 15-17. It is then that the kind of friends a child has selected will lead to behavior that may or may not be acceptable to important adults in his reference group. These are all the adults in his envi-ronment, such as parents and teachers and his peers. A reference group is any group whose norms are accepted and emulated. A reference group could be the family, congregation or class. For many people the family is the principal ref-erence group. Others may view their family with skepticism and use their friends and associates as their reference group.

It is easily observed that children, even before gaining access to adolescent friendship, will seek friends who behave as they do. Hence aggressive students seek other aggressive students and delinquent adolescents seek out other delin-quents. Research has shown that these associations come about because those who develop these friendships create their own social environment. Conse-quently, early aggression or delinquency or positive conduct such as school involvement all lead to later friendships with those of a similar bent.[466]

---

465. Peggy Giordano, Stephen Cernkovich, Theodore Groat, Meredith Pugh and Steven Swinford, "The Quality of Adolescent Friendships; Long Term Effects?" *Journal of Health and Social Behavior*, 39, (1998): 55-71.
466. Ross Matsueda and Kathleen Anderson, "The Dynamics of Delinquent Peers and Delinquent Behavior," *Criminology*, 36, (1998):269-398.

These associations then lead to a shared identity through interaction with valued others. These experiences allow youngsters to develop social competence and techniques used to include some and exclude others. Social conformity is learned, as well, in friendship groups. Some of these friendship groups become bullies in school and oppress other children. While bullying is usually attributed to boys who compete for athletic prowess, it is equally common among girls who compete for popularity.

It is an axiom of social psychology that aggressive children are popular among their peers. In fact, some observers argue that adolescents need to be aggressive to be popular. Popularity results in a sense of invulnerability among adolescents and the transfer of invulnerability into power. That power is produced by the wish of other adolescents, particularly in school, to be allowed to join a clique or "in-group" who are generally deemed "cute," "cool" and "talented." All this is interpreted among junior and senior high school students as "popular," because those who are deemed to belong to the "in crowd" are widely known and sought after as friends. Playing football and performing as a cheerleader allow boys and girls to wear uniforms (which are generally close-fitting) in class on days when sports events take place.[467]

Once a student has gained popularity, he or she must now maintain that status. This can be difficult because popularity depends on speaking to others, and acknowledging those who seek to spend time with the popular students without being labeled a "phony." A "phony" is someone who tries too hard to be friendly and thereby loses the popularity so difficult to attain.

As youngsters move up in the grades, attractiveness to the opposite sex becomes more and more important. Therefore, good-looking girls who are liked by boys and who date "important" boys are seen as popular. The same is true of boys who can date the best-looking girls in school.

In high school, extracurricular activities are a major conduit to friendships, as are parents, in the sense that parents decide where a student lives and where he attends school. Location makes a big difference in the development of adolescent friendships, because residence and schooling are so closely tied together. Both reflect the socioeconomic condition of adults, and both reflect race. Friendships are not random but depend on opportunities to meet. Friendships are more

467. Patricia Adler, Steven Kless and Peter Adler, "Socialization to Gender Roles: Popularity Among Elementary School Boys and Girls," *Sociology of Education*, 65, (1992):169-187.

influential at the high school level than in college. In secondary schools friendships are heavily dependent on race and gender. Most children, whether Afro-Americans, Euro-Americans or others, feel most comfortable with friends of their own race.[468]

It is evident that integrated neighborhoods and integrated schools can exist. However, integrated friendships are almost unknown. In fact, there is a *de facto* racial segregation in most schools. As children get older, this segregation increases, although athletics and classroom activities bring children of different races together *de jure*.

Because many Afro-Americans devalue schooling, friendships between children in the Afro-American community can lead some children away from school success that they might otherwise enjoy. Asian-American children generally have strong family backing in favor of schooling (whether Chinese, Japanese, Korean or Vietnamese). Therefore, children of those ethnic groups are more likely to succeed in school than either Euro-Americans or Afro-Americans and their friends are most likely to favor learning. The same thing is true of Jewish Americans, of whom 80% attend college and who hold more graduate degrees per capita than any other ethnic group in America. Although these peoples differ in language and culture, they all support education *ipso facto*.

Gender is even more important in formulating friendships than ethnicity. While boys base friendship on shared activities, particularly athletics, girls tend to base friendships more on "disclosure," or discussion of such private matters as boyfriends.[469]

THE EFFECT OF SOCIAL CLASS ON ADOLESCENT PERCEPTIONS

Social class is then a major force in the thinking of adolescents. Ellen A. Brantinger, professor of education at Indiana University, found that adolescents are not only aware of social class differences, but that they lump together low achievement, problematic behavior and low social class as well as good behavior,

468. M.L. Clark and Marla Ayers, "The Role of Reciprocity and Proximity in Junior High School Friendships," *Journal of Youth and Adolescence*, 17, (1988):403-11.
469. Laurence Steinberg, Brad Brown and Sanford Dornbusch, *Beyond the Classroom: Why School Reform has Failed and What Parents Need to Do*, (New York: Simon and Schuster, 1996).

high class status and refined conduct. In part this class consciousness is derived from the tracking system found in American high schools. That tracking system segregates good students from weak students and generally also segregates the poor from the more affluent. Those left at the bottom of the system recognize their position in the scheme of things, leading to resentment and in many cases to the "dropout" who leaves school as soon as possible.

According to Brantlinger, high-income students who do well in school generally report that they expect to be liked by teachers and that their relationship to teachers is good. The reason is not only that teachers are well aware of the income of their students' families but also that students from high-income families are more likely to meet the expectations of teachers. American high schools tend to offer a curriculum that invites students to attend college. That is much more likely among high- and middle-income students than working-class children. Therefore, the expectations of family and the expectations of teachers match for middle- and high-income students; much of what is expected in school is taken for granted within these social classes.[470]

Middle-income students believe that teachers like them; this is natural, because their families are the social equals of teachers. Children from the educated middle class live in the same neighborhoods as their teachers; their parents and their teachers are often acquainted and may even have attended the same college together.

High-income students, says Brantlinger, view teachers as social inferiors and may make critical remarks about teachers' personalities and teaching ability ("talks with an accent," "appears ignorant," "dresses like a dork"). High-income students also believe that they can manipulate teachers and "get away" with rule violations. They do not complain about discipline because they are seldom given more than the mildest penalties. In fact, high-income students expect teachers to respect them and to favor them. High-income students are also indifferent to individual teachers.

Brantlinger compared the attitudes towards teachers of high-income students to that of low-income students. That comparison yielded considerable differences in the perception of teachers. Many low-income children in her study felt that teachers were rejecting because of their poverty. Even high-achieving low-income students have that perception. Low-income students feel powerless

---

470. Ellen A. Brantinger, "The Social Class "Embeddedness of Middle School Students: Thinking About Teachers" *Theory Into Practice*, 33, no.3 (Summer 1994):191-198.

to relate to teachers — and with good reason. Teachers are members of American society and teachers know the difference between the poor and powerless and the wealthy and influential. The rejecting conduct by teachers makes teachers important in the lives of poor children. Poor children often feel that teachers don't want to help them but blame them for failure to understand the subject matter. Teachers often "make short shrift" of students without family influence or power. Low-income children worry about their status with teachers and perceive many teachers to be unfair and biased against them. As a consequence, low-income students remember most vividly those teachers who helped them, who favored them and who treated them kindly.

Because teachers are responsible for failing them and disciplining them, low-income students often resent teachers but not the system. At the same time, low-income students are also critical of themselves for not meeting school expectations. In sum, Brantlinger concludes that, "The perceived culpability and merits of students, in turn, legitimate stratification in school and society."[471]

Some low-income students may leave school early because their experiences in the typical American high school are humiliating and emotionally painful. Dropping out has numerous negative consequences in almost every instance (despite stories about Thomas Edison and other success stories who did not prosper in school).

Every study of school "dropouts" has shown that low attendance and low test scores, as well as student mobility, are good predictors that a student may leave school early. Student mobility refers to the changing of schools for reasons other than promotion. Studies have shown that one half of students who move from one school to another do so not because they changed their residence but because they are discouraged in the school they are attending. Such discouragement usually follows low grades, the label of "trouble maker" and other performance failures by both the school and the student.[472]

Drop out rates are of course dependent on both the characteristics of a school and the characteristics of students. When a student leaves a school voluntarily, his action is called a "drop out." Schools can, however, discharge students because of poor behavior, poor attendance or being over age.

---

471. Ibid. p. 196.
472. Carolyn Riehl, "Labeling and Letting Go: An Organizational Analysis of How High School Students Are Discharged as Dropouts," In: Aaron M. Pallas, Editor, *Research in Sociology of Education and Socialization*, (New York: JIA Press, 1999) pp. 231-268.

Characteristics of students which are associated with dropping out include ethnicity, family attitudes, socio-economic status and academic success. Academic success is dependent of engagement in school. Those students most engaged in school activities are least likely to quit while those least engaged are most likely to leave. Furthermore, a study of student turnover in 51 high schools in California demonstrated that student-teacher ratio and teachers' advanced degrees had a positive effect on the student drop out rate.[473]

Dropping out of school is a predictor of unemployment in later years. The reasons for this association are that many of those who leave school early have poor reading skills, that they are frequently living in a single parent household, that they were involved in anti-social behavior and that they were exposed to violence.

ADOLESCENT DEVIANCE

Not all adolescents go to school. Some adolescents, although enrolled in school, become delinquents. Some of those who become delinquents are violent while others confine their criminal activities to stealing and other non-violent offenses.

Adolescence is by definition a state of anxiety and role conflict. The reasons for this conflict are that adult culture pushes in one direction and youth culture pushes into another. This is visible in the area of sexual activity. Adult culture seeks to influence adolescents to be abstinent and to delay parenting, even as peers promote sexual experimentation, which often leads to teen pregnancy.

Pregnancy is of course a route out of adolescence and into adult status. So is violence. It has been estimated that in large American cities one quarter of all adolescents have been exposed to violence by witnessing someone being shot or killed. Such experiences are positively related to violent behavior as well as to hostility and depression in children and adolescents.[474]

---

473. Russell Rumberger and Katherine M. Larson, "Student Mobility and the Increased Risk of High School Drop Out," *American Journal of Education,* 107 (1998):1-35.

474. Tama Leventhal and Jeanne Brooks-Gunn, The Neighborhoods they Live in: The Effects of Neighborhood Residence on Child and Adolescent Outcomes." *Psychological Bulletin,* 126 (2000):309-337.

Hostility and depression, like other emotions, are not only psychological conditions. They are also related to culture and social structure. The best example of a culturally induced emotional state is *anorexia nervosa*, a self-imposed starvation found almost exclusively in teenage girls and young adult women. This condition exists only in Western industrialized societies, while in Japanese society there exists a condition called *taijin kyofusho*, which is described as "a morbid dread of causing embarrassment to others."[475]

It is reasonable to expect that if emotional conditions can be induced by the majority culture, that this is also true of subcultures. A subculture is a group that is set apart from the majority culture by a culture pattern not accessed by others. An example is that part of the American people who cannot speak English and therefore speak a foreign language. Likewise, there is in the United States a durable subculture of delinquency. That subculture of adolescents is involved in group violence, theft, vandalism and other crimes committed by adolescents between the ages of 15 and 17 in western societies.

Needless to say, anxiety and frustration can result from failure to do well in school. Those who are unsuccessful in school and in the area of upward mobility and socio-economic competition have reason to associate with one another so as to counteract the anxiety that such failure must provoke. The sociologists Robert Merton and Albert Cohen have explained the relationship between school failure and delinquency, based primarily on the earlier work of Emile Durkheim, who developed the concept of anomie. According to Durkheim, there are societies, like the United States, in which there is a great deal of confusion and contradiction as to social norms or expectations. In such societies some people, including adolescents, do not know what is expected of them. Merton applied the concept of anomie to all kinds of deviant behavior and particularly to delinquent gangs. Merton argues that in US society some people unhappily realize that they will never be able to achieve the ideal: the popular goals such as money, conspicuous consumption, a college education or political and economic power.[476]

Because of this realization, which can occur among children who have failed in school, some will turn to criminal or delinquent behavior because they

475. John Hagan, "Defiance and Despair: Subcultural and Structural Linkage between Delinquency and Despair in the Life Course," *Social Forces*, 76, no.1 (September 1997) :119-134.

476. Robert Merton, "Social Structure and Anomie," *American Sociological Review*, 3, (October 1938):672-682.

have become convinced that one must win, by whatever means possible. Of course there are other avenues of adaptation, and some who consider themselves "losers" may exhibit retreatism or renunciation of the competitive community, for instance by joining a hippie commune, or a convent. Retreatism involves the rejection of socially approved goals and culturally achieved means of attaining them. Retreatists have not internalized the usual success goals such as money or fame. They are unwilling to "play" the game. Instead they retreat by joining a retreatist community and/or they retreat through the use of drugs and alcohol. Others join groups engaged in loud and aggressive political protest while yet others conform as best they can to the low status they must endure.

Some adolescents seek to escape middle-class demands by sharing a mutual set of values based on smoking, using alcohol and other drugs, and truancy. These status offenses allow some adolescents the opportunity to create their own social status hierarchy based on defiance of authority and contempt for the demands of teachers.

Then there are some youngsters who join delinquent gangs consisting of school failures and/or school dropouts. According to Cohen, these delinquent gangs tended to be malicious and motivated by spite, anger, hostility and revenge. He further argued that delinquent gangs are non-utilitarian in that they steal and vandalize things they didn't want and didn't use. Delinquent gangs, wrote Cohen, believe that their actions are right precisely because the majority society views such actions as despicable and offensive. Cohen then explains how youngsters become malicious and negativistic because of their inability to meet the demands of middle-class values.

According to Cohen, these values are: ambition or "getting ahead"; individual responsibility; skills and achievement; postponing gratification or hard work; rational planning, not gambling; manners and courtesy; control over physical aggression, not violence; wholesome recreation like sports, not drinking bouts, and respect for property.[477]

It is evident that delinquent subcultures have become a permanent feature of American society because school failure almost always guarantees unemployment or "dead end" jobs and even feelings of despair at a later age. This does not deny that there are some school dropouts who have "made it big." There are a few who left school early and then became millionaires and even billionaires.

---

477. Albert Cohen, *Delinquent Boys*, (New York: The Free Press, 1955)p.97.

That, however, is so unusual that it becomes the stuff of legends and cannot be normally expected.

Those who recognize that because of their failure to be successful in school their socioeconomic prospects are very poor and they can therefore be motivated to engage in delinquency. By associating with delinquent gangs and therefore entering the subculture of delinquency, they can forget their economic distress during the time they are involved in juvenile delinquent gangs. The sociologist John Hagan has shown that delinquent behavior precedes poor employment or unemployment, so that delinquent youths do not usually foresee the economic consequences of their school failure or their delinquency. Delinquency is a legal term referring to the crimes of young people under a legislated age such as 17 or 18. Defiant of adults, disadvantaged in their resources and facing few possibilities of upward mobility, most of those who are in that situation seek to solve their problems by joining gangs, who have their own status system, their own winners and losers, their own successes. These successes can consist of becoming known for physical violence, for sexual conquests, for drinking large amounts of alcohol or using drugs. Although youngsters who have failed in school and joined such gangs know that their chances are poor, they can, for a time, practice denial and hide within the confines of the gang from the realities that must envelop them later.[478]

Youths who have engaged in the fun and freedom that gang life allows may well enter the working world without much regret. In fact, there is a counter-school subculture of people who laugh at education and who seek to defy school at all cost. Fighting and thieving is enjoyable to many who engage in these activities, because the thought of defying school authorities is hard to resist. "Getting away with something" is truly a "high" among many of those who have abandoned school, as is conflict with the law, i.e. the police. All this leads to later problems in staying employed, problems not usually visible to youngsters at the time they leave school. Because entry-level adult employment usually means physical labor, for recent school dropouts, it also confirms their masculinity, as road work or construction requires "heavy lifting" and hard muscles. Incapable of foreseeing the future, many such youngsters believe they are invincible and not subject to grief and pain.[479]

---

478. John Hagan, "The Search for Adolescent Role Exits and the Transition to Adulthood," *Social Forces*, 71, (1993):955-980.

479. Paul Willis, *Learning to Labor: How Working Class Kids get Working Class Jobs*, (New York: Columbia University Press,1977).

Young employees who are generally single enjoy the money and the things money can buy for the first time since leaving school. Clothes, cars, nightlife and girls are all available to them for the first time, unlike those who remain in school and labor over homework and take orders from their mothers.

It is only at midlife, after the erstwhile youngsters are no longer young, that the "sleeper effect" of school failure becomes grossly visible. Trapped in a "dead end" job, often in an industry that is losing jobs, these former adolescents may have families to support or have contracted debts they cannot meet, and in any case they face a future that resembles the present, at best, without any hope of escape from drudgery and poverty. Low wages and unstable jobs are the usual consequences of school failure, which can easily lead to despondency and a loss of confidence in one's ability to ever achieve success in terms of the competitive American culture.

There are, of course, delinquents who stay in school, renounce delinquency with age, and in many cases end up as well off as those who remained in school and were never delinquent.

THE UPPER CLASS ADOLESCENT

Although it seems almost impolite to suggest that there is an upper class in democratic America, there is; and, furthermore, they constitute a minority. This has been most adequately demonstrated by E. Digby Baltzell, himself a well-born American and author of *Philadelphia Gentlemen, The Protestant Establishment, Puritan Boston and Quaker Philadelphia* and other books describing the American elite from the inside. Baltzell discusses at some length the elite schools in New England and Pennsylvania.[480]

Included in the so-called "elite" schools are sixteen boarding schools founded between 1778 and 1906. The oldest of these is Phillips Andover, located in Massachusetts, and the most recently founded is Kent, located in Connecticut. Whatever the merits of such boarding schools, the tuition alone indicates the level of income and wealth the students represent. At Andover Academy the annual fee for the 2003-2004 school year was $23,400 for "day students" and $30,100 for those who require room and board. At Kent, the fees are

---

480. E. Digby Baltzell, *Puritan Boston and Quaker Philadelphia*, (New York: The Free Press, 1979)p.275.

$25,900 and $33,000 respectively. These high schools are usually called academies, so as to distinguish them from the public high schools attended by almost everyone else, and referring to the ancient Greek school where Plato taught. Originally these schools were exclusively masculine and were church related. Most of these schools are now co-educational and no longer require a religious orientation.

Sociologists describe the upper-upper class in America as those who are born into that class and who have inherited immense wealth. These families constitute less than 1% of the American population. Members of the upper-upper class live in exclusive neighborhoods like Beacon Hill in Boston, Rittenhouse Square in Philadelphia, the Gold Coast in Chicago or Nob Hill in San Francisco. They find each other listed in books like *The Social Register*. Begun in 1887, the *Social Register* now includes about 40,000 families in all parts of the country.

This elite resembles a caste more than a class, because a class is accessible to those who can come up with the money and power. A caste is a group into which one must be born. The true elites view as outsiders anyone who is not "in" by birth, no matter how wealthy. Traditionally, upper-upper class parents urge their children to marry into similar families. It is for this reason that the *Social Register* lists families and not individuals.[481]

It is noteworthy that the Social Register never mentions anyone's occupation or place of business. That may be because achievement is not at issue; it is also hard to define the "job" of someone who is independently wealthy. Only the names of the family members and their addresses and telephone numbers are given, alongside the schools attended and club memberships.

The American upper-upper class has long believed that due to education, including good taste and the association of other elitists, they were the bearers of American civilization and the natural rulers of the United States. For example, George William Curtis wrote in his 1897 book, *The Public Duty of Educated Men*, that the people needed to hear the thinker and the scholar. He meant that these thinkers and scholars, educated at private academies, should be the leaders in politics and should be the officeholders, instead of the demagogue and the shouting rabble.[482]

---

481. John C. Macionis, *Sociology*, p.278.
482. George William Curtis, *The Public Duty of Educated Men*, (New York: Charles E. Merrill and Co. 1897).

Such views motivated the founding of the boarding schools their sons and now also their daughters were to attend. In addition to wishing to keep their children from contamination by the "rabble," elitists also wanted to be sure that their children would be accepted by "the best" colleges, meaning Harvard University, Yale University or Princeton University.

It is not surprising that American politicians, including presidents, are often the product of such schools as Groton Academy and Harvard College or Andover and Yale. For example, Franklin D. Roosevelt, 32nd President of the United States; his Undersecretary of State, Dean Acheson; Ambassador Averill Harriman; and Francis Biddle, US Attorney General in the Roosevelt cabinet, graduated from Groton Academy. These schools are now open to a limited number of scholarship students; indeed, some students come from the black community and other ethnic communities found in all American cities. Nevertheless, the "old school tie" still ties, as seen by the candidates for the presidency and vice presidency of the United States in 2004. President George W. Bush graduated from Phillips Andover Academy and Sen. John Forbes Kerry graduated from St. Paul Academy in New Hampshire; both graduated from Yale University.

Until recently, it was common for the men who entered a diplomatic career to be graduates from elitist boarding schools and universities. When President Calvin Coolidge appointed Joseph C. Grew to become an ambassador of the United States, he, like 75% of all ambassadors, was a graduate of an elitist boarding school. The foreign service was at one time called "the club." From the very beginning, the United States has been dominated by White Anglo Saxon Protestant elites, and they do not always act in way that recognize all men being "created equal."[483]

After World War II, and especially after the upheavals of the 1960s, the elite boarding schools relaxed their rigid requirements somewhat. Nevertheless, even today those who enter the elite schools are generally assured wealth, status and power. They enter the most prestigious colleges, are appointed to the best jobs, become chief executive officers, serve on corporate boards, and become directors of foundations and organizations. There can be little doubt that America, like England, has a ruling class whose membership is closed to all but a fractional few. Moreover, "when openings occur on government advisory boards

---

483. Edward N. Saveth, "Education of an Elite," *History of Education Quarterly*, 28, no. 3, (Autumn, 1988):382.

or when a new administration is appointing cabinet members, government officials turn to the inner circle of business leaders."[484]

Although the elite boarding schools did not become accessible to girls until the 1970s, the life of upper class girls did not resemble that of the usual American high school student even before the 60s gender revolution. An excellent example of this kind of privileged youth is the life of Barbara Pierce Bush, First Lady of the United States during the administration of her husband George H.W. Bush. She is a relative of the 14th President of the United States, Franklin Pierce.

Her father, Marvin Pierce, was the president of the McCall Corporation. Educated at Ashley Hall, a private boarding school in South Carolina, she met George H.W. Bush, a senior at Phillips Andover Academy, when she was sixteen. Even as a child she held elementary school teas using Tiffany silverware. She also had a pony stable. Later she became a student at exclusive Smith College.

The life of Barbara Pierce Bush, except as First Lady, is not uncommon among those who are born to privilege. Even in preschool and elementary school, the upper class child is likely to attend a private day school. Adolescents are usually sent to a boarding school and then attend Harvard, Princeton or Yale universities — they used to go to "finishing school." These schools leave a distinctive mark upon their students, which may be seen in their vocabulary, inflection, style of dress, tastes, values and manners.[485]

Upper class children are also regularly taught by private tutors and are also given classes in dancing and other social skills in the elementary years, with a view of teaching children "proper" manners. Horseback riding, music and foreign languages are also taught by private instruction, as is tennis. All this leads to the "old boy" and "old girl" networks, which are then continued by membership in social clubs restricted to the same elite.

The culminating event of upper class adolescence is the "debutante" ball, which is sponsored by the elite families of Palm Beach and numerous American cities. Debutantes attend "coming out" parties wearing white evening gowns; they dance first with their fathers and then with eligible bachelors invited from a list of upper-class men.

---

484. Peter W. Cookson and Caroline Hodges Persell, *Preparing for Power: America's Elite Boarding Schools*, (New York: Basic Books, 1985)p.168.
485. G. William Domhoff, *Who Rules America Now?* (New York: Touchstone Books, 1983)p.24.

Their separate status thus insured, adolescents of the upper-upper class are as far removed from the lives of ordinary young people that they almost live on a different planet.

Thus, social class in America can make the difference between the abyss of unemployment, addiction and an early death and a life of privilege and power, constant praise and self-assurance and all that which aristocracy has always enjoyed at the expense of those who labor.

SUMMARY

Status and role are universal and are therefore also found in high schools among adolescents. Conspicuous consumption is used to label social class among youngsters, as is physical appearance and sports prowess. Upward mobility is very important to high school students, as it is to all Americans, although some students "drop out" and enjoy the initial freedom that work and money brings them.

The school system is in part responsible for success and failure as it is generally college oriented and leaves behind those not attuned to academic study and the postponement of gratification.

If we are to examine the gaps between sectors of American society, we must acknowledge that the generation gap is but one of many. The children of the elite upper-upper class are excluded from the normal high school struggles described above. They face their own challenges at private academies, among their own kind, and they usually go on to succeed in dominating the business and political arena in the United States.

INDEX

Printed in the United Kingdom
by Lightning Source UK Ltd.
104802UKS00001B/93